COLECCIÓN TÁMESIS
SERIE A: MONOGRAFÍAS, 306

THE FICTION OF JUAN RULFO

IRONY, REVOLUTION AND POSTCOLONIALISM

AMIT THAKKAR

THE FICTION OF JUAN RULFO

IRONY, REVOLUTION AND POSTCOLONIALISM

TAMESIS

First published 2012 by Tamesis, Woodbridge

ISBN 978 1 85566 238 4

Tamesis is an imprint of Boydell & Brewer Ltd
PO Box 9, Woodbridge, Suffolk IP12 3DF, UK
and of Boydell & Brewer Inc.
668 Mt Hope Avenue, Rochester, NY 14620, USA
website: www.boydellandbrewer.com

A CIP catalogue record for this book is available
from the British Library

The publisher has no responsibility for the continued existence or accuracy of
URLs for external or third-party internet websites referred to in this book,
and does not guarantee that any content on such websites is,
or will remain, accurate or appropriate

Papers used by Boydell & Brewer Ltd are natural, recyclable products
made from wood grown in sustainable forests

Printed in Great Britain by
CPI Antony Rowe, Chippenham and Eastbourne

CONTENTS

ACKNOWLEDGEMENTS

I would like to thank the Arts and Humanities Research Board for funding the research which made this book possible. It was initially inspired by Professor William Rowe, at Birkbeck College (London), who encouraged me to pursue the line on irony which is its main focus. I must also express profound gratitude to Dr Chris Harris, at the University of Liverpool. The focus in this book on postcolonial contexts in Rulfo's work is largely a result of his persuading me of their importance and he has made tireless efforts to help me advance the project.

I am grateful to Víctor Jiménez, Director of La Fundación Juan Rulfo, for highly authoritative guidance and assistance during my research in Mexico. For their hospitality and warm friendship, I would like to thank Raúl and Miriam Ramírez and Iván Daniel. Roberto García Bonilla, of the Mexican culture department, CONACULTA, deserves special mention for friendship, expert advice and encouragement. I would also like to pay tribute to El Colegio de México for high-quality academic support. The use of their library resources and consultation with their staff, particularly Yvette Jiménez de Báez, Martha Elena Venier and Pablo Lombó, contributed to a very productive stay. In addition, the Archivo General de la Nación and the Hemeroteca of Mexico City provided me with essential primary sources for the socio-historical context of Rulfo's work. In England, three institutions have played a major part in helping me to finish this work: Sydney Jones Library (Liverpool), the Institute of Latin American Studies (London) and the Department of European Languages and Cultures (Lancaster).

Most importantly, I would like to pay tribute to all of my family, particularly Naomi, Sebastian and Leo, as well as my brother Bimal and sister-in-law Rajal, my parents Mahendra and Chandra, and Naomi's parents Ken and Julie, for loving support of my commitment to the project

Introduction: Form and Content, Text and Context

Interpretations of literature tend to hover in the space between form and content (or form and 'meaning'). The question of balance is an immediate concern for literary critics and one looks to others for guidance. According to Susan Sontag, the analysis of form in a text is far more important than the pursuit of meaning: 'the function of criticism should be to show *how it is what it is*, even *that it is what it is*, rather than to show *what it means*'.[1] Nonetheless, in many works of literary criticism, meaning is the very focus and it is easy to end up favouring meaning over form. Sontag argues that this can be avoided: 'The best criticism, and it is uncommon [...] dissolves considerations of content into those of form.'[2] With these words in mind, I aim to examine the content of Juan Rulfo's work through the form of irony, the discreet employment of which is one of the signs of what Sontag would (admiringly) call a 'stubborn' author. For Sontag, interpretation is made all too easy by those authors who are so uncomfortable with the rawness of their art as form that they insist on gifting to us its content:

> Sometimes a writer will be so uneasy before the naked power of his art that he will install within the work itself ... the clear and explicit interpretation of it. Thomas Mann is an example of such an overcooperative author. In the case of more stubborn authors, the critic is only too happy to perform the job.[3]

She proceeds to cite Kafka as an example of a 'stubborn' author, detailing the ways in which the content of his work can be read as social, psychoanalytical or religious allegory, depending on one's approach.[4] Given the range of inter-

---

[1]   Susan Sontag, 'Against Interpretation', in *A Susan Sontag Reader* (London: Penguin Books, 1982; first published 1964), p. 104.

[2]   Sontag, p. 103.

[3]   Sontag, p. 99.

[4]   The two categories, stubborn and overcooperative, may be present in a single author: one might say that the less successful works of Fuentes (the longer novels) tend to consign him to the group of 'overcooperative' authors, while the shorter works, such as the stories and shorter novels, make him a 'stubborn author'.

pretations available of Rulfo, it is clear that, as with Kafka, this is a 'stubborn' author; indeed, Gerald Martin refers to his work as 'worthy of Kafka'.[5] Rulfo's 'stubbornness' is marked by a kind of irony which forces his readers to establish less-than-obvious ironic connections not only between the two 'internal' elements of a text, form and content, in a centripetal direction, but also between text and 'external' context, in a centrifugal direction.

It is principally in the centrifugal dimension that we are most in danger of over-interpreting. For example, the same critic who has deemed Rulfo 'worthy of Kafka' seemingly overstates the case for the application of European critical formulae to Rulfo's novel:

> Rulfo's novel operates on both the nation (Mexican/Latin American) and individual (universal) planes, and … a critical vision compatible with the new Marx and the new Freud underpins the entire narrative. Without such a framework it becomes indecipherable and spirals away into labyrinths of 'magic' and 'mystery'.[6]

The use of the word 'indecipherable' here is potentially misleading and provocative but, rather than overstating his case, what Martin is suggesting is simply that a politicised reading facilitates an evaluation of the social and ethical context of Rulfo's work. Without this political evaluation, Western interpretations based principally on 'magic' or 'mystery' can obscure or even cheapen the context. This is why, when dealing with *Pedro Páramo*, Martin considers Rulfo's work in the context of the Mexican Revolution and the experience of peasants in Mexican history, asserting that 'social relationships … govern this apparently most ethereal of novels'.[7] Sontag herself would have found it hard to disagree with the notion that most modern novels deal with social situations that have a context in political systems and historical processes and that there is 'meaning' here to be pursued. But her gripe seems to be that we should assess this context at the *expense* of form, the latter being far more important as it represents what the work of art *is* rather than what it *means*. Having considered both critics, we have here the kernel of the problem: how does a work of interpretation approach a political context that undeniably exists while giving due appreciation of the form? It is the premise of this book that, by investigating the 'centripetal' and 'centrifugal' ironies in Rulfo's texts, we have a flexible methodology which allows us to study (literary) form with reference to a (political) context and vice-versa.

---

5   Gerald Martin, 'Narrative Since 1920', in *A Cultural History of Latin America*, ed. by Leslie Bethell (Cambridge: Cambridge University Press, 1998), p. 175.

6   Martin, 'Narrative since 1920', p. 175.

7   Martin, 'Narrative Since 1920', p. 176.

Yet, given the historical and literary circumstances at the time of the publication of Rulfo's novel and short stories (the 1950s), it is curious that political approaches to his work have been thin on the ground and that scant attention has been paid to the employment of irony in revealing the politics of his fiction. Rulfo's work appeared after a period of over thirty years since the inauguration of General Álvaro Obregón's post-Revolutionary regime in 1920. In those years, Mexican literature had grappled with the complex issues spawned by the Revolution through genres such as 'the novel of the Revolution', indigenist literature and regionalist fiction. This literary output failed to produce a format or style which had satisfactorily engaged with the general feeling of disappointment in the outcome of the Revolution. Perhaps this was because the disappointment was not fully tangible; but perhaps it was also due to an overinsistence on conveying 'realistically', 'naturalistically', 'historically' the detail of the Revolution rather than dealing *metaphorically* with its significance and how it should be presented as a work of art. According to John S. Brushwood, it was only with the publication of Agustín Yáñez's *Al filo del agua* in 1947 that this trend was broken: 'The transformation of reality in this novel stands out against a background created by some fifteen years of fiction that favoured objective representation rather than artistic transformation.'[8] If Yáñez's groundbreaking novel of 1947 paved the way, in some respects, for a metaphorical treatment of the Revolution, Rulfo's own work is often seen as a further step towards the modern novel of the Boom. Authors of the 1960s, such as Carlos Fuentes and José Fernando del Paso, inspired by Rulfo's techniques, went on to construct successful critiques of post-Revolutionary society with challenges made through form as much as through content. Despite its association with this key juncture in the literary and political development of Mexico, the relationship between literary form and political content in Rulfo's work has generally escaped the kind of close scrutiny I present here.

One major exception can be found in Carlos Blanco Aguinaga's essay 'Realidad y estilo de Juan Rulfo', written in the year that *Pedro Páramo* was published (1955), in which we find positive encouragement to pursue a formal critique based on political context, an approach conspicuous by its absence in most of the following 35 years of criticism on Rulfo.[9] One collection of articles, published in 1981 by *INTI: Revista de Literatura*

8　John S. Brushwood, 'Literary Periods in Twentieth-Century Mexico: The Transformation of Reality', in *Contemporary Mexico: Papers of the IV International Congress of Mexican History*, ed. by James Wilkie, Michael C. Meyer and Edna Monzón de Wil (Berkeley: University of California Press, 1976), p. 671.
9　Carlos Blanco Aguinaga's essay is reproduced in *Para cuando yo me ausente*, ed. by Juan Rulfo (Mexico City: Grijalbo, 1982), pp. 175–203.

Hispánica, proposed three major approaches to Rulfo's work (the formalist, the mythical, the philosophical), none of which address the political interpretation called for by Blanco Aguinaga.[10] This balance is partly redressed in another important collection of criticism on Rulfo, a special edition of *Cuadernos Hispanoamericanos* published in 1985, in which political approaches abound, for example 'La ley, la culpabilidad y la indiferencia en los cuentos de Juan Rulfo' by William Rowe, and '*Pedro Páramo*: texto e ideología' by Julio Calviño Iglesias.[11] In 1986, Wiliam Rowe gave a sensitive treatment of form and politics in his critical guide to *El llano en llamas*, an inspired edition of the Grant & Cutler series, frequently cited in many of the chapters in this book.[12] Political and formal contexts were even more clearly established by two influential essays on Rulfo, one by José C. González Boixo in 1989 and the other by Peter Beardsell in 1990. In the introduction to the Cátedra edition of *Pedro Páramo*, González Boixo devotes an entire section to context, making the point that there are clear geographical and temporal parameters to the 'telón de fondo' of Rulfo's 'visión infernal': 'sus historias se ubican en un lugar y en un tiempo delimitados con bastante exactitud – [la] región de Jalisco … y la época de la revolución y post-revolución'.[13]

The spatial and temporal context outlined here by González Boixo is made even more specific in Beardsell's essay, a richly contextualised critique which takes into account 'historical' referents such as *caciquismo* and the Cristero War along with 'universal' themes such as solitude and death.[14] But Beardsell is aware also of the essential irony of the text, which resides in the contradiction between, on the one hand, its apparent nature as 'a dialogue of the dead' and, on the other, the humorous atmosphere it creates. There is also, in this essay, encouragement to pursue themes associated with the legacy of colony, which is the dominant aspect of meaning treated in this book. The pointers to irony and postcolonial contexts in Beardsell's work are followed up in the most recent collection of articles on Rulfo, a special edition of the *Revista Canadiense de Estudios Hispánicos* in 1998 (Volume XXII, No. 2). In an article by Jean Franco, 'Rulfo y el *ressentiment*', a determined case is made by a leading exponent of 'sociocrítica' to look at Rulfo's work

[10] *INTI: Revista de Literatura Hispánica* (Providence: Providence College), 13–14 (Spring–Fall 1981).

[11] *Cuadernos Hispanoamericanos* (Madrid: Agencia Española de Cooperación para el Desarrollo), 421–23 (July–Sept 1985).

[12] William Rowe, *El llano en llamas* (London: Grant & Cutler, 1986).

[13] José C. González Boixo, 'Introducción', in *Pedro Páramo* by Juan Rulfo (Madrid: Cátedra, 1989), p. 16.

[14] Peter Beardsell, 'Juan Rulfo: *Pedro Páramo*', in *Landmarks in Modern Latin American Fiction*, ed. by Philip Swanson (London: Routledge, 1990), p. 83.

'como el contrapunto de la narrativa nacional'.[15] In the process, several good insights are made on this and on the various ironies in Rulfo's work.[16] Despite discussing these in relation to Deleuze and Nietzsche, among others, there is no explicit attempt – no doubt due to limitations of space – at a coherent strategy for organising these ironies in *relation* to the political context, much less to the value of the form of irony as a vehicle for this relationship.

Thus, the current critical corpus on Rulfo leaves one with the feeling of tentatively suggested ironies and political contexts in his work. The central argument of this study, meanwhile, is that Rulfo's fiction is both ironic and political: not only does the irony operate on a fictional level within itself, i.e. centripetally, but it also alludes to political circumstances in a centrifugal direction, principally towards what I call the 'colonising' discourse of the post-Revolutionary state. The subtlety of this dual operation accounts for the power of the work because it allows for two levels of understanding, one which caters for those who have no knowledge of the historical context and the other for those who have acquired some understanding of it. Having successfully travelled the world in dozens of translations, including countries as diverse as Norway, Japan and Greece, Rulfo's fiction has an appeal which transcends the boundaries of his native region of Jalisco. Though it may be successful in each language for different cultural reasons, some of this appeal can surely be attributed to the power of the less politically-specific *centripetal* irony at work in his writing. Notwithstanding this 'universal' appeal, as other critics have pointed out, Rulfo's writing is the product of a specific time and place, the study of which enriches the work. Anybody who has read Rulfo once will certainly be encouraged to reread his work having acquired some awareness of its historical and geographical context. Subsequent readings furnish unexpected layers of irony and make others much more clearly perceptible than in the first. Peculiarly, then, the two elements of the text (form and content) are meaningful and ironic in direct proportion to the reader's understanding of the external context. This is to say that the more one understands outside the text, the more one understands within it, and the less – in the words of Sontag – 'stubborn' the author becomes. Form, in the shape of irony, is always the key to unlocking the text in this way.

Formal analysis, then, is the basis of the study here but I intend to move away, chapter by chapter, from form per se in order gradually to emphasise textual content and, crucially, context. I have no doubt as to the ambitious-

---

[15] Jean Franco, *Revista Canadiense de Estudios Hispánicos* (Montreal), XXII:2 (Winter 1998), 274–75.

[16] Franco, pp. 275–82. A good example is Franco's assertion that women in the story 'Anacleto Morones' use a form of irony called 'socarronería', a kind of dry sarcasm, as their revenge against men, even though these women are hardly spotless themselves.

ness of an approach to literature which simultaneously integrates an analysis of contiguous historical process. One of the most successful critics to have taken this approach was the great Carlos Monsiváis, although the field of his vision tends towards the majestically panoramic, rather than the rigorously specific. In this study, I hope to test a type of literary examination which allows not only for the analysis of fiction 'in its own right' ('practical criticism') but also a thoroughgoing treatment of its socio-political context ('historical criticism'). Indeed, I sincerely hope that, in this study, fiction will help to interrogate politics itself, encouraging debate on the nature of post-Revolutionary rhetoric and its ideological evolution: not only do I wish to suggest a new way of looking at Rulfo, and a new way of looking at irony, but also a way of looking at historical processes which takes account of the critiques that they engender in fiction.

Juan Rulfo and Fictional Irony

To meet Susan Sontag's challenge of identifying first what a text is, rather than what it means, as discussed in the introduction, this chapter will approach Rulfo's work through fictional irony: its philosophical development, its purposes and its operation. The best starting point for this study is the author whose work inspired my interest in Rulfo's use of irony, Hayden White. I will return to his work in further chapters but, for now, I should mention that it provides a vital philosophical background to our subject. For White, the irony and scepticism of late Enlightenment thought had been contested by Rousseau, Hegel and Comte with what he calls 'naïve' conceptualisations of the world, creating 'the self-confident tone of early nineteenth-century historiography'. Between 1830 and 1870, historians and novelists consequently aimed at objectivity and realism but 'succeeded only in producing as many different species of "realism" as there were modalities for construing the world in figurative discourse'. An ironic posture towards truth was then invited by Marx's 'revealing the ideological implications of *every* conception of history' (emphasis added), the philosophical expression of which is Nietzsche's idea that all is potentially truth or fiction, thus creating the 'ironic condition' in historiography and art.[1] By the early twentieth century, the epistemological grounds for realism had been thrown into doubt, making the fictional writer question what one can actually 'know' except the chaos of the world.

Juan Rulfo was one of many twentieth-century writers whose work marked a rupture with the realist, objective and 'naïve' viewpoint of the previous century described by White. Outside Mexico, the beginnings of this new type of fiction had already emerged in works such as Fyodor Dostoyevsky's *Crime and Punishment* (1866), in which the irrationality of the human mind is given a privileged vantage point. Other writers, such as James Joyce and Franz Kafka, had also experimented with techniques which challenged traditional, ninenteenth-century structures by giving form to the inexplicable.[2]

---

[1]   Hayden White, *Metahistory, The Historical Imagination in Nineteenth-Century Europe* (Baltimore: Johns Hopkins University Press, 1973), pp. 39–41.
[2]   For a contextualised placement of Rulfo's fiction in literary history see Norma Klahn,

Just as European authors forged ahead with new novelistic techniques, by the 1930s, literature in the Americas (including the United States, with authors such as William Faulkner) had begun to evolve into a similar force of radical innovation through the work of writers such as Machado de Assis, Jorge Luis Borges, Alejo Carpentier and Miguel Ángel Asturias. Hispanoamerican literature, in particular, was experiencing a revolution in which scepticism towards realism and objectivity was a keynote, making it as much a revolution of philosophy as it was of style. After all, as Norma Klahn states: 'La novela realista sólo se podía dar en un mundo explicable.'[3]

The revolution in literary style and philosophy itself needs to be understood as a gradual process and against the backdrop of social and technological changes which made such a revolution inevitable. As Philip Swanson has argued, given 'the stimulus of social development in the form of European immigration, rapid modernisation and urban migration [...] some kind of major change on the literary scene was inevitable'.[4] Thus, according to Swanson, the keynote of scepticism was intrinsically connected to such literary movements as regionalism, social realism, magical realism and neo-indianism. According to Carlos Fuentes, the twentieth century is a period when Spanish American fiction becomes a way of asking questions instead of pretending to know all the answers to such changes: 'se inicia un tránsito del simplismo épico a la complejidad dialéctica, de la seguridad de las respuestas a la impugnación de las preguntas'.[5] It is my contention here that fictional irony, and, more particularly, Rulfo's irony, is very much in keeping with the spirit of the sceptical approach to realism, objectivity, knowledge and modernity identified by the aforementioned critics. This is the philosophical context of Rulfo's irony, and I shall return to it, but what is the fictional context? What, specifically, is the relationship between Rulfo's irony and the 'mechanics' of fictional irony (the way it functions)?

Fictional Irony

D. C. Muecke's *Irony* (1970) begins with a look at the original Greek *eiron*, figure who is, according to Theophrastus, 'evasive and non-committal,

'La ficción de Juan Rulfo: nuevas formas del decir', in *Toda la obra* (Mexico City: Fondo de Cultura Económica, 1997), pp. 521–30.

3   Klahn, p. 522

4   Philip Swanson, 'Introduction: Background to the Boom', in *Landmarks in Modern Latin American Fiction*, ed. by Philip Swanson (London: Routledge, 1990), p. 5.

5   Carlos Fuentes, *La nueva novela hispanoamericana* (Mexico City: Joaquín Mortiz, 1969), p. 13.

concealing his enmities, pretending friendship, misrepresenting his acts, never giving a straight answer'.[6] With subsequent reference to fictional texts exclusively from the European canon, Muecke develops this contrast between appearances and reality in the *eiron* to conclude that features of all modern fictional irony are: '(i) a contrast of appearance and reality, (ii) a confident unawareness (pretended in the ironist, real in the victim of irony) that the appearance is only an appearance, and (iii) the comic effect of this unawareness of a contrasting appearance and reality'.[7] In the light of the above discussion on nineteenth-century realism, the main problem with this view of irony is that it presupposes an epistemologically-secure world in which 'reality' can be taken for granted by a god-like writer, 'creating an independent world but also ... playing with its inhabitants'.[8] This is a kind of irony in which the writer is intervening in the production of meaning as opposed, as we shall see with Rulfo, to encouraging the *reader* to produce meaning.

Judging by Muecke's choice of examples, the model of author-as-god in irony is most relevant to Western comedic irony. In this type of irony, the author almost visibly determines the fate of the characters, nudging us with 'nods and winks' and directing us ever closer to a reality where meaning is clear and non-negotiable. This view of irony as an editorially-intensive technique would be contested by Northrop Frye, for whom the discussion should also begin with the concept of the *eiron*, although with markedly different conclusions. It is in Aristotle's *Ethics* that we actually meet the figure of the *eiron*, 'a self-deprecating or unobtrusively treated character in fiction, usually an agent of the happy ending in comedy and the catastrophe in tragedy.'[9] By deprecating himself, this character becomes invulnerable and thus ironic in the sense that, on the face of it, he 'means' very little but, in fact, he is more powerful than his victim, the *alazon*, 'a deceiving or self-deceived character in fiction, normally an object of ridicule in comedy or satire, but often the hero of a tragedy.'[10] For example, in the case of *Oedipus Rex*, which I shall discuss later, we could argue that the blind prophet Teresias is the classic *eiron* whilst his incredulous, ostensibly more powerful interlocutor – Oedipus himself – is the *alazon*. Frye proceeds from his discussion of the role of the *eiron* to argue that irony has become the art of 'saying as little and meaning as much as possible or, in a more

---

6 D. C. Muecke, *Irony* (London: Methuen, 1970), p. 14.
7 Muecke, p. 35.
8 Muecke, p. 38.
9 Northrop Frye, *The Anatomy of Criticism, Four essays by Northrop Frye* (Princeton: Princeton University Press, 1957), p. 365.
10 Frye, p. 365.

general way, a pattern of words that turns away from direct statement or its own obvious meaning'.[11]

According to Frye, the ironic fiction writer must eliminate all editorial intrusion and let the text speak for itself, so that 'complete objectivity and suppression of all explicit moral judgements are essential to his methods'.[12] There are therefore two types of irony, naïve and sophisticated:

> Irony is naturally a sophisticated mode, and the chief difference between sophisticated and naive irony is that the naive ironist calls attention to the fact that he is being ironic, whereas sophisticated irony merely states, and lets the reader add the ironic tone himself.[13]

This is comparable to Sontag's stubborn/cooperative binary discussed in the introduction but, in the case of Rulfo, an extreme of sophistication and stubbornness is reached where a certain onus is placed on the reader to fill the gaps. As William Rowe explains:

> What the reader is told in Rulfo's stories is limited almost entirely to what the characters are aware of. But in order to grasp the full meaning of a story, the reader has to go beyond the characters' view of their world. The incompleteness and partiality of the characters' perceptions, the general atmosphere of obscurity, invites in the reader an urge to complete and explain. We thus become involved in constructing a fuller picture out of limited information.[14]

In Rulfo's work, then, the quest for authorial 'objectivity' is eschewed in favour of the attempt to privilege the 'knowledge' of his characters. In this situation, so-called ironic 'detachment' is brought about not by the presumptuous objectivity of realism but by the author's attempted withdrawal from the construction of meaning, even with themes as disturbing as incest, murder and vengeance.[15] In the short story 'Macario', for example, Rowe explores the meaning of an extraordinary amnesia, which is ironic in that it subverts our assumptions about the psychological effect of violence: the protagonist

---

[11] Frye, p. 40.

[12] Frye, p. 40.

[13] Frye, p. 41.

[14] Rowe, p. 9.

[15] With the term 'detachment', I am referring to the traditional view that the ironist must be somehow distanced from 'reality': 'There is yet another feature of irony which appears regularly in discussions of irony. We can choose from among a number of terms: detachment, distance, disengagement, freedom, serenity, objectivity, dispassion, "lightness", "play", urbanity' (Muecke, p. 38). Again, however, Muecke tends to see the traits listed here as essential ingredients of (Western) objectivity in relation to a comedic irony.

fails to remember whether he strangled somebody or not and consequently insists that his godmother must have been right to have said he did. For Rowe, 'the notion of an objective reality breaks down. How far can we or should we supply the missing objectivity?'[16]

Thus, whereas the implication in Muecke's analysis of objectivity is one of authorial superiority, allowing the author to 'play' with his characters and judging them in the process, Frye's model of ironic positioning and Rowe's 'missing objectivity' mean that the author's right to judgement and analysis is deliberately curtailed. The irony of a 'sophisticated' fiction writer like Rulfo is related less to the idea of author-as-god than to that of author-as-*dead*, for this situation puts responsibility on the reader to produce rather than accept meaning, to make sense of the often miserable scenes with which Rulfo presents us. For example, fragmentation in *Pedro Páramo* forces us to re-order people's lives in a journey of meaning personal to each reader. Similarly, the cycle of violence presented in 'El hombre' is given no 'rational' cause-and-effect explanation and it is up to the reader to interpret this, whilst the absence of interlocutors in 'Acuérdate' and 'Luvina' forces the reader to *become* the interlocutor.

The reduced presence of the author is therefore an ironic posture towards traditional fictional irony, such as that of Voltaire's *Candide* (1759), where the author is a god-like presence, gifting the reader his ironic vision of the world through comedic satire. Rulfo's work cannot easily be called satirical, except in a few instances, for this is a form of irony in which the targets are much more overt as a result of the interpreting presence of the author. If the overarching editorial position of Rulfo is one of reduced presence, what tools do we, as readers, need in order to produce meaning given that these are not provided by the author in a direct and explicatory style, as they are in satire? Clearly, a more self-sufficient, independent ability to perceive irony is required but can we expect this from every reader? If so, would everyone have the same sense of what irony is and of how to respond to it? In everyday life, irony is common in the way we refer to everyday events but, as Clare Colebrook argues, if 'irony is saying something contrary to what is meant', it would be impossible to delimit:

> This definition is so simple that it covers everything from simple figures of speech to entire historical epochs. Irony can mean as little as saying, 'Another day in paradise', when the weather is appalling. It can also refer to the huge problems of postmodernity; our very historical context is ironic because today nothing really means what it says. We live in a world of quotation, pastiche, simulation and cynicism; a general and all-encom-

16 Rowe, p. 11.

passing irony. Irony, then, by the very simplicity of its definition becomes
curiously indefinable.[17]

There is indeed a modern tendency to overuse the term 'ironic', lazily
applying it to any image, text or occurrence which is not what it seems. In
everyday American conversation, the term can simply mean 'unfortunate';
for example, the fact that it rains on a wedding day in Alanis Morissette's pop
song 'Ironic' (1996). On the other end of the scale, huge complications arise
with Richard Rorty's ideas on postmodern irony where there is no 'criterion
of wrongness' because everything is a 'language game'.[18] In order to steel
ourselves for a difficult process of definition which will only truly mature in
the last chapter and conclusion of the book, we will begin here by describing
types of irony traditionally associated with *fiction*, rather than everyday life
or epochal theorising. In a literary work, we may reasonably argue that these
are the principal tools that the reader will use to make sense of any ironies.
In the work of Rulfo, at least four types of fictional irony can be found:
dramatic, cosmic, situational and verbal.

Dramatic Irony

This form of irony occurs when the reader is made aware of a set of circumstances of which a character is ignorant. It is frequently employed in theatre
as it affords the audience a priviliged perspective, as Colebrook explains:

> [A] sense of detached superiority is achieved by dramatic irony, in which
> the audience knows more about a character's situation than the character
> does, foreseeing an outcome contrary to the character's expectations, and
> thus ascribing a sharply different sense to some of the character's own
> statements.[19]

The audience is thus placed in an exalted position, 'looking down' on the
situation while the character, like a mouse trapped in a scientific laboratory,
remains unaware. The ironist author gives us a panoramic view of events and,
in the atmosphere of a theatre, this bond creates a conspiratorial relationship
between author and audience for one is keeping some very important information from a character who is 'physically' on stage and psychologically real.
For this reason, it creates a relationship between author and audience that I

---

[17] Clare Colebrook, *Irony*, New Critical Idiom Series (London: Routledge, 2004), p. 1.

[18] Richard Rorty, *Contingency, Irony and Solidarity* (Cambridge: Cambridge University
Press, 1989), p. 75.

[19] Chris Baldick, *The Concise Oxford Dictionary of Literary Terms* (Oxford: Oxford
University Press, 2001), p. 130.

call ironic complicity, an understanding which is tacit rather than voiced and is based either on humility (in tragedy) or flattery (in comedy).

In comedy, complicity is established by flattering the reader with a comfortably superior viewpoint. When Don Quijote attacks a row of wind-mills, the amusement is derived from a superior sense of the border between reality and fantasy.[20] In this particular instance, comedic dramatic irony is more likely to encourage the reader to share a god-like perspective on events with the author, in keeping with Muecke's model of irony, and requiring a certain distance to be kept between reader and character. In tragedy, on the other hand, complicity is experienced as a sensation in which the reader feels powerless before the character's situation. For example, in the story of Oedipus Rex, it becomes apparent to the audience well before it becomes apparent to the protagonist that the prophecy of the blind Teiresias (the *eiron*, according to Frye's reading of the term) will come true: inadvertently, the king has condemned himself when he sentences to death the man who has visited a plague on his kingdom. The audience is incapable of preventing the inevitable and there is a consequent sense of humility before the events of the world, mirroring the subsequent humility of Oedipus Rex and, implicitly, the latent humility of the author.

In the work of Rulfo, dramatic irony – where it exists – tends towards the tragic. Reading Rulfo's work is indeed an emotionally exhausting and humbling experience during which one feels a kind of 'compassion fatigue' due to a sense of powerlessness. One of the clearest instances of tragic dramatic irony is in Don Fulgor's persuasion of Dolores to marry Pedro Páramo. The reader (but not Dolores) is aware that the *hacendado*'s intention is simply to acquire her financial assets and therefore eliminate the debt to her family.[21] The psychological presence of Dolores is indeed very strong: she is central to the story, endearingly human and psychologically convincing (why would a woman of her standing not want to marry the most important man in town?). Thus, when we see her weep with joy, we feel the guilt of an eavesdropper who knows more than they should. We mimic in this scenario the same ironic

---

[20] This is not to say that the reader's position is *always* entirely secure in this work. According to Michael Scham, Cervantes's irony 'expresses a suggestive skepticism: […] the awareness that rational and insane responses to the world are separated more by degree than kind'. Indeed, this can lead to varying uses of irony: 'While much of the humor is satirical in nature, finding resolution in the ultimate control of the narrator and the superior knowledge of the reader vis-à-vis the characters, in other instances, there is a lack of clear resolution and restoration of order, a lingering disorientation.' See '*Don Quijote* and the Art of Laughing at Oneself', *Bulletin of the Cervantes Society of America*, 29:1 (2009), 31–55 (p. 33).

[21] Juan Rulfo, *Pedro Páramo* (Madrid: Cátedra, 1989), pp. 104–06. The novel was first published in 1955. All subsequent references will be to this edition with the page number identi-fied directly after the quotation.

tension and complicity that exists in dramatic irony in plays. However, the sense of powerlessness before the content is offset by the empowering effects of a pared-down, 'stubborn' text in which meaning is to be explored. Thus, the complicity is partly constructive as the reader is expected to understand more from the written word than is immediately apparent: we feel powerless to help Dolores to see the true intentions of Pedro but, more constructively, we come off our laurels and consider the tragedies caused for a community which lives in the grip of a single man.

Similarly, in the story 'Talpa', there is a constructive dramatic irony in our knowledge of the reason for the decision of the narrator and his sister-in-law, Natalia, to take Tanilo, his brother, on a pilgrimage. We know that the narrator and Natalia have had an affair and that they wish to take Tanilo there not because it will cure him but because the long hot journey will in fact kill him. Ironic complicity derives not only from our understanding of Tanilo's position (at his expense) but also from our knowledge that the quest of the narrator and his lover is doomed. We are given to understand, from the very beginning of the story, that Tanilo's death, despite being the outcome initially desired by the narrator and Natalia, does not produce the expected happiness for the two lovers. Thus, the narrator becomes both the *eiron* (ironist) and the *alazon* (victim) in a single story, forcing the reader, as Rowe suggests we should with Rulfo's fiction, to 'move from looking through the characters to looking at them'.[22] Through this constructive type of dramatic irony, the reader feels not the comfort of understanding a single interpretation of the text, as he or she would in comedic dramatic irony, but the confusion of a complicit relationship marked instead by impotence before the tragic ironies of that text. The discomfort generated is deliberate for, as we shall see in later chapters, this sense of powerlessness accords with the theme of peasant vulnerability vis-à-vis local power structures. It is reinforced by another key tool in Rulfo's narrative technique: cosmic irony.

Cosmic Irony

For Colebrook, cosmic irony is '[where] the expectations of a character or community are thwarted by life's events, events which often seem to pass judgement on life or that seem to be the outcome of fate'.[23] In contrast to comedic dramatic irony, the ironist here is not strictly the author: the ambitions of a character are foiled by God, destiny or fate to the extent that these are effectively the ironists, and all of us (not just the characters) their victims.

---

[22] Rowe, p. 9.
[23] Colebrook, p. 179.

In this sense, it is much closer to tragic dramatic irony, as described above, but without the need to give the reader any privileged, panoramic view of the plot, for this form of irony is not dependent on the 'keeping' of knowledge from a character and is therefore not so strictly reliant on plot, narrative structure or complicity. Instead, knowledge of the *limits* of knowledge, and therefore of the 'unknowable' and unpredictable forces of life, is what marks out cosmic irony and its effects on characterisation. In the Western canon, cosmic irony pervades centuries of fiction from Greek to Shakespearean tragedies to some of the novels of Thomas Hardy, where the protagonists, frequently doomed from the outset, endure painfully inevitable outcomes, largely because of their ignorance of key information. As Paul Turner has noted, a certain obsession with what he calls 'agnosia', a position of 'not-knowing' influenced by readings of Greek literature, pervades most of Hardy's work: 'One of his favourite ploys was to prolong the reader's ignorance, not just of facts, but of identities.'[24] Cosmic irony is thus concerned with unknown, incomprehensible or unpredictable forces produced by fate, destiny, nature, the human condition, God or (according to this book) man-made discourses. These can all be seen to foil the plans and ambitions of a protagonist in any interpretation of fiction based on cosmic irony.

There is a certain grotesque quality to this irony in which human existence itself becomes an ironic victim. In the work of Rulfo, one of the most obvious examples of cosmic irony is in the situation of Juan Preciado in the novel *Pedro Páramo*. This is a character who has but one aim when we meet him in the first pages of the novel: to meet his father and to make him pay for abandoning himself and his mother, Dolores. Yet there is clearly a force working against this aim, one which bears some relation to the idea of fate and destiny, for the portentous caws of the ravens in the first few pages and the holes in the portrait of his mother seem to point towards an inevitable failure. His ambition turns on him and, instead of fulfilling his destiny by avenging his mother, or at least meeting his father and discovering his roots, he meets death and narrates his story from the grave. The journey is counter-epic in the sense that it subverts the reader's expectations of a journey of triumph over adversity. It is therefore an ironic comment on human existence, pointing up the grotesqueness of life through images of death, tales of exploitation and unfulfilled lives.

Both in this novel and in *El llano en llamas*, a Catholic God, paradoxically characterised by absence, is also seen to play a role in the destiny of characters. For example, the story 'Es que somos muy pobres' exhibits a

---

[24] Paul Turner, *The Life of Thomas Hardy*, Blackwell Critical Biographies (Oxford: Blackwell, 1998), p. 3. There is further discussion of Greek influences on Hardy in Chapter 1 of Turner's book, 'How I Built Myself a House', pp. 5–12.

strong undercurrent of fatalism where the force thwarting ambition appears to be a merciless God, although the cosmic 'ironist' in these stories could also be interpreted as a more amorphous Catholic discourse. Thus, we could say that, in the story 'Talpa', Tanilo is trapped by a Catholic discourse which encourages faith in miracles: he is virtually dragged, already festering with pustules which reek of death, to Talpa. His hope is therefore indicative of a kind of cosmic irony in which, as I shall demonstrate in this study, not only God, fate or nature but also human discourses can upend the expectations of characters. Tellingly, this discourse of miracles is supposedly exploited by Natalia and the narrator to quicken the death of Tanilo. However, they discover that it is they who have been fooled, a fact which indicates to the reader that the discourse, like nature, fate or any deity, is more powerful than any individual.

Situational Irony

Situational irony is less grand in scope than cosmic irony but similar to the extent that there is a discrepancy between a situation expected and that which eventually arises: a character may find him- or herself in a position which is paradoxical or the opposite of that which they had intended. However, no external, cosmic force is necessarily to blame; rather, the ironic situation is a result of personal failure or, as Jonathan Tittler puts it, 'a paradoxical circumstance, one that is contrary to expectations or to reason itself'.[25] Here, the sense of an author being the ironist is much stronger than in cosmic irony as ambition and failure are deliberately juxtaposed in specific narrative choices, creating much of the dramatic tension that makes it enjoyable. In *The Tempest*, Prospero teaches the uncouth Caliban the English language in order to civilise him with the result that he learns how to curse; Hoffmiller, the protagonist of Stefan Zweig's *Beware of Pity* (1939), agrees to marry a crippled woman out of pity only to end up in a much more pitiable situation of his own; in *A Place of Greater Safety* (1999) by Hilary Mantel, the revolutionaries of the French Revolution become as corrupt, divided and abusive of power as the *ancien régime* they replace. Although these European examples might engender rather tenuous cosmic readings, they conform more recognisably to a pattern in which the paradoxes of everyday life are more important than ontological questions. The tone of cosmic irony thus tends towards the tragic ('Why is life so cruel?') whereas that of situational irony is more banal ('Isn't it strange how … ?').

---

[25] Jonathan Tittler, *Narrative Irony in the Contemporary Spanish-American Novel* (Ithaca and London: Cornell University Press, 1984), p. 18.

Situational irony also has a long history in Latin American writing, one exponent being the colonial Mexican writer Sor Juana, Inés de la Cruz, especially in her poem 'Hombres necios que acusáis', in which men are accused of creating the very faults they fear in women. More recently, in Borges's story *Emma Zunz* (1949), the heroine, apparently taken advantage of by a sailor in Buenos Aires, has in fact exploited him to fake an attempted rape. Examples in Rulfo's work abound: in 'Nos han dado la tierra', illiterate peasant soldiers discover that the only way that they are able to complain is by writing a letter to the Government; in 'Anacleto Morones', the fugitive protagonist's flight from his village only invites the village to find him; in *Pedro Páramo*, the sinner Padre Rentería must suppress his guilt over his own unabsolved sins in order to absolve the sins of others. Indeed, many of the characters in Rulfo's fiction find themselves in some kind of situational paradox in which ambition and failure are counterposed. This not only intensifies the drama but also, as we shall see, makes more urgent the need for the reader to produce meaning, particularly with reference to context.

Verbal Irony

There are many techniques in verbal irony: pun, understatement, hyperbole, bathos, sarcasm, amongst others.[26] Many of these may well be used in spoken language as well as in the written word, though, in both cases, and to varying degrees, literal meaning diverges from 'invisible', intended meaning to the extent that, as Katharina Barbe puts it, 'we differentiate between sentence meaning and speaker [or writer] meaning'.[27] For example, after a governor's wordy and irrelevant speech in the wake of an earthquake in Rulfo's short story 'El día del derrumbe', we hear a campesino cry '¡Exacto! Usted lo ha dicho.' The sentence meaning may be 'Exactly! You've got it!' but the speaker meaning, or at least the meaning we presume to be intended by Rulfo, is something along the lines of the opposite.[28] In fact, a much less direct verbal irony is more common in the work of Rulfo, as we see in the

---

[26] Sarcasm is a controversial inclusion. According to Muecke, irony only exists where we 'feel the force of both the apparent and real meanings'; so sarcasm cannot be ironic because 'the sarcast's tone so unequivocally conveys the real meaning that there can scarcely be any pretence of being unaware of it' (Muecke, p. 51). I include it here because there is still a clear distance between the words used and the meaning intended in sarcasm. It is perhaps simply a more direct member of the same family of ironical devices, much more obvious but not necessarily less effective in demanding a response which involves constructing meaning.

[27] Katharina Barbe, *Irony in Context* (Amsterdam and Philadelphia: John Benjamins, 1995), p. 15.

[28] Juan Rulfo, *El llano en llamas* [1953] (Madrid: Cátedra, 1997), p. 156. Subsequent page numbers in brackets refer to the same edition.

story '¡Diles que no me maten!' where a character killed thirty-five years ago is called 'Juvencio Nava', a fragmented pun suggesting the words 'juventud' and 'navaja', reinforcing the feeling in the story that justice – through the actions of Nava's son – is catching up with the offender.

In order to explore how a verbally ironic communication can indicate and/or develop a literary relationship that is beyond the scope of direct state-ments, it is useful to look more closely at how it functions independently of writing, in ordinary speech, and especially to study the difference between irony and lies. I shall begin by considering the ironic potentialities of a single, relatively ordinary sentence: 'He is a nice chap.' This sentence is uttered by a person A to a person B in relation to C, who is not present. We assume that the subject, 'he' (C), is known to all and that the word 'nice' connotes values such as kindness, generosity and warmth. The use of the word 'chap' (light-hearted and colloquial) also indicates a certain breaking-down of distance between the speaker and listener.[29] In short, such simple and direct sentences can indicate or even generate a relationship of trust based on an explicit and mutually recognised grasp of meanings. For the purposes of irony, this sentence nevertheless represents a reductive approach to language in which there is little room for manoeuvre. If, on the other hand, the same sentence is not the true opinion of the speaker, it may be a lie, in which the speaker has used the wrong signifiers to describe the signified. Nevertheless, the intention is still to imply that these signifiers are correct: A wants to persuade B that C is trustworthy, knowing that he actually is not (with the purpose, say, of encouraging B to lend money to C). The lie is still an attempt at communica-tion of a specific, 'reductive' meaning and it still relies on a trust in language whilst the lie is not discovered: the intention is not to invite questioning of words but trust, in the hope of achieving a (malevolent) purpose. In contrast to the case of irony, the literal meaning and the intended meaning in both lies and direct statements are the same, even if the 'truth' is the *opposite* of the literal meaning in lies.

If the same words are uttered ironically, the speaker has also deliberately used the wrong signifiers to describe the signified (as in the case of lies). However, this time, the intention is not to make the listener *believe* his words but to make him or her *question* them: it is assumed by the speaker that the listener will not accept the literal meaning of the communication. With an ironic intonation and expression, A can tell B that C is 'a nice chap' with the aim *not* of encouraging him to lend money to C but actually to

---

[29] We can never be sure that the meanings associated with the word 'chap' will ever completely coincide in the minds of two people, although they might agree on a dictionary definition. To some extent, then, in order to make any interpretation work, we have to assume a 'temporary fixity' of meaning.

discourage him from doing so. If B recognises the ironic intention of A, it is because he has refused to accept the validity of the signifiers employed; he has questioned them. Whereas, in the case of the direct statement and the lie, the meaning is reductive because it is reduced to a literal reflection of the meaning of the sentence (even though the liar has in mind the opposite of this literal meaning), here the sentence is open to the *production* of meaning (beyond literal meaning) even if, as in the case of sarcasm, the words are to be taken simply as the polar opposite of their direct, literal significance. The ironic statement is therefore a complex form of communication which depends on an existing or potential bond between speaker and listener. This bond is based less on an acceptance of the reflective value of a word than on a recognition of its unreliability. So, although irony relies on both trust *and* language, as do direct statements and lies, it differs because it is based not on what somebody says but on the implications of the *manner* of their saying what they say and, to some extent, precisely on what they do *not* say. Ironic complicity is therefore reinforced through the small misdemeanour of deliberately 'misusing' language, or catechresis.[30] Language in such a relationship is not necessarily taken to mean what it apparently means and this fact needs to be accepted by both individuals; if it is not, the attempt at communication breaks down.

This complicity can be defined as follows: an understanding on the part of both speaker and listener, firstly, that literal meanings must be doubted; secondly, that the intentions of this disruption to the normal course of communication will be clear to both (though not necessarily to anybody else); thirdly, that the complicit communication may be based on a convergence of values between A and B (being 'on the same wavelength'); and, fourthly, that this communication is indeed deliberate and the ironist is not intending to 'double bluff' anybody. Thus, language itself is not as important as the *relationship* between A and B, especially the extent to which they are 'on the same (ironic) wavelength' and share the same 'referents' independent of the words in question. The question of shared ironic referents is indeed key to an understanding of Rulfo's irony and this is the subject of the next section: if Rulfo and his reader are strangers (to varying degrees), how is a relationship of trust formed? What are the shared referents and where are they? Which of these referents exist solely in the text and which in the context? How do referents in text and context interact with each other and what is the reader's relationship with them? This is a key problem because it helps us to approach the slippery nature of 'context' which, though an ever-changing and unstable

---

[30] More thoughts on this process of 'misusing' language will be presented in the next chapter.

accessory to understanding a text, is vital to the writer's irony as it helps to ensure the reader is on the same ironic wavelength.

Ironic Referents in the Centripetal–Centrifugal Continuum

In Rulfo's work, there is always much more to the written word than the literal, as Felipe Garrido points out: 'hay lecturas más profundas o más complicadas, más sútiles que permiten ir descubriendo progresivamente nuevos planos, nuevos niveles, tal vez no sospechados en un principio'.[31] Some of the clearest examples of the existence of these 'deeper' readings lie in the story 'Nos han dado la tierra', in which we find four ironic referents:

(i)   The words of the title, which are not necessarily to be taken at face value as it is evident that the fertile land the peasants were promised has not been delivered to them.

(ii) The epic form, which is undermined in Rulfo's story with a counter-epic of frustrated ambition.

(iii) The peasants' futile demands for land, a type of cosmic irony where their fatalism seems to represent submission to a divine force as well as to the state discourse which seeks to replace it.

(iv) State propaganda, which promoted the notion that the peasants received their due share of land after the Revolution.

These four referents span the entire centripetal–centrifugal spectrum. The first referent (especially the word 'tierra') operates within the text itself in an ironic 'motion' that is centripetal, for the infertile land that the peasants are given is described within the text. It could be argued that the second referent is centrifugal since the epic is a form which exists 'outside' this particular text; yet it could also be argued that this referent is principally centripetal in that it is literary: the epic is an extremely common root form for many literatures and the reader will not normally be unaware of expectations associated with it. The third referent, the peasants' demand for land, could be said to be centripetal, in the sense that these peasants exist as characters within the text, but it is perhaps best understood centrifugally: the characters exist in the fiction but represent figuratively a wider rural population – not included in the text – who were also disappointed by the non-fulfilment of revolutionary promises. The fourth referent is principally centrifugal as it presupposes the juxtaposition of the text with the information machine of

---

[31] Felipe Garrido, '*Pedro Páramo* y *El llano en llamas* de Juan Rulfo', in *Para cuando yo me ausente*, ed. by Juan Rulfo (Mexico City: Grijalbo, 1982), p. 23.

propaganda which exists outside the fiction: government speeches, school text books and the official press. It must be stressed, then, that no example is entirely centripetal or centrifugal: the centripetal irony in (i) depends on a centrifugal understanding, however vague, of the importance of fertile land to a Mexican peasant; the centripetal irony in (ii) relies on a basic awareness of the narrative form of the epic in literature; the centrifugal irony of (iii) is reinforced by the frustrated land demands of the characters within the text itself; the centrifugal irony of (iv) can only function with the text itself, which provides the basis for juxtaposition. Thus, centripetal and centrifugal ironies are not opposites but work along a continuum. Despite this, it is of heuristic use to mark out the general differences between these two ironic 'motions' in order to facilitate subsequent clarity on the discussion of the functions of irony. Again, an example sentence will be analysed in different ways.

In the following sentences, the irony in the second sentence is centripetal because it is dependent on the information, the ironic referent, which precedes it in the first: 'John tends to kill people at random. He's a nice chap.' The irony can therefore be contained within the two sentences, just as it can be contained within the confines of any given text. In Voltaire's *Candide*, the ironic referent is introduced by the philosopher Pangloss in the first chapter: 'It is clear, said he, that things cannot be otherwise than they are for since everything is made to serve an end, everything necessarily serves the best end.'[32] The rest of the novel is an attempt to undermine this notion by a process of *reductio ad absurdum* so that Pangloss's initial statement cannot be taken as the opinion of the author. The notion itself originates in the thinking of Leibniz but preknowledge of Leibniz hardly enhances the appreciation of the irony of the novel, as the object of irony is adequately summarised in the thoughts of Pangloss expressed in the first chapter and periodically thereafter. It is indeed often repeated at times of comical disaster, as an ironic counterpoint to these disasters. Therefore, the novel principally works 'inwards on itself', requiring the reader to spot ironic targets *within* the fiction, albeit with little effort, even if external targets also exist.

In the novel *Cinco horas con Mario* (1966) by Miguel Delibes, external referents are more important. In this work, the ironic referent is Carmen, the conservative, adulterous wife of the dead Mario, the liberal to whom she lectures during his wake on the evils of adultery, among other issues. Here, one referent is clearly defined: Carmen. Without explicit statement, the writer's message is that this woman is hypocritical; but the most important part of the message is that the society she represents is also hypocritical.

---

32 Voltaire, *Candide* [1759] (New York: W. W. Norton, 1991), p. 2. Translated by Robert M. Adams.

However, the words which he uses to convey this message are, in the main part, those of Carmen herself, which, if they are to be taken at face value, are regurgitated fascist propaganda – certainly not the actual opinions of the author.[33] The communication of the real opinion of the author via irony then becomes heavily dependent on both the efficacy of his techniques (the degree of 'ironic spin' (see below)), and the 'preknowledge' of the reader, who must be aware to an extent of the persecution of the left in Spain under Franco, its distrust of literature in general, its xenophobia and its use of empty slogans in propaganda. Without this knowledge, a layer of the irony is lost – the layer which takes its referents from 'outside' the fiction, from history and culture. Unlike that of *Candide*, then, this is an irony that works towards the 'outside', using the text as its centre, and thus relies on foreknowledge to an extent.

What if this foreknowledge does not exist? What else can the writer rely on to communicate an ironic message? Here the matter of ironic 'spin' is crucial. If the simple sentence 'John is a nice chap' is to be ironic (with no introduction or preceding, 'explanatory' sentence), there are only two feasible possibilities: either it presumes knowledge of John's true character on the part of the listener or it depends heavily on ironic inflection. There are two inter-related elements which are crucial to the functioning of centrifugal irony: the efficacy of ironic inflection, that is the technique used to convey the irony (for example, voice intonation and facial expression), and the ability of the listener to perceive the irony. The latter is dependent not only on foreknowledge but also on his or her receptiveness to and/or need for ironic inflection. For example, the sentence 'Hitler was a nice chap' barely needs to be emphasised ironically. On the other hand, if the listener has never heard of Hitler, he or she might need a little ironic suggestion. The ironist must judge the awareness of the recipient and deliver just the correct degree of ironic 'spin'. It is important to recognise too that the ironist is an ironist whether or not the recipient has understood the irony. For example, if the sentence 'Hitler was a nice chap' is uttered by a left-wing historian to an anti-Semitic fascist, it is possible that the latter, without a context or sufficient ironic 'spin', will miss the irony; but the opinion of the ironist clearly still stands and this opinion remains distinct from the words she or he has used.

Therefore, we distinguish between ironic communication and ironic perception: irony exists in both but, in the former, both perception and communi-

---

[33] According to Santos Sanz Villanueva, *Cinco horas con Mario* is 'uno de los alegatos más contundentes de nuestras letras contra el conservadurismo de las clases medias crecidas en el humus del nacionalcatolicismo'. See 'Miguel Delibes', in *Ensayo, Novelistas españoles del siglo XX* (Madrid: Fundación Juan March), August–September (2003), 3–14 (p. 9).

cation of that perception have taken place while, in the latter, the original perception remains even if the communication of it has been lost or, at the very least, complicated. Returning to fiction, for example, what if a reader does have foreknowledge but misses the intent of ironic inflection? In the novel *Memorias póstumas de Brás Cubas* (1881) by Machado de Assis, the attempt to present an ironic vision of the elite classes of Brazil was hampered by the fact that only elites were able to read and also because, although there would undoubtedly have been exceptions amongst the readership, the techniques used to convey the irony – which anticipated the modernism of the twentieth century – were too innovative to be widely appreciated and understood at the time. As Stephen M. Hart indicates, there is in this novel a certain breach of the 'rules' of communication via fiction, mirroring the deceit in the context of the theme of love: '[...] what is remarkable about this novel is that the deceit should also filter into the contract between reader and writer'.[34] An additional complicating factor in the communication of ironic meaning in this novel was perhaps the unwillingness of the highly privileged sectors of society to accept criticism, ironic in itself given that one of the targets of Machado's irony is their blind, complacent faith in themselves and their status. The book was largely forgotten until years later when it became considered a forerunner of the modern Latin American novel. It has since been accepted as a work of irony, proving that immediate, successful communication of ironic perception is not essential to the existence of irony. Thus, excluding the efforts of the author of this study, the absence of a specifically ironic interpretation of Rulfo's work does not preclude the existence of irony in his fiction.

The successful communication of ironic perception depends largely on the input of the reader and a careful balancing act that must be performed by the author. Part of the attraction of reading irony is the satisfaction the reader enjoys from discovering a second layer of meaning to the superficially obvious, the act of reconstructing meaning from the parts put before the reader. This is a technique which engages the author, text and reader in a kind of dialogue. We are asked to reject what we are being told on a paper-thin superficial level and to reconstruct the meaning ourselves, almost on an authorial level. The reader reacts positively to this challenge and enjoys plumbing the depths of the fiction through the unstated. The trick for the author, however, is this: if the gap between what is being said and what is meant to be discovered is too great, the reader will miss the intent; without a significant gap, however, there is no challenge for the reader and, therefore,

---

[34]   Stephen M. Hart, *A Companion to Latin American Literature* (Woodbridge: Tamesis, 2001), p. 132. See Chapter 2 of the present study for further discussion of the mechanisms of this deceit.

no enjoyment. It is along this tightrope, indeed, that the 'wobbles' associated with postmodern irony lie.

Postmodernism and the Politics of Irony

There is, for Richard Rorty, a sense in which all expressions of language are subject to contingent forces or contexts and that, therefore, no expression of language can lay claim to 'truth'.[35] This philosophy promotes, as Colebrook puts it, a belief not in objective truth or 'transcendental social judgement' but instead in 'the uncontrolled proliferation of language and texts'.[36] Insofar as the philosopher or writer needs to abstain from 'transcendental social judge-ment', we can be sure – as we have seen from the lack of 'editorial intrusion' – that Rulfo's irony is consistent with this technique of detachment and, as we shall see, in its non-insistence on the 'finality' of Western terms of reference. However, any consequent relativist insistence on the validity of *all* forms of language, without any ethical mediation, is dangerously close to Derrida's postmodern 'freeplay' in which, as Peter Barry recently noted, 'there are no absolutes or fixed points, so that the universe we live in is "decentred" or inherently relativistic'. The problem with such an approach is that ethical 'fixed points' can also fall by the wayside because, as Barry suggests, 'there is no longer any authoritative centre to which to appeal for validation of our interpretations'.[37] In her discussion of the violence in novels and films like Brett Easton Ellis's *American Psycho* (1991) and Quentin Tarantino's *Reservoir Dogs* (1992), Colebrook demonstrates one particular manifestation of the dilemma: 'Even if we were to decide that such works were ironic, how do we avoid the enjoyment, repetition and reinforcement of violence that these texts also make possible?'[38]

Linda Hutcheon makes this point in a different context by referring to a museum exhibit in Canada in which a white woman is seen to be 'teaching' indigenous people about washing clothes, the intention being to make visitors reflect on the condescending values of Western culture. However, the caption was minimal: 'Taken in Nigeria about 1910, this pharaoh shows missionary Mrs Thomas Titcombe giving African women "a lesson in how to wash clothes".' The intended verbal irony signalled by the quotation marks was barely or wrongly perceived by some and the irony was lost, with the result that complaints were made. This suggests a major problem in minimalist

---

[35] Rorty, p. 73.

[36] Colebrook, p. 156.

[37] Peter Barry, *Beginning Theory, An Introduction to Literary and Cultural Theory* (Manchester: Manchester University Press, 2002), p. 67.

[38] Colebrook, p. 158.

postmodern irony for, in this case, although colonialist thinking is intended to be presented ironically, the paradoxical result is a colonialist statement which fails to be questioned, thereby turning itself into a *validation* of colonialism. Indeed, for many African people, this exhibit was yet another example of colonial patronising. Referring to Bhabha's ideas on ambivalence, Hutcheon points out that this is an understandable reaction:

> If colonial discourse contains both colonizer and colonized, caught in a problematics of indeterminacy and ambivalence, then does this sort of irony re-enact (even as it critiques) 'an ambivalent mode of knowledge and power'. Does this particular irony embody Manichaean dualisms or subvert them? Or, does it depend on who is doing the interpreting?[39]

Drawing on Hutcheon's thoughts on the same event, Colebrook makes the following point in agreement: 'Unlike Rorty, Hutcheon recognises that such gestures of irony, far from avoiding the old myths of the West as the privileged viewpoint of reason, once again allow the West to speak in the absence of others.'[40]

For this reader, however, there is a possible solution to this dilemma. The centrifugal irony, i.e. the references to colonial patronising in the museum exhibit's caption that were intended as ironic, can only work if *centripetal* irony (or 'traditional irony' in Colebrook's terms) has been employed in order to produce interpretative possibilities beyond the literal. Centripetal irony is not postmodern: it is the bare mechanics of dramatic, verbal, situational and cosmic irony in the ways that I have described above. It takes simple literary mechanisms, which are on no account exclusively Western, to question language (as well as configurations of language such as romance, the epic, the tragedy, the comedy), and it therefore *prepares* the reader for centrifugal irony, which is more minimalist and closer to what is called postmodern irony. Indeed, if this centripetal irony is done well, there is no limit to the field of referents in centrifugal irony: it could be the rhetoric of a government or particular president, a discourse such as feminism or colonialism, or even – as with Rorty – all linguistic creations with their own separate contexts. Along the centripetal–centrifugal continuum, some referents are more centrifugal than others but all are accessible given enough readings of a text and enough effort to contextualise by attempting to inhabit other

---

[39] Linda Hutcheon, *Irony's Edge: The Theory and Politics of Irony* (London: Routledge, 1994), p. 193.
[40] Colebrook, p. 159.

contexts, as Eagleton proposes,[41] instead of simply ironising context altogether, as Rorty advises.

Thus, we may ask, what if the caption to the exhibit in the Canadian
museum to which Hutcheon refers had been prefaced with the following,
admittedly blunt, centripetal verbal irony: 'White woman teaching indigenous
people about hygiene, *of which they are clearly and completely ignorant*'?
The second clause is so clearly sarcastic as to encourage doubt about the
first, yet the intention of the original caption's postmodern irony to relativise
ethics is unaffected. Thus, verbal centripetal irony can be used *in the service*
of centrifugal irony. Another example is the ear-cutting scene in *Reservoir*
Dogs: its jaunty soundtrack, 'Stuck in the Middle with You' by Stealers
Wheel, is so incongruous as to induce in the viewer a sense of critical doubt
(rather than naked enjoyment) about the violence here and in the entire film.
Therefore, the re-enactment of the discourse being ironised is only a danger
to the extent that centripetal irony has not prepared the recipient for the questioning of that discourse. Indeed, as I shall proceed to argue in this book, the
violence in 'Acuérdate', 'El día del derrumbe', 'La cuesta de las comadres'
and *Pedro Páramo* is laden with centripetal ironies that serve the purposes
of the centrifugal ironies in those texts. Rulfo's work therefore successfully
meets the challenge of walking the ironic 'tightrope': the centripetal irony in
the texts mentioned is overt enough to alert the reader to the fact that there is
more to be understood from the text than meets the eye but covert enough to
train the reader to read between the lines in order to view that extra-textual
context for her- or himself, rather than simply having it spoon-fed.

---

[41] Terry Eagleton, *The Idea of Culture* (Oxford: Blackwell, 2000), p. 50.

2

Centripetal Irony in 'Nos han dado la tierra' and 'El día del derrumbe'

In Rulfo's fiction, there are few uncomplicated, linear narrative structures; the characters' lives are not dwelt upon, well-introduced or fully-drawn; sentences are kept to a syntactic minimum and dialogue, particularly, is given without much explanation. The result is an almost Borgesian disturbance of the reader's orientation which establishes, in turn, a certain aporia, or doubt, ensuring that we are alert to meanings beyond the literal. In many instances, these meanings are transparent, particularly where the ironic referent lies within the fiction itself (centripetally) but, as discussed in the previous chapter, Rulfo's irony also points to referents outside the scope of the fiction (centrifugally), chiefly the 'rhetoric of revolution' described later in the book. This referent is arguably more complex and inviting of critique but centripetal referents are just as important as they help to establish the ironic rapport of complicity between reader and writer which, in turn, facilitates the transfer of meaning in centrifugal irony. Therefore, in this chapter, I shall examine the operation of centripetal irony in two of Rulfo's short stories, particularly in their relationship with traditional modes of emplotment.

Hayden White argues that, on a 'deep level of consciousness', historians – as well as fiction writers – make use of four poetic modes of configuration (tropes) based on aesthetic or moral grounds with no epistemological basis: romance, comedy, tragedy and irony.[1] Romance represents a victory of 'good over evil, virtue over vice and light over darkness and of the ultimate transcendence of man over the world in which he was imprisoned by the Fall'.[2] On the other hand, comedy and tragedy are seen as qualifications of the naïve belief of romance in redemption; both accept conflict as inevitable but offer different consolations: in comedy, the reconciliation of social and natural forces symbolised in festive occasions at the end of narrative accounts; in tragedy, an enhanced awareness for those who have survived the struggles depicted, including the spectator or reader, of the harshness of

---

[1]   White, p. x.
[2]   White, p. 9.

'the law governing human existence which the protagonist's exertions against the world have brought to pass'.[3] In irony, however, this spirit of redemption is opposed by 'diremption', an apprehension of man as a *captive* of the world, its slave rather than its master, incapable of overcoming the darkness which has befallen him.[4] Irony therefore subverts established norms based on resolutions: 'stories cast in the Ironic mode ... gain their effects precisely by frustrating normal expectations about the kinds of resolutions provided by stories cast in other modes'.[5] If comedy and tragedy qualify romance, irony qualifies all of these as it indirectly asserts the naivety of *any* apprehension of the world (including irony) which assumes the ability of language to grasp 'reality'. It therefore represents 'a conviction that the world has grown old [and] "paints its gray on gray" in the awareness of its *own* inadequacy as an image of reality'.[6]

Whether it is presenting man as 'captive of the world', subverting established configurations of language or challenging language itself, the irony described by White is distinctly centripetal as it is characterised by an awareness of the inadequacy of literary norms rather than any specific socio-historical context. I would argue that, in 'Nos han dado la tierra' and 'El día del derrumbe', Rulfo's irony hints at this inadequacy by undermining forms associated with the tropes examined by White, namely the epic (associated with romance) and farce (associated with comedy) respectively. The romantic epic has been so prevalent in all fiction, Western or non-Western, that this irony operates on an unconscious level and the irony is therefore more centripetal than centrifugal. For David W. Price, the epic has in the past been considered the source of all narratives, and the relative merits of any narrative form, whether fictional or historical, in any given period has often rested on how justifiably it can claim to be the heir to this form.[7] If Price is correct, we can assume the reader reads with certain expectations of the epic, whether these are gleaned from the Bible, the *Bhagavad-Gita*, Homer's *Odyssey*, the Aztec migration myth or any story in which there is a journey in which some form of triumph over obstacles is key. Thereafter, such expectations become operative as assumptions that are not necessarily brought into the conscious mind but inform an act of interpretation, thus constituting an

---

3   White, p. 9.
4   For White, if irony is the 'linguistic protocol in which scepticism in thought and relativism in ethics are conventionally expressed', satire is its 'fictional form'. For my purposes, this is unnecessarily confusing: irony is indeed a sceptical mode of apprehending the world, with 'satire' being merely one (not the only) fictional form of this. See White, pp. 37–38.
5   White, p. 8.
6   White, p. 10. Emphasis by White.
7   David W. Price, *History Made, History Imagined, Contemporary Literature, Poiesis, and the Past* (Urbana: University of Illinois Press, 1999), pp. 19–20.

interpretative framework or norm. In my interpretation of the story 'Nos han dado la tierra', the challenge to the romantic epic is mediated through bathos and catachresis.

Bathos and Catachresis in 'Nos han dado la tierra'

The 'tierra' in the title of this story is not immediately ironic because the reader does not yet know its referent; rather, the irony begins in the first paragraph with a questioning tone, established through bathos: 'Después de tantas horas de caminar sin encontrar ni una sombra de árbol, ni una semilla de árbol, ni una raíz de nada, se oye el ladrar de los perros' (39). The repetition of 'ni' and the rhythm of the three objects which are not found make this first sentence monotonous and almost self-negatory, a tone reinforced with the word 'nada', which appears four times in the first hundred words. On the same first page, 'nada' is associated with the word 'nudo', suggesting that the small knot of a minority who have survived the futile trek across the plain feel negated, made 'nada': 'Hace rato, como a eso de las once, éramos veinti-tantos; pero puñito a puñito se han ido desperdigando hasta quedar *nada* más este *nudo* que somos nosotros' (39).[8] This self-negating tone acquires further ironic value in relation to the *delegado*'s promise of fertile land, as that internal referent comes into ever-sharper focus in the rest of the story. The bathos in this vision of growing nothingness culminating in the nega-tion of the self therefore has a function: it is a form of verbal irony directed specifically against a *configuration* of language, the epic model of fiction in which the norm is a progression, the very inverse of bathos, towards triumph over obstacle. I shall return to this function of bathos but, for the purposes of the current argument, I would like to explore how it is aided by another key tool in Rulfo's ironic armour: catachresis.

Irony, according to White, undermines language in configurations such as romance, comedy and tragedy by '[pointing] to the potential foolishness of all linguistic characterizations of reality as much as to the absurdity of the beliefs it parodies'.[9] The emblem of the 'sophisticated' trope of irony, rather than the more 'confident' metaphor, metonymy or synecdoche, is catachresis, or linguistic 'misuse', such as in the 'manifestly absurd' mixed metaphor 'blind mouths'.[10] The dictionary sense of the term is the misapplication of words, due to an erroneous perception of their meanings and to their prox-imity in sound, for example, luxuriant for luxurious. For literary purposes, and for ours here, it is any word or combination of words in which language

[8]   Emphasis added.
[9]   White, p. 37.
[10] White, p. 34.

is *deliberately* 'misused' in a way that alerts the reader to the questionability of any literal interpretation, thus inducing aporia.[11] For example, the deliberate and illogical juxtaposition of senses in a phrase such as 'blind mouths' puts the reader on a plane of meaning production that invites questioning of language itself. This is a kind of verbal irony where no obvious target or referent is apparent, yet the reader's orientation has been undermined, forcing her or him to interpret and assess the text more independently, much as a similar 'misuse' of a linguistic configuration, such as the epic here configured as a journey of nothingness, can disorientate and force an interrogative posture towards the epic form as a whole.

The concern of this argument now is to examine the precise relationship between bathos and catachresis in 'Nos han dado la tierra'. As mentioned previously, the principal motif of the epic is the journey, with attendant connotations of struggle and romantic conquest, whether spiritual, moral or physical. Here, the journey is a process of almost masochistic self-denial and the conquest is that of empty, infertile territory, all of which is expressed through bathos but also, and perhaps most clearly, in an example of catachresis on the second page:

> Cae una gota de agua, grande, gorda, haciendo un agujero en la tierra y dejando una plasta como la de un salivazo. Cae sola ... Y a la gota caída *por equivocación* se la come la tierra y la desaperece en su sed. (40, emphasis added)

Here, there is catachresis in the deliberate misapplication of the phrase 'por equivocación' or 'by mistake', which is strictly illogical and certainly not metaphorical (there is no 'como si'). Yet, it could not possibly be taken literally and, whilst it seems to be verbally ironic, it has no obvious 'target': who could have made this 'mistake' and why? The raindrop itself? Such a phrase forces us to confront the language used, to ask questions of it. In this case, we discover through our own interpretation that the function of this disturbingly cruel use of 'por equivocación' is to reassert the feeling of wasted effort which pervades the entire story: the motif of triumph over obstacle, a vindicated journey, is replaced with the sense of a pathetic and humiliating error. Just as the raindrop falls mistakenly on the Llano, the peasants – equally pathetically and insignificantly – have been 'dumped' here. If a mistake has been made, it appears to be made by nature itself or, in another potential interpretation, possibly by the Aztec sun god Huitzolopochtli, which

---

[11] In Baldick, *Concise Oxford Dictionary of Literary Terms*, p. 17, aporia is 'a point at which a text's self-contradictory meanings can no longer be resolved, or at which the text undermines its own most fundamental presuppositions'.

would add a strong note of cosmic irony to the story. A further interpretation could attribute this cosmic force to the state, rather than nature, for it is the state which has apparently dumped the peasants here. These interpretations can only convert the catechresis into the more confident emblem of a 'metaphor' if, and only if, in the absence of an obvious target for this misuse of the words 'por equivocación', and due to the lack of editorial intrusion, we the readers (and not the writer necessarily) make the effort to *look* for these possible metaphors. Through the application of catachresis, therefore, we are encouraged to discover meanings for ourselves.

Just as catachresis forces us to create meanings, bathos in this story forces us to discover the reason for this journey of hope against hope. We discover this reason only half-way through the story. The story doubles back to a time before the journey began and we find out that the peasants had been offered land by the government apparently in return for participation in a military struggle. Thus, the information we receive is offered back-to-front: we are told *of* the journey before we are told of the reason *for* the journey. Having first allowed the reader, through bathos and catachresis, to experience the sense of pointlessness which the peasants themselves feel on an immediate level, Rulfo encourages us, half-way through the story, to view the government *delegado*'s comments with scepticism. When the *delegado* glibly announces that they have been granted 'todo el llano grande' – the vast, infertile plain described in the first two pages – we are able to understand more completely the emptiness of meaning in this grand characterisation. The peasants, meanwhile, begin to separate the literal meaning ('lots of land') from the meaning perceived ('no land because it is all too dry') in a process that mimics catachresis. What we do with Rulfo's seemingly incongruous use of the phrase 'por equivocación', the peasants do with the *delegado*'s illogical use of the word 'tierra'. That is to say that both the peasant and the reader respond with puzzlement, questioning and (re)interpretation.

The *delegado*'s use of the word 'tierra' is a disingenuous allusion to the letter of the law ('any land') rather than its spirit ('fertile land'). The response of the peasants is unconcealed disappointment and they request instead 'la tierra buena' (41). But the supplication falls on deaf ears and the *delegado*'s faintly disguised mockery continues: 'No se vayan a asustar por tener tanto terreno para ustedes solos ... son miles y miles de yuntas' (42). The peasants continue to protest but the *delegado* shuts them out: 'no nos quiso oír' (42). The response to this non-communication is not further supplication or complaint but another instance of verbal irony, this time by the peasants themselves, in the almost sarcastic use of the word 'tierra': 'Así nos han dado esta tierra' and, later, 'Ésta es la tierra que nos han dado' (42). However, this is not truly sarcasm for there is no bitter or aggressive comedy here. Instead, it seems that the peasants are gradually reinterpreting the word 'tierra', or expanding their understanding of it, and somehow resigning themselves to this new interpretation. The word 'tierra' here is like an echo, devoid of its literal meaning and consequently of any substance: the peasants fill the gaps just as we do with the words 'por equivocación'. In the story itself, meanwhile, communication has simply been stifled, recalling an earlier description of the difficulty of talking on the plain:

> Uno platica aquí y las palabras se calientan en la boca con el calor de afuera, y se le resecan a uno en la lengua hasta que acaban con el resuello.
> Aquí así son las cosas. Por eso a nadie le da por platicar. (40)

The only other possibility for productive communication is the written word, as the *delegado* says of their protests: 'Eso manifiéstenlo por escrito' (42). He surely knows that these peasants are illiterate and barely likely to risk the little they do have by challenging the government officially. This particular piece of advice delivers a cruel, situational irony: the peasants can only complain in writing; but they cannot write.

After this interlude referring to a time previous to the journey, the feeling of bathos in the text is 'fulfilled' at the end as the group relinquish their rights to the land they have been given and head for the town they finally reach. Their future remains uncertain, thus providing an end which also jars with that of the classical epic in which triumph of one sort or another is the final note. The one character who refuses to submit to the fate of the peasants is Esteban, who has carried his hen the entire length of the journey, not for sustenance but 'para cuidarla' (43), carefully holding it and waving hot air into its mouth in a pathetic effort to save it from asphyxiation in the heat. Earlier in the story, we are told how even lizards shun the heat of the plain to hide in their nests. We are therefore invited to consider the further situational irony that, while the government sends citizens to lands from which animals recoil, Esteban touchingly looks after his hen to the last. However, he is seen as eccentric, at best, for doing so and the implication is perhaps that one either submits or becomes insane for resisting. There is none of the consciousness-raising cathartic effect associated with tragedy; instead, the sense of 'finality' in such an ending is replaced by a question mark, which brings to mind Carlos Fuentes's remark about how the twentieth-century Latin American text has come to be a way of asking questions, through 'la complejidad dialéctica', rather than providing answers in the form of 'el simplismo épico'.[12]

---

[12] Carlos Fuentes, *La nueva novela hispanoamericana* (Mexico City: Cuadernos Joaquín Mortiz, 1969), p. 13.

The precise nature of the questions asked by the text depends on the path a given interpretation takes, which can change from reader to reader, but there is no doubt that the word 'tierra' is central to this story. On a centripetal level, Rulfo reveals the abuse of the word by the *delegado*, shattering its link to expected meanings: the land given is not useful, as the peasants are led to expect, but utterly hostile to cultivation. On this centripetal level, the catachresis in the word 'tierra' elicits both in the peasants and in Rulfo's reader forms of perception that focus on the ironic rather than literal nature of the word. Of course, in the centrifugal dimension, Rulfo's 'tierra' can be placed in the context of meanings associated with and operative within the rhetoric of Revolution, as in the battle cry '¡Tierra y Libertad!', where 'Tierra' is understood as an economic resource, a factor of production (useful land), as well as a corollary of freedom. Yet, in this story, 'tierra' is shown to have another, emptier meaning, one which equates to nothingness. Within the confines of the text, it stands as an almost silent denunciation of the rhetoric of the *delegado*, whether or not the reader is aware of the wider, historical referent which is the rhetoric of the Mexican Revolution. Rulfo thus generates a powerful centripetal irony conveyed through the incomprehension of the peasants and the cruel reference to a single drop of rain that can only fall on the Llano 'por equivocación'. This catachresis may only be a hinge that opens a door from the centripetal to the centrifugal dimension but its existence is crucial to both.

Comedy and the Rhetoric of Revolution in 'El día del derrumbe'

In 'El día del derrumbe', a governor visits a rural town in the aftermath of an earthquake during the post-Revolutionary period. The language and farce in this story point to a comic mode of configuration, as I argue below, but, instead of the reconciliation expected of endings in the trope of comedy, there is a brawl. In 'Nos han dado la tierra', a kind of verbal irony related to catachresis is the response to the mockery of the *delegado*; in this instance, we are a stage further removed from communication in that, while the governor's speech is ironically devoid of real meaning (as are the words of the *delegado*), so too is the response of the audience and particularly that of the drunkard shouting '¡Exacto!' The result of non-communication in the first story is an atmosphere in which talking makes one feel as though one were suffocating, especially in the heat of the plain. Here, the metaphor for a breakdown in communication is not suffocating heat but a riot: 'La cosa es aquello, en lugar de ser una visita a los dolientes y a los que habían perdido sus casas se convirtió en una borrachera de las buenas' (154).

In the very first page, the comedy trope is signalled by a discussion relating to the date and place of the earthquake. This conversation is so absurd as to be comic (how do the two characters manage to forget the date and place of such a catastrophic event?) but if, for Shakespeare, Molière and Dickens, comedy ends in festive reconciliation which affords the feeling of finality, in Rulfo's story, we have a kind of counter-comedy, subverting the expectations associated with this narrative form, just as 'Nos han dado la tierra' does with those associated with the romantic epic. For even the version of comedy that is farce usually ends with some resolution but, in this case, when the drunkard pulls out a gun and starts shooting, there is a catastrophic lack of communication. This centripetal challenge to the comic mode, specifically to its need for resolution, is much more than a manifestation of Hayden White's largely centripetal 'diremption'. As hinted by the ironic icing on the cake which is the playing of the national anthem during the riot, it prepares us for Rulfo's (centrifugal) critique of the rhetoric of Revolution, which is satirised quite openly in this story, to the extent that the subversion of the comic trope runs parallel to the subversion of post-Revolutionary rhetoric.

As with 'Nos han dado la tierra', a great deal of the onus is placed on the reader to interpret the irony. 'El día del derrumbe' unfolds through a dialogue between two men, Melitón and an unnamed narrator. The circumstances of the two characters are not dwelt on by Rulfo: we are not told their age or anything else about their background save that Melitón was once a municipal president and, in the last paragraph, that the narrator has a wife and a child who was born on the same day as the earthquake. Neither are we given details of the audience or the circumstances in which the dialogue takes place. The lack of information means that we are forced to readjust our focus from the characters to the story they are telling. We have, in effect, become eavesdroppers receiving information and surmising what is not told in order to inform further information we are given. This is no minor challenge for Rulfo's readers as, having read the title 'El día del derrumbe', they find in the first few lines that the narrator is unable to give the basic information of which year (either the last or the year before) and in which town (either Tuzacacuense or Pochote) he experienced the earthquake, though he thinks he can remember that people ran towards a church when it began. Thus, the comedy of the story, like the tragedy in 'Nos han dado la tierra', lies initially in the space between our expectations, based on the title, and what we then read. This comic configuration is reinforced not only by the farce at the end, but also more subtly by the humorous language of the unnamed narrator, the details of the story and the technique of juxtaposition.

As we shall see, the ironic device of juxtaposition, particularly, enables Rulfo to critique centripetally a formulaic, cliché-ridden post-Revolutionary rhetoric with the result that any reader who is unaware of this discourse is immediately apprised of its vacuousness. The narrator, on the other hand, employs a localised, colloquial lexis ('catrincito', 'chacamotas', 'lambiscones', 'melcocha' etc.) and his expression is lively and subtle, the verbal irony particularly pointed and dry when referring to the objective of the governor's visit: 'En viniendo él, todo se arregla, y la gente, aunque se le haya caído la casa encima, queda muy contenta con haberlo conocido' (152). We then appreciate the implicit situational irony in the narrator's description of the visit during which, instead of helping victims, commiserating gravely with the inhabitants and suggesting rebuilding plans, the governor nonchalantly sits down with his entourage for a slap-up meal of tortillas and guacamole in view of a highly excited crowd:

> La gente que estaba que se le reventaba el pescuezo de tanto estirarlo para poder ver al gobernador y haciendo comentarios de cómo se había comido el guajalote y de que si había chupado los huesos y de cómo era de rápido para levantar una tortilla tras otra rociándolas con salsa de guacamole; en todo se fijaron. Y él tan tranquilo, tan serio, limpiándose las manos en los calcetines para no ensuciar la servilleta que sólo le sirvió para espovorearse de vez en cuando los bigotes. (152–53)

The satirical target here is unclear for we have, on the one hand, a supposedly naïve and excitable audience and, on the other, the delicate, educated manners of a feasting governor who ignores them. The question of who to laugh at is not at all clear at this stage and this is partly due to the lack of any obvious editorial intrusion. There are no pauses so we are never allowed to stop to engage with a mediating author and our resulting involvement in the text gives us the illusion that we are interpreting its content by ourselves. The description thus conforms to irony in Frye's terms as 'a dispassionate construction of a literary form, with all assertive elements, implied or expressed, eliminated'.[13] Of course, Rulfo is implying a moral judgement through the narrator's words but the point is that the authorial voice does not penetrate the dialogue in any clearly attributable form. Such editorial commentary would be a type of 'empirical' data and the lack of it implants the story in the field of myth, fable and oral history. Indeed, when Melitón is asked by the narrator to recite the governor's speech, it is because he is 'bueno para eso de la memoria' (153), suggesting the vitality of oral history. In a narrow sense, oral history is unreliable, for we know by now that the narrator is not sure of the date or place of the earthquake; however, we begin to adjust our interpretation of his recollections from an interest in the details to a fascination – instead – with the seemingly alien *values* of the governor.

There is now an even greater distance between what we expect from the story's title and what we are now reading, for it all seems to have less and less

---

[13] Frye, pp. 40–41.

to do with the earthquake itself. This is, of course, similar to our experience of 'Nos han dado la tierra', even if the distance here is comedic rather than tragic. In the same way that we are encouraged to ascertain new meanings in the gap between our expectations and reality in 'Nos han dado la tierra', here we are invited to explore meanings within the comedic space between, on the one hand, the title of the story and, on the other, the events that follow as well as the style in which it is presented. The 'emprical facts' of history which constitute one (limited) referential field, and which we initially expect in this story in the form of dates and places, seem in the end far less important than details such as the recollection that people ran towards a church. Once we accept this aversion to accuracy as valid and, indeed, revealing, the narrator's unreliable memory is not important for, even if people did not in fact run towards a church, it is clearly what the narrator *believes* they would have done in such a situation. Rulfo is therefore communicating a historical truth which is, in this case, to do with religious beliefs.

In Ricoeur's terms, this is a poietic story, a text which, according to Price, 'instead of merely copying the real [...] attempt[s] to annihilate it by expanding the referential field in order to effect what Ricoeur calls a mimesis that is a poiesis, a creative construction that grounds the possibility of critique'.[14] The truths of fiction belong to a second-order referential field of the imagination which casts aspersions on the first-order referential field of historical 'fact' described in 'empirical' terms as dates, places, deeds and motives. The chief method by which Rulfo achieves this critique of the first-order referential field is by ironic juxtaposition, a key technique of what Frye calls 'sophisticated' irony and the 'avoidance of direct statement': 'The practice of cutting out predication, of simply juxtaposing images without making any assertions about their relationship is consistent with the effort to avoid oratorical rhetoric.'[15] Whilst Rulfo employs this technique himself, it is not with any lofty implication that only his privileged, educated position allows him to do so; for he readily allows his rural, uncouth narrator to employ the same technique, for example in the passage quoted above where he contrasts the excitable rural crowd with the urbane governor during the meal. Yet, the structure of the story belies Rulfo's careful, authorial control of the irony. For example, it is through the juxtaposition of the title, which is dramatic and specific, with the first few lines of dialogue, in which we are denied drama and specificity, that one ironic referent becomes clear: our very own understanding of what constitutes history.

On a less general level, as mentioned previously, Rulfo also encourages

---

14 Price, p. 45.
15 *The Anatomy of Criticism, Four Essays by Northrop Frye* (Princeton: University of Princeton Press, 1957), p. 61.

the reader to consider the contrast between the mystifying rhetoric of Revolution and the narrator's clear and humorous narration. His mastery of juxtaposition not only helps to critique general perceptions of history but also, more specifically, the post-Revolutionary rhetoric of those who pretend to have control over it, though – crucially, for the argument in this chapter – without requiring the reader to have any direct knowledge of this discourse from the first-order referential field. The nonsensical syntax and vocabulary of the governor's rhetoric, which should really include condolences to victims and offers of support, becomes apparent to us as soon as he is invited to speak. Here, we are dependent on Melitón's memory, which is clearly not verbatim (and need not be for the reasons given above) but spiced with affectation and humour:

> Conciudadanos – dijo –. Rememorando mi trayectoria, vivificando el único proceder de mis promesas. Ante esta tierra que visité como anónimo compañero de un candidato a la Presidencia, cooperador omnímodo de un hombre representativo, cuya honradez no ha estado nunca desligada del contexto de sus manifestaciones políticas y que sí, en cambio, es firme glosa de principios democráticos en el supremo vínculo de unión con el pueblo, aunando a la austeridad de que ha dado muestras la síntesis evidente de idealismo revolucionario nunca hasta ahora pleno de realizaciones y de certidumbre. (155)

Melitón's memory configures the governor's words as a mish-mash of the kind of rhetoric to which the peasants had been exposed in the aftermath of the Revolution, in other words language designed to persuade people that the radical goals of the 1917 constitution are being met. The very first word ('conciudadanos') invites inclusion of the audience while the following words evoke a jarring, alien, revolutionary ideology: 'honradez', 'principios democráticos', 'unión con el pueblo' and 'idealismo revolucionario'. These words stand out as mere soundbites in a syntactically incomprehensible speech which bears little relationship to the issues which must concern the inhabitants of the town: casualties, ruined buildings and homelessness. Instead, the speech is justification for a single person to be dined by the very people who need this help: of course, he is a man full of promises 'rememorando [su] trayectoria' and he once accompanied a presidential candidate to this area, don't you know! Thus, we interpret the governor's speech as a deliberate attempt to pound out soundbites while glorifying himself and avoiding real issues. This is true even when he belatedly discusses the topic of aid:

> Concurrimos en el auxilio, no con el deseo neroniano de gozarnos en la desgracia ajena, mas aún, inminentemente dispuestos a utilizar munífica-mente nuestro esfuerzo en la reconstrucción de los hogares destruidos,

hermanalmente dispuestos en los consuelos de los hogares menoscabados por la muerte. (156)

The language here is designed to enable the 'fudging' of the issue of aid at a later date: 'neroniano' is a word which will go over the heads of everyone; 'nuestro esfuerzo' is an effort, not a promise; and 'dispuestos' is disposed, not 'resueltos' (determined). Nevertheless, in an example of situational irony, the speaker seems spurred on by two instances of incomprehension which he takes for support – first, the applause which punctuates the speech, and second, the sporadic cries of '¡Exacto!' from a drunk who has clearly not understood it. Thus, he strides from obfuscation to hyperbolic offers of support which, though grandiose, ring decidedly hollow in the context of an uncomprehending audience, whilst the words 'esta hecatombe nunca predecida ni deseada' sound somewhat fatuous in the wake of an earthquake:

> Os ayudaremos con nuestro poder. Las fuerzas vivas del Estado desde su faldisterio claman por socorrer a los damnificados de esta hecatombe nunca predecida ni deseada. Mi regencia no terminará sin haberos cumplido. (156)

The emptiness of this rhetoric is even clearer when juxtaposed with the honest, humorous and unfettered language of the narrator. The rhetoric of the governor, as we have seen, is impersonal and humourless and therefore devoid of power. On the other hand, Melitón and the narrator communicate to their audience on an informal, imaginative level:

> – Traía geólogo y gente conocedora, no crean ustedes que venía solo. Oye, Melitón, ¿como cuánto dinero nos costó darles de comer a los acompañantes del gobernador?
> – Algo así como cuatro mil pesos.
> – Y eso que nomás estuvieron un día y en cuanto se les hizo de noche se fueron, si no, quién sabe hasta qué alturas hubiéramos salido desfalcados. (152)

The use of phrases such as 'no crean ustedes que', 'Oye', 'algo así como', 'y eso que', 'quién sabe qué' are colloquial and help to make the rhythm of the language mimic that of natural conversation. This is the medium through which, in the space of a few lines, the two characters demonstrate powerfully the *waste* of money involved in the governor's visit. This waste we contrast with the complete absence of a clear commitment to *pledge* money for victims of the earthquake, in the speech of the governor. Thus, the juxtaposition of two types of language becomes in itself a vehicle for conveying a message about the values of the post-Revolutionary regime. The governor must believe he has used fine, educated and therefore powerful language, even though he has merely given the impression that the simple renewal of Revolutionary promises represents their fulfilment.

While the governor seems unable to communicate to his audience and the latter give out drunken, uncomprehending messages to him, between Melitón and the narrator an effective dialogue unfolds in the story in the sense that it gradually discloses the 'truth' about the day of the earthquake. This type of truth is not one that can be obtained through the archival study of speeches or even the horror stories of the victims, for it lies within the second-order referential field that can best be accessed by literature, especially when it creates an interpretative space in which expectations are subverted, in this case the resolution and reconciliation expected of comedy. The 'truth' is the existence of hypocrisy, greed and egotism on the part of the governor and, on the part of the narrator, warmth, humour and imagination as well as a certain callousness (we learn at the end that he left his wife – not untypically, it might be added – to look after the birth of their son by herself). Thus, the conversation created by Rulfo serves as a type of model, an attempt to encourage communication and interpretation through the medium of informal dialogue using local norms rather than meaningless and predictable alternatives, whether these be literary forms such as comedy or political discourses such as post-Revolutionary rhetoric. It barely needs repeating that the reader requires no recourse to centrifugal, extra-textual referents to come to this conclusion.

The Rhetoric of Revolution 'Outside' the Text

One of the best exponents of centripetal/centrifugal motions of irony is Machado's *Memorias póstumas de Bras Cubas* (1881) which, in a foreword to a translation published in 1982, Rulfo praises particularly for its use of irony.[16] There are two distinct projections of the protagonist: Bras Cubas the dead narrator and Bras Cubas the living character qua character, the nineteenth-century Brazilian pseudo-aristocrat. The relationship between the two is enriched by a reading of Roberto Schwarz's discussion of ideology in *Misplaced Ideas* (1992). Against the philosophical background of Comtian positivism, political relationships were modernised without disrupting the system of favours which governed socio-economic relationships in general, thus providing a 'smoke screen' of rationality for any arbitrariness. This is what Schwarz terms 'an ideology of the second degree': one which not only fails to reflect reality but also, unlike European liberalism, fails adequately

---

[16] Juan Rulfo, Foreword, in *Memorias póstumas de Bras Cubas* (Mexico City: SEP-Universidad Nacional Autónoma de México, 1982), pp. 1–4.

to disguise it. Nonetheless, the elites, although unaware of the true nature
of the smoke screen, rigorously maintained it, feeding a shifting ground of
misleading ideas: 'Thus one could methodically call dependence independence, capriciousness utility, exceptions universality, kinship merit, privilege
equality, and so on.' This unconscious pretence was nurtured in the elitist
newspapers which professed Enlightenment ideals, in the architecture which
masked old buildings with superficial European façades and even in the more
formal behaviour of the Court. It was apparent also in the way that writers
like Silvio Romero attempted to establish the 'national spirit' by replacing
one European literary fashion, romanticism, with another, realism.[17]

In such an atmosphere, imported modes of behaviour, speech and style
became the signs of a national charade apparent only to a minority of individuals that included intellectuals such as Machado de Assis. In his novel,
then, Bras Cubas the dead narrator critiques the deficiencies of the literary
modes of romanticism and realism, the prevailing trends of Machado's time,
thereby satirising not only the romanticist and realist narrative of Bras Cubas
the character, indicating in the process the futility of *all* such configurations,
but also the character himself and the class he represents at a specific time in
Brazilian history. The result is an internally contextualised satire in which the
targets are obvious (to all but the targets themselves), although they are even
more clearly distinguished with centrifugal references to history.

In the work of Rulfo, we are not handed a split character with whom to
form such a discerning understanding of language, on the one hand, and
specific ironic targets, on the other. Yet, if we do not gain such an understanding, I would suggest that some of the power of his work is lost. It is in
Rulfo's linguistically intensive style of irony, less overtly satirical than that
of Machado but awash with verbal ironies, that the author's intent is clear. As
we have seen, the two texts we have analysed demonstrate *within themselves*
that they are cast in an ironic mode. We can see that no fore-knowledge of
referents outside the stories is required in order to understand their ironic
content. Unlike more satirical fiction, such as that of Machado de Assis,
this does not mean that Rulfo has had to make his ironic referents clear to
the reader; indeed, the latter, far from being allowed to share in the understanding of the irony without effort, is expected to produce ironic meaning.
Thus, in Frye's terms, we can characterise Rulfo's irony as 'sophisticated'
(lacking editorial intrusion) and, in the context of White's schema, we can see
that there is a rejection of established narrative norms and that 'diremption'
replaces redemption in romance (in the form of the epic) and in comedy (in

---

[17] Robeto Schwartz, 'Misplaced Ideas: Literature and Society in Late-Nineteenth-Century
Brazil', in *Misplaced Ideas: Essays on Brazilian Culture* (London and New York: Verso, 1992),
pp. 23–27.

the form of farce). By implication, of course, there is a rejection of historical narrative in general.

Nevertheless, there is clearly more to the irony than this, for Rulfo's work contains 'concrete' historical references. For Price, the value of a historical novel is not in its ability to 'unveil the hidden power structures of history or reveal the institutional forces that shaped the past, nor … seek to discover the slow evolutionary processes of history'.[18] This is the task, more commonly associated with what we may call conventional history, that draws on the first-order referential field mentioned in the above discussion. Instead, 'true narrations' are those which 'engage in speculations that make possible a *critique* of accepted versions of history, a critique that challenges us to refigure our images of the past and configure possible histories for the future'.[19] Thus, in order to explore Rulfo's irony a stage further, we must accept that his texts refer to an *extra-textual* 'reality' which belongs to what is commonly termed 'history'. In the case of 'Nos han dado la tierra', for example, there is a clear reference to the post-Revolutionary programme of agrarian reform and, in 'El día del derrumbe', the obvious empirical referent is revolutionary rhetoric itself.

The centrifugal referents in Rulfo's work lie hidden in the type of rhetoric found in the governor's speech in 'El día del derrumbe' and in the *delegado*'s mockery in 'Nos han dado la tierra': the sanctity of the Mexican Revolution and the institutions it produced; post-Revolutionary land reform and educational initiatives; the dismantling of local economic power structures and the attack on provincial Catholicism. The forms in which these ideas manifest themselves include, among others, revolutionary speeches, government posters, murals, school text books and the secularisation of national calendars. The picture is never complete, therefore, with centripetal irony alone yet, as we have seen, the mechanics of centrifugal irony demand that a rapport of trust and shared outlook exist between reader and writer and this depends on centripetal irony. This trust is perhaps easy enough to generate with somebody who is from a similar location and politically likeminded but can it transcend cultural boundaries?

As I stated earlier, Rulfo's work has been translated across the world in countries as different as Norway, Greece, China and Japan. The translator of the Japanese version, Akira Sugiyama, in an interview with Víctor Jiménez, gives one clue as to how trust can be generated across such diverse cultures through recognisable themes: '[Cuando] uno lee a Rulfo en Japón recuerda un mundo perdido, y es muy interesante para nosotros. Nos hace recordar

---

18 Price, p. 45.
19 Price, p. 47. Emphasis added.

el mundo que existía también aquí en otro tiempo, o que todavía sobrevive en algunos lugares.'[20] I would suggest that, in addition to this thematic resonance in countries outside of Mexico, Rulfo's work forms initial relationships with such diverse readerships through form, specifically by means of the kind of centripetal ironies we have examined in this chapter. For example, when Jiménez asks about the difficulty of translating Rulfo's style, 'lleno de todas esas alusiones', Sugiyama posits that Rulfo's famously sparse prose has a certain resonance too: '[Es un estilo] lacónico, y muy intuitivo, que obliga al lector a usar toda su imaginación [...] Hay un parentesco, entonces, en la manera de expresarse de Rulfo y la expresión en japonés.'[21] For the purposes of my argument, however, the main attraction that Rulfo's fiction has for readers from every background is the intuitive feeling that centripetal readings are not enough, that the work needs to be revisited and that each time it is revisited, something new is gleaned as a result. More specifically, and as we will see in the chapters that follow, the more we know about the rhetoric of revolution, the more complex the irony becomes.

---

[20] Víctor Jiménez, 'Juan Rulfo en Japón', in *Los Murmullos, Boletín de la Fundación Juan Rulfo* (Mexico City: Quadrata) 1 (1999), 14–35 (p. 21).
  [21] Ibid., p. 20.

3

Centrifugal Irony and 'La Unidad Nacional'

My main concern thus far has been centripetal irony in Rulfo's work. In this chapter, and in the chapters that follow, the focus will shift towards centrifugal irony and the revolutionary rhetoric which is its target. This rhetoric has at least been referred to within the two stories discussed so far ('Nos han dado la tierra' and 'El día del derrumbe'). But, if we are to examine Rulfo's complex deployment of irony even more closely, a much deeper understanding of this referent (in the form of post-Revolutionary speeches, posters, murals, textbooks etc.) is crucial. An appraisal of Mexican revolutionary rhetoric which has been particularly helpful to me is that provided by Edwin Williamson:

> In effect, appeals to the spirit of the Revolution could function as a transcendent sanction for political power ... The state thereby acquired a mystique which the illiterate multitudes found easier to sympathize with than such bloodless liberal abstractions as 'the sovereignty of the people'.[1]

Of the various aspects of this 'transcendent sanction for political power', I would like to start with the most obvious: nationalism. In this chapter, I shall examine the ways in which Rulfo's fiction ironises campaigns for national unity in the rhetoric of the post-Revolutionary government (1920–55).[2]

   In the post-Revolutionary period, cultural nationalism was a political and economic goal of successive governments and therefore a key element of the rhetoric of revolution. However, it seems a half-hearted and cosmetic project in hindsight, as Blanco Aguinaga points out: 'Los murales, el cine, las novelas que podían haber tenido sentido en tiempos de Cárdenas, no

---

[1]   *The Penguin History of Latin America* (London: Penguin, 1992), p. 391.
[2]   The inaugural year of Álvaro Obregón's government, 1920, is seen by most historians as the start of the post-Revolutionary period. In retrospect, the institutional phase of the revolution has been said to begin in 1946, though this would not necessarily have been obvious at the time that Rulfo was writing his work (1940s and 1950s). For this reason, I define the 'post-Revolutionary' period as 1920–55, that is to say, up to the date of publication of Rulfo's second and final major work, *Pedro Páramo*.

son ya sino retórica frente a la realidad.'[3] Indeed, many of Rivera's murals of the 1920s are incongruously optimistic portrayals of a Marxist past and future; the national ballet projected, and continues to project, a stereotyped and folkloristic image of the indigenous population, as well as the peasantry in general; the school textbooks of Cárdenas's administration displayed in both text and illustrations a democratic and socially just vision of Mexico that was impossible to achieve; the governments of the 1940s and 1950s, finally, were quite unabashedly duplicitous in their insistence on, and conflation of, national unity and 'cooperation' between employers and workers. Throughout, concepts concerning ethnic solidarity, 'family' and rural support for the party were key to this rhetoric.

These unifying efforts were necessary in the tense and volatile atmosphere created by the Revolution but they are critiqued in the ironic prose of Rulfo. In 'La cuesta de las comadres', the permanence of violence, patriarchal hierarchy and disunity in the countryside is implicitly contrasted with the revolutionary, democratic and unifying aura of the word 'reparto'. In 'Acuérdate', the hollowness of a national unity campaign based on the concept of the national family is exposed in a tale which stresses the lack of dialogue in a violent, patriarchal society. In fragment 48 of *Pedro Páramo*, where we shall begin, Rulfo's portrayal of an indigenous community is entirely at odds with the nationalistic, participatory and economically vibrant image projected by the government. Although Rulfo makes use of centripetal verbal, situational and cosmic ironies in these texts, the main thrust of the irony is centrifugal because the referents lie in the rhetoric of the post-Revolutionary government. As we have seen in the previous chapter, centripetal irony performs the function of awakening the reader's interest in what is not said in the text and thereby facilitating the transfer, on more detailed readings, of the centrifugal irony which undermines the even more subtle subtext of post-Revolutionary rhetorical strategies. For example, in the case of the people of Apango in *Pedro Páramo*, where I shall start, it is the rhetoric of an *ethnic* unity which is ironised.

Ethnic Unity: Integration and the Indigenous People of Apango in Pedro Páramo[4]

Here, the word 'integration' will be used to denote the degree to which an ethnic minority group has adapted to life in a country without entirely losing

---

3   Carlos Blanco Aguinaga, 'Introducción', in Rulfo, *El llano*, p. 14.

4   Some parts of the analysis of this fragment first appeared in Amit Thakkar, 'One Rainy Market Day: Integration and Indigenous Peoples in the Fiction and Thought of Juan Rulfo', in *(Re)Collecting the Past: History and Collective Memory in Latin American Narrative*, ed. by

its own sense of identity and culture. 'Assimilation' and 'acculturation' are taken to mean that that group is gradually being 'taken over' entirely by, or voluntarily taking on, the dominant culture. In the 'integration' model, both ethnic minorities and the receiving community interact culturally to produce a pluri-cultural society which, within a common legal, economic and political framework, respects diversity and does not attempt to enforce the majority culture. The liberal nationalists and positivists of the nineteenth century saw no place for the integration of the culturally-backward Indian or the racially-tainted *mestizo* in the national image of Mexico. They were keen instead on a carefully monitored *assimilation* to a European image of the nation and, notwithstanding the rise of the Indian president Benito Juárez, there were limited routes of access to power for non-whites.

In the 1920s, the post-Revolutionary government promoted a national identity which foregrounded the *mestizo*, hailed as 'la raza cósmica', a national icon symbolic of the country's mixture of races, by the first education minister of the newly formed Secretaría de Educación Pública (SEP), José Vasconcelos. In Vasconcelos's cultural hierarchy, 'high' civilisations such as that of the Greeks were paramount and exemplary, modern European peoples followed and Indian civilisations were at the bottom.[5] This concept of Indians was a throwback to the views of positivists such as Andrés Molina Enríquez in that the indigenous population, for these writers, represented an obstacle to economic progress and modernity, particularly in their passivity and their persistence with ancient working practices.[6] Vasconcelos took the idea of the Indian as obstacle to economic progress and added, with 'reckless stereotyping', a notion of the Indian as obstacle to cultural enlightenment, although culture and economics were never far apart in the indigenist debate which ran throughout the twentieth century and continues today.[7] *La Raza Cósmica* was therefore an assimilating rather than integrative theory in that Indians were expected to conform to the cosmic race: they would be redeemed once they had acquired the qualities of the *mestizo*, these qualities being a combination of the physical robustness of the Indian and what Vasconcelos called 'la mente clara del blanco'.[8] Indeed, it is a

Victoria Carpenter (Oxford: Peter Lang, 2009), pp. 191–216. They are reprinted here by kind permission of Dr Carpenter and the publishers, Peter Lang.

   5   For a short description of this theory, see José Vasconcelos, 'La Raza Cósmica', in *The Mexico Reader, History, Culture and Politics*, ed. by Gilbert M. Joseph and Timothy J. Henderson (Durham, NC: Duke University Press, 2002), pp. 15–19.
   6   Anne T. Doremus, *Culture, Politics and National Identity in Mexican Literature and Film, 1929–1952* (New York: Peter Lang, 2001), pp. 133–34.
   7   Joseph and Henderson, p. 15.
   8   José Vasconcelos, *La Raza Cósmica* [1925], in *Obras Completas II* (Mexico: Libreros Mexicanos Unidos, 1957), p. 923.

point not often mentioned that Vasconcelos's concept of beauty extended
to a romanticisation of the Spanish language from the elitist viewpoint that
clear and precise diction signified culture: 'La simple dicción clara supone
ya un refinamiento, una comprensión que es timbre de aristocracia mental
y preparación para la bella literatura.'[9] The contribution of the Indian to
Mexico's destiny was thus reduced to a vague notion of stout physical
strength whilst their language, religion and culture were presumed to be
either unnecessary or a veritable hindrance.

Notwithstanding this notion of the Indian as obstacle to culture, or at best
an object in need of redemption through assimilation to 'la raza cósmica',
there was a counter-movement, encouraged by the writings of Manuel Gamio,
particularly in *Forjando Patria* (1916), and Alfonso Caso's essay 'El indio
mexicano es mexicano?' (1948), which tended towards an idealised view
of the Indian as noble savage, exploited by the *mestizo* and white man, but
also to be redeemed by the Revolution through *mestizaje*.[10] The economic
backwardness in this case is seen as a result of white and *mestizo* disre-
spect, exploitation and outright cruelty towards the Indian rather than an
innate indigenous resistance to the forces of reason represented by European
modernity.[11] Thus, the Indian – along with Vasconcelos's *mestizo* – was also
celebrated in the 1920s: indigenous art and handicraft became fashionable in
the 1920s; folklore ballets (sponsored by the SEP) won national and international acclaim; Rivera's later frescoes would foreground the countryside and
its indigenous roots, rejecting the classical, universal motifs encouraged by
Vasconcelos in the early 1920s.[12] This process of 'integration-by-celebration'
was sustained throughout the 1930s, taking on a more economic and educational impetus with Cárdenas.

In the 1940s, during President Manuel Ávila Camacho's 'unidad nacional'
campaign, the Indian was also targeted in government posters as a vital cog in
efforts to industrialise and modernise the countryside. In one, a smiling indigenous boy is foregrounded against a backdrop of the ancient and the future: a
pyramid in the distance and, in between the boy and the pyramid, a modern
tractor ploughing a fertile field. The caption sentimentalises a relationship
between 'nosotros' and indigenous people whilst talking of 'redeeming' the

---

9   José Vasconcelos, *De Robinson a Odiseo* [1935] in *Obras Completas II* (Mexico:
Libreros Mexicanos Unidos, 1957), p. 1559.
10 Manuel Gamio, *Forjando Patria* (Mexico City: Editorial Porrúa, S.A., 1960). Caso's
essay appears in *El Ensayo Mexicano Moderno*, ed. by José Luis Martínez (Mexico City: Fondo
de Cultura Económica, 1958).
11 Doremus, pp. 133–36.
12 Doremus, pp. 136–37.

indigenous people, whom it describes as 'indios mexicanos', all of which betrays a certain discomfort in the message of integration:

> Cuando nos sentimos en contacto con las capacidades creadoras de riquezas y de arte de la raza indígena, comprendemos en toda su significación la fuerza de justicia del anhelo de la Revolución de redimir e incorporar a una elevada vida nacional al indio mexicano.[13]

In similar vein to government posters, tourist brochures and posters in the United States promoted 'mexicanidad' or 'lo mexicano' as exotic, and the humble, compliant Indian was accordingly seen as the most commercially-marketable image of a country known all too much for violence and insta-bility. As Alex Saragoza puts it, 'the diverse nature of Mexico's indigenous culture distilled into a predominantly Aztec or Mayan reference as the pyramid became the icon of the country's indigenous heritage'.[14]

Therefore, integration here is a very convincing but dangerously misleading illusion. This is not the kind of 'interactive' integration discussed earlier, for the image of the Indian portrayed on almost every level was one that betrayed a lack of understanding of the indigenous and consequently encouraged stere-otypes as commodities: the alien was transformed into the exotic and the exotic happened to be commercially viable. Yet, so-called exotic groups still did not see themselves as 'exotic', or indeed as commercial assets, for they did not necessarily think in these terms. From a modern perspective on the word 'integration', one would expect a level of economic *exchange* between the *mestizo* and indigenous communities, based – as I have described – on common roles as citizens while respecting diversity. Here, however, integra-tion is dictated by economic *expediency* – if the Indians can be convinced that they represent Mexico, they will dutifully perform their Indianness in posters and hopefully in dances and music performances held in hotels and on beaches. They may also take a greater part in the industrialisation programme by not opposing with violence the incursion onto their lands by ever-expanding haciendas. Even the work of Mexican anthropologists such as Caso in the 1950s, who praised indigenous communities for their sense of community and suggested that they be 'integrated' as central figures in the national unity campaign, tended to emphasise the value of the Indian in terms of artistic production, which is to say in terms of their clear economic

---

13   Archivo General de la Nación, Colección Carteles, Ávila Camacho: C/993/75.
14   Alex Saragoza, 'The Selling of Mexico: Tourism and the State, 1929–1952', in *Fragments of a Golden Age: The Politics of Culture in Mexico Since 1940*, ed. by Gilbert Joseph, Anne Rubenstein and Eric Zolov (Durham, NC: Duke University Press, 2001), p. 100.

import.[15] Thus, the 1930s, 1940s and 1950s saw an attempted assimilation of the indigenous not just to 'high' Western culture but to capitalist values, or at best a half-baked integration, one of state convenience based on the assumption that the economic ways of the dominant culture were still the most correct and important for the successful 'integration' of the indigenous people in the Mexican Revolution. In this way, the indigenous people were converted into commodity-objects represented stereotypically for the purposes of Western-style capitalist industrialisation.

In Rulfo's work, there is only one passage in which the indigenous population is featured. The passage appears in *Pedro Páramo*, in fragment 48, which belongs to the thread in which the efforts of Pedro Páramo to court Susana are narrated.[16] As such, it is deep in the section where voices are heard by the dead Juan Preciado and Doroteo, where Comala's past is represented in snatches of disparate but connected accounts. I would argue, therefore, that it is important to our appreciation of Comala in general. It begins with the words 'Es Domingo' and then makes use of the present tense, normally used for routines, indicating strongly the ritualistic importance of the indigenous people arriving to set up their Sunday market:

> Es Domingo. De Apango han bajado los indios con sus rosarios de manzanillas, su romero, sus manojos de tomillo … Tienden sus yerbas en el suelo, bajo los arcos del portal, y esperan. (155)

The scene which ensues recalls two of Diego Rivera's 1920s murals: *El tianguis* and *La lluvia*. The picture being set up here is one of local colour, a folkloristic view of the market. Certainly, the government encouraged the celebration of market days as important symbols of the nation's prosperity and the vibrancy of *interaction* between the indigenous communities and the rest of the population. *El tianguis*, Rivera's depiction of a bustling town on market day with indigenous commodities being sold to crowds of people, occupies a large part of the murals on the ground floor of the SEP. The attire of the *mestizo* at the front of the crowd marks him out from a seemingly homogenous crowd as a tax collector, suggesting a fruitful economic exchange between a *mestizo* nation and an indigenous rural population. During the 1930s and 1940s, indeed, rural produce and market days were promoted in government posters and official agricultural calendars.

The reader discovers there is little of this energetic, 'bustling' quality in this market. In fact, Rulfo's scene ironically, and more tellingly, evokes the mood of *La lluvia*, in which a group of indigenous peasants are huddled together

---

15 Doremus, pp. 137–38.
16 See González Boixo, in his introduction to Rulfo, *Pedro Páramo*, p. 28.

in the foreground under covers made of palm leaves as the rain descends on their fields in the background. The impression is of a rural community at one with its climatic conditions and, by extension, with nature itself, sheltering from the rain, aware of its productive uses and economic benefits, and protected by state soldiers. As one caption to the picture states, 'los elementos heterogéneos de los tres planos – mujeres, niños, soldados con 'capotes' de hojas de palma, montañas escalonadas como pirámides y nubes cargadas de lluvia – se unen en perfecta unidad tonal y rítmica'.[17] In Rulfo's rain scenes, there is a similar sensitivity to the rhythms of nature, one example being the story 'Es que somos muy pobres', in which the rain destroys the economic prospects of a family: 'lo único que pudimos hacer, todos los de mi casa, fue estarnos arrimados debajo del tejaván, viendo cómo el agua fría que caía del cielo quemaba aquella cebada amarilla tan recién cortada' (55). The rhythm of rain and the anguish it causes are subtly projected through the rapid alliteration of double 'a' sounds (caía, quemaba, aquella, cebada, amarilla, cortada), and the picture of the family huddled beneath a shed is almost a mirror image of Rivera's *La lluvia*, except that the rain representing the external force of nature here is destructive.

It is the rain that defines fragment 48 of *Pedro Páramo* from the very beginning: 'Una lluvia menuda, extraña para estas tierras que sólo saben de aguaceros' (155). The destructive capacity of this rain is made clear: it is shown to have ruined the economic significance of the day, for the men of Comala must tend to their fields and redirect the channels that the deluge produces away from their precious *milpa*, or fields of corn, the staple commodity of the rural economy and probably its main export to the urban world.[18] Thus, the rain, the essential ingredient of fertility, is ironically also a symbol of destruction, infertility and economic ruin when excessive. It is not disadvantageous solely for Comala: it also means that market day is effectively over for the indigenous people of Apango. This is made clear in a scene in which Indians shelter under their awnings, contrasting starkly with Rivera's *El tianguis* and *La lluvia*, images in which rain is a *productive* force. The indigenous people of Apango are in tune with their natural environment and community to the same degree that the figures in Rivera's mural are but the state-representing soldiers are absent, as is the creative, productive face of the rain: Tláloc, the rain god, is as unhelpful to the indigenous as he is to the rest of the population.

Initially, then, the reactions of the two communities to the economically

---

[17] Luis Cardoza y Aragón and Antonio Rodríguez, *Diego Rivera, Los murales de la Secretaría de Educación Pública* (Mexico City: SEP, 1986), p. 137.

[18] Interestingly, the Indians are associated with herbs, as if their presence is merely auxiliary to the staple maize.

destructive force of the rain are similarly negative. The *mestizo* peasants of
Comala here are desperate, unaided victims of natural problems whilst the
indigenous people anxiously await customers, trembling, 'no de frío sino de
temor' (155). However, once it becomes obvious that there will be little trade
today and their makeshift straw awnings become increasingly heavy with
rainwater, the Indians begin to converge in a festival atmosphere: 'Platican,
se cuentan chistes y sueltan la risa ... Piensan: "Si al menos hubiéramos
traído tantito pulque, no importaría"; pero el cogollo de los magueyes está
hecho un mar de agua. En fin, qué se le va a hacer' (156). The final remark
is one that reflects the stereotypical fatalism of the rural population and their
cheerful surrender to natural forces, rather than the 'fatalismo atemporal' to
which Blanco Aguinaga refers as the norm for other Rulfian characters.[19]
At the end of the day, the indigenous people pick up their stalls and pass
by the church to pray to the Virgin, just as their solitary customer Justina
had done after buying an expensive branch of rosemary. The intermediary
role of the Church in cultural interaction is not dwelt upon here: perhaps the
reader is expected merely to reflect on the fact that these two communities
do have a need for spiritual comfort which happens to coincide in Catholicism, though this cannot form the basis for integration. The encounter with
this solitary customer, moreover, implies mistrust between the Indian and
mestizo communities: '[Justina] se detuvo en el primer puesto, compró diez
centavos de romero, y regresó, seguida por las miradas en hilera de *aquel
montón de indios*' (156).[20]

While Justina leaves, complaining of rising prices, the people of Apango
are more than prepared to accept their misfortunes: '"Ahí será otro día",
dijeron. Y por el camino iban contándose chistes y soltando la risa' (156).
The merriment of the indigenous people is reflected in the grotesque sound
of boiling water, with onomatopoeic sounds ('b' and 'rr') which increasingly
seem to mimic their laughter:

> Justina Díaz, cubierta con paraguas, venía por la calle derecha que viene de
> la Media Luna, *rodeando* los *chorros* que *borbotaban* sobre las *banquetas*.
> (156)

> Allá afuera ... se sentía como si el agua hirviera sobre el agua estancada
> en la tierra ... Los caños *borbotaban*, hacían espuma ... El agua seguía
> *corriendo*, diluviando en incesantes *burbujas*. (158)[21]

---

19 Blanco Aguinaga, 'Realidad y estilo', p. 186.
20 Emphasis added.
21 Emphasis added in both quotations.

In Susana's room, meanwhile, there is a feeling that Comala and its inhabitants are beginning to drown in a kind of hellish quicksand of boiling rainwater. The rain, the symbol of both fertility ('... hilvanando el hilo de la vida', 157) and destruction, drowns out sounds, the signals of life ('La lluvia amortigua los ruidos', 157). In the following fragment, in which Bartolomé's ghost visits Susana, it seems to boil in its own heat: 'Y después sólo la lluvia, interminente, fría, rodando sobre las hojas de los plátanos, *hirviendo* en su propio *hervor*' (159, emphasis added). The violation of logic here recalls the catachresis in the single drop which falls 'por equivocación' in 'Nos han dado la tierra'. The rain thus almost mocks the land and people it falls on and, as the Indians return to Apango with little material profit from their market day in Comala, their laughter too seems to mock the inhabitants of the town, as if the last laugh will be on the *mestizos* and their dying town, perhaps on those who do not surrender to natural forces but instead to the market forces which nature might disrupt from time to time.

Therefore, the reactions of these communities to the rain and an economically unproductive day are ultimately different. That of the indigenous people of Apango is indicative of a mentality which easily disassociates itself from (literal) market forces. The rain falls, they worry briefly about the problem and then go on their way with a joke and a story. Meanwhile, the town, which depends on stable crop production, is plunged into a minor crisis represented metaphorically by the mental instability of Susana. Most significantly, once the *tianguis*, symbol of economic mediation, is removed, these differences become more stark. Is it the case that the only possible form of cultural interaction between these two groups is an economic one? If so, how inspiring or effective is this form of interaction to the indigenous community given that they seem to accept their economic misfortune so passively? The feeling that emerges from the fragment, then, is one of an indigenous people who are difficult to place in the context of modern, liberal economic thinking, a feeling which does not jar with Rulfo's own respectfully cautious attitude towards the indigenous people: 'Nunca empleo a los indios porque para mí es imposible entrar y llegar a profundizar en la mentalidad indígena.'[22] This statement, from – apart from anything else – an educated, urbanised man who lived most of his young life in the countryside, suggests the complications of any national unity initiative which aims to incorporate the indigenous people in the process of modernity. Indeed the remoteness of indigenous people is paradoxically suggested by Rulfo's placing of this fragment at the heart of the novel. By fragment 48, we have already been struck by how remote Comala

---

[22] Antonio Palicio, 'Juan Rulfo: la revolución cubana desencadenó el "boom" americano', *ABC*, 22 April 1982, p. 31.

is from the imagined community of the Mexican nation, but, by the end of this fragment, having seen the indigenous people leave Comala as easily as they descend on it, we have a sense of double remoteness: an indigenous community on the margins of a peasant community on the margins of a national community.

This scene is therefore centrifugally ironic for there are evident implications of this schism for the national unity campaign and, in particular, for all efforts at indigenous integration since the days of Vasconcelos, whether cultural or economic in focus. Indeed, even today, the level of illiteracy and indifference to state initiatives among many of the indigenous people reflects an indifference to capitalist modernity which sometimes explodes into open hostility, as in the Chiapas rebellion of the 1990s. It is significant that among the grievances of the Ejército Zapatista de Liberación Nacional were 'hunger, misery and marginalisation' and 'the brutal exploitation we suffer in the sale of our products'.[23] In the context of this story, then, the smile of the indigenous boy in Ávila Camacho's national unity poster appears less accommodating and more bemused: he seems to inhabit an externally-choreographed world in which his own stereotypical dress is supposed to merge seamlessly with the tractor and well tended fields representing a foreign world of industrialisation and economic 'integration'. The pyramids and indigenous headgear represent a cultural integration based on stereotyping, with the type of easily identifiable, easily marketable symbols represented in some of the government's tourism brochures. Fragment 48 of *Pedro Páramo* thus evokes an impasse that is relevant today: the capitalist, economic incentive is not necessarily a useful basis for economic interaction, given that cultural attitudes to life, and particularly economic life, seem to be very different between *mestizos* and indigenous peoples.

Family Unity: Communication and Violence in 'Acuérdate'

A central aspect of post-Revolutionary rhetoric was the concept of the Mexican family. In the context of national 'revolutionary' unity, Obregón's definition of 'all the working classes' as a family in his 1919 manifesto is significant: 'day-labourers, workers, professionals, small agriculturalists, ranchers and shop-owners – constituting the great majority of the *Mexican family* ...'[24]

---

[23] 'EZLN Demands at the Dialogue Table', from *Shadows of Tender Fury: The Letters and Communiqués of Subcomandante Marcos and the Zapatista Army of National Liberation*, translated by Frank Bardacke, Leslie López, and the Watsonville, California, Human Rights Committee (New York: Monthly Review Press, 1995), pp. 155–62. Quoted by Joseph and Henderson, p. 639.

[24] Álvaro Obregón, 'The Revolution was Fought for Democracy', in *The Meaning of the*

(emphasis added). Later, in the wake of a second world war in which many national sovereignties were at stake, the word 'patria' became a key term in describing the importance of family. For Ávila Camacho, this notion of patria would support a national unity based on a concentrated aim: 'La justicia social reclama el progreso armónico de toda la comunidad; debemos, pues, sentirnos todos unificados en un fin.'[25] His national unity campaign was based partly on a sentimental depiction of the homeland: images of the country-side portrayed in government rhetoric remained faithful to a kind of neo-colonial vision of peace, order and tranquillity. In 1943, an article published in the editorial section of the government's official daily voice, *El Nacional*, described the nature of family and its relationship with the notion of 'patria' in these very terms:

> La patria es también ese cielo, esas montañas, esos campos, ese vasto mar que bate nuestras costas. Y todo esto no está fuera de nosotros, está dentro. Llevamos en nuestra naturaleza física como un eco del suelo materno, y en nuestros corazones el recuerdo radiante, imborrable de su imagen.[26]

As I stated earlier, such distinctly feminine concepts of the 'patria' as the 'motherland' (as opposed to the 'fatherland') were useful for the invocation of spiritual loyalty in a country where devotion to the mother had become institutionalised. In the 1930s, Mother's Day began to rival festivities held in honour of the Virgin of Guadalupe. In one school textbook, 'the Mexican mother' was venerated as a worker in her own right, 'una obrera sin límite en su labor'.[27] Her tireless and unappreciated care for her children was acknowl-edged and so was her love: 'su trabajo y su amor sostienen y vivifican nuestro hogar'.[28] In 1938, *Excelsior* devoted a spread in its photo-section to 'Madres Prolíficas' and their enormous families. It also offered prizes to the most prolific mother as well as to the first woman to give birth on 10 May.[29] The economic motives behind this cult of fertility were quite openly offered: the editorial of the same newspaper in 1938 addresses the scarcity of population in rural areas, while suggesting that the promotion of Mother's Day was part

Mexican Revolution, ed. by Charles C. Cumberland (Boston: D. C. Heath, 1967), p. 10.

[25] Ávila Camacho, in a speech quoted on p. 14 of Jesús Orozco and Francisco J. Núñez, 'Ideología y Programa de Gobierno en los discursos de Toma de Posesión de los Presidentes de México 1928–1982', *Huella: cuadernos de divulgación académica* (Mexico City: Ediciones del ITESO, 1983).

[26] C. Wagner, *El Nacional*, 5 June 1943, p. 3.

[27] Secretaría de Educación Pública (SEP), *Serie SEP 3er año* (Mexico City: SEP, 1938), p. 82.

[28] SEP, p. 82.

[29] *Excelsior*, 12 May 1938, p. 5.

of a general need to hold up the honest, large and hard-working family as a proletarian ideal: 'Se buscará ... los medios más adecuados para la más efectiva protección de la familia proletaria.'[30]

To complete the effect, the urban Revolutionary state would be an unequivocally male provider of a kind of revolutionary 'virility'. The people are 'the Mexican family', the nation is described as the 'Motherland' but Obregón also refers to 'the fruits of those good seeds which the Revolution sowed and which have been irrigated by torrents of blood from unknown men ...'.[31] Such imagery was reinforced with frescoes such as Rivera's *La sangre de los mártires revolucionarios fertilizando la tierra* (1926–27) in which the martyred Zapata and Otilio Montaña lie beneath a fertile field, connoting economic prosperity and ideological vigour. The concept of the Mexican family was used also to pair the countryside with the city in a 'fraternal' vision of national togetherness, recalling Rivera's *El abrazo* (1923). Indeed, during the presidency of Lázaro Cárdenas (1934–40), the call for national unity was given a fresh spin, with the emphasis on worker collectivity and action in both 'fields and factories':

> In the fields and factories [Cárdenas] ... urged atomized workers and peasants to unify their fragmented organizations into leagues and centrals; he took a hand to healing their quarrels. He met peons, migrants, unemployed, workers, women, and youth with the same slogan: 'Get organized!'[32]

A major aspect of his campaign therefore entailed the projection of a countryside and peasantry unified in support of the new president, the new government and its 'socialist' aims and goals. With President Manuel Ávila Camacho (1940–46), the terms of this arrangement between countryside and urban state changed. The rural economy lay in the hands of an elite landed class and the banks, at a time when state involvement in the economy was selectively played down. This tactic of private investment encouraged by the state was dressed up as a necessity if barren areas of the countryside, such as those which inspired the northern landscape of Rulfo's fiction, were to be brought into the national economy.[33] Such tactics in fact manifested them-

---

[30] *Excelsior*, 12 May 1938, p. 5.

[31] Obregón, p. 12.

[32] Donald C. Hodges and Ross Gandy, *Mexico: the End of the Revolution* (Westport: Praeger, 2002), p. 73.

[33] 'Grandes extensiones de México, y ahí están evidenciándolo incontables llanuras del Norte solas y estériles, requieren para incorporarse a la vida agrícola, no de la magia administrativa de una subvención oficial sino de la fuerza financiera privada que haga de esos campos zonas productoras, sustento de negocios por sí mismos, con una solventación lograda a virtud de actos concretos, esto es trabajo escueto y analtecedor.' Jesús Orona Tovar, *Miguel Alemán:*

selves 'on the ground' in job losses, reduced wages and greater power for the rural *empresario*, all of which resulted, in turn, in rural exodus and agrarian unrest in the 1950s. The national family was quietly put aside as the importance of political unity with the Church and, more importantly, 'family' unity *within* the party took precedence. Even in this context, the family as a social unit was still considered to be more potent than the urban state in alleviating the dire economic circumstances, despite the fact that these circumstances were created largely by state policy: peasants, according to Ávila Camacho, were to be taught 'el hábito de ahorro, disciplina capaz de alentar el crédito y de afianzar el presupuesto y la vida de la familia'.[34] The idea, it seems, was to shift the burden of socio-economic integration onto the citizen, while the state took care of the more profitable sectors of the economy.

Symptomatic of the state's failure to communicate with the peasantry and address its grievances was its objectification of the countryside as an idyllic pre-Revolutionary paradise. When, for example, the outgoing governor of the Federal District, Isidro Fabela, was invited to a celebratory dinner in his home town of Atlacomulco, a friend read a passage from a story by Fabela in which the pastoral imagination was somewhat pronounced.[35] This passage is taken to prove that Fabela is 'un hombre de la tierra, de esta tierra del Estado de México, fértil y risueña ... un amante del campo y de su vida reposada y simple'. Fabela's own memories are even more telling in their suggestion of a somewhat misplaced nostalgia for hierarchical order:

> Yo quiero a este pueblo bendito porque en su escenario rural aprendí a amar con respetuosa y misericordiosa simpatía, al rústico aldeano y al tímido peón, que me daban los buenos días con medroso talante y me besaban la mano a la despedida, diciéndome con voz de ancestral sumisión:
> – Adiós, señor.[36]

In fact, none of this picture of pastoral bliss chimes with a reading of Rulfo's fiction. Such idyllic visions of the countryside could only impede meaningful communication between the urban state and rural communities, where the rhetoric of family unity was irrelevant as large numbers of youngsters were

---

Retrato y radiografía de un optimismo (Sinaloa: Partido Institucional Revolucionario, 1951), p. 19.

[34] *Excelsior*, 2 September 1944, p. 1 and p. 12.

[35] 'Entre el rústico caserío, esfumado poco a poco por el bello agonizar del día, se deslizan los rebaños impacientes, camino de sus chiqueros, balando en inarmónica dulzura, mientras los pastores, con una cría recién nacida bajo el brazo y una lugareña canción en los labios, abren las trancas de la corralada, donde la turba, nerviosa y descomedida, se precipita buscando el último rincón.' *El Nacional*, 17 May 1945, pp. 1–8.

[36] *El Nacional*, 17 May 1945, p. 8.

forced to leave their families in search of work in the cities. In the story 'Acuérdate', there is an acute sense of rural alienation and the disintegration of community life, subtly represented by a title and refrain which suggests obliquely the absence of community memory and of state–citizen dialogue. The first two paragraphs are disarmingly humorous and tinged with the impression of a pleasant, bucolic life. We are told of a humorous-sounding ditty called the 'rezonga ángel maldito'; the narrator tells of affectionate nick-names and epithets like 'el Abuelo', 'la Berenjena', 'la Arremangada', 'el Urbano' and 'la Natalia' and there is a quaint, rustic touch of humour about the young girl who has an attack of hiccups during Mass. The relaxed move-ment of the narrative from one member of the family to the other evokes the image of a wise, old man recounting the folklore of a village.

One might imagine, at this stage, the idyllic rural settings of the *comedia ranchera*, such as those of the highly popular films of Jorge Negrete, *Ay, Jalisco, no te rajes* (1941) and *Allá en el rancho grande* (1949), which depict nostalgically, and with a good deal of humour, the social relationships and hierarchies which prevail in the Mexican countryside:

> Es un cine vuelto hacia el pasado. Incluso el presente es un tiempo perfectamente identificable con el pretérito. Una intemporalidad atrofiada predomina. Añora la belle époque del paternalismo porfiriano. Se arraiga en haciendas semifeudales donde la lucha de clases se resuelve en el agra-decimiento y la generosidad. La mansedumbre del peón gracioso excita el arrepentimiento del patrón villano.[37]

Such movies resorted to folklorising the countryside in order to appeal to the nostalgic demands of the audience: cockfighting, horse-racing, tradi-tional songs, mariachis, bar-room brawls and traditional costumes for females were all common features.[38] Indeed, the blurb for one film about the era of Díaz – 'Si me viera Don Porfirio' – is candidly nostalgic in its equation of 'grandeza' with the ultimate strongman of Mexico: 'Hoy Gran

---

[37] Jorge Ayala Blanco, *La Aventura del Cine Mexicano en la Epoca de Oro y Después* (Mexico City: Editorial Grijalbo, 1993). Furthermore, they tended to glorify the machista ethos with a division between those who were in and those who were not: 'en la comedia ranchera, o se es un macho tremendamente simpático o se es un personaje sometido al macho, a merced de sus desmanes, nulo y sin defensa' (p. 56).

[38] For 'folklore', I take W. Dirk Raat's summary of the thoughts of the folklore scholar Jan Harold Brunvand (leaving aside the problematic area of the distinction between folk and popular culture): 'an unofficial and traditional, noninstitutional part of culture ... [encom-passing] ... all knowledge, values, attitudes, and beliefs transmitted in traditional form by word of mouth, customary behavior or material forms (for example, artifacts)'. This is quoted from 'The Mexican Pet and Other Stories: Folklore and History', in *Twentieth Century Mexico*, ed. by Raat and William Beezley (Lincoln: University of Nebraska Press, 1986), pp. 44–45.

Estreno. ¡Sentimental evocación de épocas inolvidables! ¡Por primera vez se presentan en la pantalla escenas auténticas de la vida de Don Porfirio Díaz, una maravillosa película que muestra en toda su grandeza el México de principios del siglo!'[39]

'Acuérdate' is, by the end at least, no such fairy tale. Aspects of the apparently humorous beginning, discussed above, already prepare us for the more tragic picture with which it ends: the infirm girl sounds 'como si estuviera riendo y llorando a la vez'; the 'rezonga ángel maldito' is recited by a dying man; *la Berenjena* loses all but two of her children at a young age and dies herself giving birth. It is chiefly in the tension between tone and content that the (centripetal) verbal irony lies. For example, the use of affectionate diminutives jars with the sad events related: one of the children is 'prieta y chaparrita', the other needed 'tantita agua con azúcar' after her hiccups and *la Berenjena* 'tuvo su dinerito' (142). Even the latter's loose lifestyle and the death of her children is gently mocked with disarmingly colloquial expression ('pues', 'se le morían', 'la canción esa'):

> Pues todos los hijos se le morían de recién nacidos y siempre les mandaba cantar alabanzas, llevándolos al panteón entre músicas y coros de monaguillos que contaban 'hosannas' y 'glorias' y la canción esa de 'ahí te mando, Señor, otro angelito. (142)

In terms of content, the poverty of her life is then demonstrated in her rummaging through garbage to find pieces of onion peel and discarded, cooked corn, 'para que se les endulzara la boca a sus hijos' (143). Within the first three paragraphs, therefore, Rulfo has introduced a tension based, on the one hand, on a verbally-hinted, idyllic vision of the countryside that many (including the state) would like to imagine and, on the other, a kind of dark underbelly which is the 'meat' of the story. This tension is disturbingly retained throughout and the rhetorical notion of a warm nuclear family is correspondingly upended with a vision of its opposite. Thus, there is already a sense of the deep misunderstandings that affect urban–rural dialogue and complicate the task of national unity

One of *la Berenjena*'s children is remembered with ironic affection as something of a cardsharp wheeler and dealer in the playground: selling toys, fruits, plants and even insects that he has picked up on the cheap or stolen from elsewhere. This is Urbano Gómez and the significance of the pun cannot be underestimated, for he reveals a certain 'urban' skill as the master of the market: 'Nos traficaba a todos, acuérdate' (143). As well as being an astute young merchant, Urbano is also a failed practician of the rural art of

---

[39] *Excelsior*, Second Section, 16 July 1950, p. 3.

favours: while inviting everyone to his impoverished sister's *tepache* stand
to drink to their heart's content, he neglects to charge them but finds that
his friends desert him for fear of having to settle their accounts.[40] Here, we
are warned of what is about to happen: 'Quizá entonces se volvió malo, o
quizá ya era de nacimiento' (144). Now, the story moves disturbingly back
to another humorous, rustic anecdote when the narrator tells us of when
Urbano is expelled after he and his cousin are caught 'jugando a marido y
mujer' behind the toilets at school (144). As the pair are ridiculed in front of
their schoolmates, he makes a vow of vengeance which resonates at the end
of the paragraph: 'Ya me las pagarán caro.' Poetically, the warning signs
reach fever pitch as his cousin's crying is intensified with the alliteration
of 'll' and 'o':

> Y después a *ella*, que salió haciendo pucheros y con la mirada raspando los
> *ladrillos*, hasta que ya en la puerta soltó el *llanto*; un *chillido* que se estuvo
> *oyendo* toda la tarde como si fuera un *aullido* de *coyote*. (144, emphasis
> added)

The final act of Urbano's childhood in the village is indeed marked by the
violence such language prefigures: his uncle nearly paralyses him with a
smack and the boy leaves angrily, 'de coraje', later to return as a symbol of
the urban world.

The interpretation of the returning Urbano as a product of the urban world
is not so farfetched when we consider how he, like the inhabitants of La
Cuesta de las Comadres, disappears into a kind of mythical exterior. In that
story, the inhabitants are described by the narrator as mysteriously wandering
into the unknown: 'Y yo también hubiera ido de buena gana a asomarme a
ver qué había tan atrás del monte que no dejaba volver a nadie ...' (46). Of
course, many of those who were disappointed by land reform or otherwise
failed in the countryside were drawn into the urban labour market as part of
the industrialisation process, which, barring oblique allusions, is a process
conspicuous in Rulfo's fiction by its absence.[41] It is likely that Urbano,
given his name and mercantilistic nature, represented part of this urbanisation process, returning only to exact his revenge. As far as the narrator is
concerned, with the word 'Acuérdate', the reader is not to forget Urbano's

---

[40] *Tepache* is a Mexican pineapple drink.
[41] 'El éxodo del campo a las ciudades, los problemas de vivienda y servicios para esta
población recién llegada, el cambio acelerado que percibimos en la construcción incesante
de caminos, presas, industrias, zonas residenciales y asentamientos espontáneos, número de
automóviles, costumbres y formas de vestir, todo lo que los economistas sintetizan en la palabra
mágica "desarrollo", son fenómenos que ya se visualizaban en los años cuarenta.' Aurora Loyo,
La Unidad Nacional (Mexico City: M. Casillas, 1983), p. 52.

violent, impoverished and rural origin in a dysfunctional family where he has sexual relations with his cousin, and his uncle admonishes him with violence. Is the implication that people's rural origins in an increasingly urbanised, impoverished and criminalised country are frequently forgotten? That these origins are not to blame for such problems? Or that they are? Rulfo, as always, leaves space for interpretation.

As in 'La cuesta de las comadres' (discussed below), the violence of a patriarchal society is perceived as a self-perpetuating phenomenon. Urbano, far from 'urbane', returns to the village as a representative of urban civilisation in the form of a policeman. The change is indicated by the words 'convertido en policía', suggesting almost a religious conversion through which a new set of values has been adopted. However, this symbol of 'urbanity' is hell-bent on revenge and certainly not prepared to enter into dialogue, just as the government of the 1940s and 1950s shuts itself off from rural problems: 'No hablaba con nadie. No saludaba a nadie. Y si uno lo miraba, él se hacía el desentendido como si no conociera a la gente' (145). This state of non-communication, as the very next line suggests, can only result in violence: 'Fue entonces cuando mató a su cuñado, el de la mandolina' (145). While, in an eerily *costumbrista* detail, his mentally-handicapped brother-in-law serenades him to the sound of church bells during a religious ceremony, shouts are heard and people run out of the church to find a scene of violence, the depiction of which is as brutal in its simplicity as that of 'La cuesta de las comadres' is in its detail: they see 'Nachito defendiéndose patas arriba con la mandolina y al Urbano mandándole un culatazo tras otro con el maúser, sin oír lo que le gritaba la gente, rabioso, como perro del mal' (145). The only way they manage to stop Urbano is when an unknown man knocks him out by hitting him on the back with his own rifle; it is telling that Urbano's violence, a result of violence, can only be stopped with violence. All of this brutality emanates from a struggle within the family, which is supposed to operate as the microcosmic unit of national unity.

Having tried and failed to relieve his guilt in confession, Urbano commits the final act of murder on himself: 'No se opuso. Dicen que él mismo se amarró la soga en el pescuezo y que hasta escogió el árbol que más le gustaba para que lo ahorcaran' (145). Thus, the protagonist completes the cycle of violence, having failed to find relief either in the family, the urban state, the rural community or the Church (through confession). At the same time, his story is representative of that of the Mexican family as a whole for he and his family are centrifugally ironic symbols of a national failure of communication and family cohesion. Frozen out of his rural community by poverty, a perceived injustice and a real violence, he finds in the urban community an answer which is brutal and repressive (the policeman) and, in the family, nothing but cause for revenge and more violence. The clash between this symbol of modernity that is the policeman and the tragic, rural figure of his poor and handicapped brother-in-law leads to a kind of chain of violence ending in Urbano's virtually hanging himself. This chain is seemingly as unstoppable as the process of urbanisation and the resultant non-communication between the state and the countryside.

The centrifugal irony in this story is of paramount importance and it is facilitated by centripetal irony. As Marta Portal demonstrates, the story initially presents us with a very rural manner of organising society: 'una pequeña comunidad que ha repartido los papeles de la representación social y ha otorgado a Urbano el de "malo" de nacimiento'.[42] Unfortunately, the resulting mockery leads to Urbano's determination to wreak vengeance as a policeman: 'Su actitud distante, su seriedad, quieren imponer el respeto. Externamente, el uniforme y la función deberían ayudarlo a conseguirlo.'[43] According to Portal, then, his ultimate inability to 'tomarlo a broma' when he is serenaded makes the story a 'parodia costumbrista'.[44] A more centripetal parody of a romantic *costumbrista* tradition, according to my thoughts in the previous chapter, would prepare us for the notion of the unreliability of realistic linguistic configurations in general. Urbano's violent reaction in a *costumbrista* scene is another source of the kind of black humour which is evident also in the tension described above between affectionate, colloquial language and the story's brutal content. It is also relevant that Urbano is misunderstood and forgotten by the discourse of both the urban and the rural community from which he emerges. While, on one level, Urbano's violence would be rejected by an urban intolerance of rural 'barbarity', on another, the rural family and community condemnation of the man is indicative of its lack of compassion and, indeed, lack of memory.

Here, we have the essence of the main centripetal verbal irony in the refrain 'Acuérdate', for it is almost absurd that the narrator should have to jog the memory of the interlocutor (who was also a 'compañero de escuela' of the protagonist) to recall a character such as Urbano. Indeed, this verbal irony accrues power as the story proceeds: the more we learn of this character's colourfulness and the eventful nature of his life, the more absurd it seems that the interlocutor should have difficulty in remembering him and the more we feel the need to interpret this absurdity by producing meaning, by becoming the interlocutor ourselves. The narrator shows some understanding of the interlocutor's forgetfulness in the middle of the story: 'Sólo que te falle

---

[42] Marta Portal, *Rulfo: dinámica de la violencia* (Madrid: Instituto de Cooperación Iberoamericana, 1984), p. 188.

[43] Portal, p. 177.

[44] Portal, p. 177 and p. 188.

mucho la memoria, no te has de acordar de eso' (144). By the end, however, his words seem to suggest an impatient reproach: 'Tú te debes acordar de él, pues fuimos compañeros de escuela y lo conociste como yo' (145). Paradoxically, the narrator is himself the product of a process which encourages the oblivion in which individuals are held, for perhaps the ultimate blame for this memory failure lies again in the unshakeability of the patriarchal system created and led by the urban state. If, for example, we go back to the beginning of the story, it is very clear in the description of Urbano's lineage that the narrator and (presumably) his interlocutor see history in patriarchal terms: 'Acuérdate de Urbano Gómez, hijo de don Urbano, nieto de Dimas ...' (142). The violence of his uncle in the absence of a father, and that of the patriarchal state represented by the policeman, also suggest that the cause of this vicious circle is a society which is directed 'from above' by a paternalistic force incapable of understanding and respecting difference, resorting instead to vilification and expulsion of anyone who threatens the sanctity of the family unit.

Thus, the result of a failure of memory and understanding from the urban world is non-communication and, eventually, violence. In this respect, the refrain 'acuérdate', as well as appealing to the reader to *become* the missing interlocutor and produce meaning from the text, could be a call directed (more centrifugally) towards the ('paternal') government to remember the ('maternal') countryside and what it really is: not the pretty, idyllic paradise, home of the nuclear family, which is suggested at the beginning of the story, and imagined by many, but a complex, divisive and violent community capable of ignoring or abandoning its own poor, 'rejects' or failures and of producing families which are anything but cohesive. The projected image of family and national values is therefore undermined with a picture of community amnesia and internal hostility. The story thus represents a kind of extended centrifugal situational irony, rather than open satire: the informed reader would be expected to construe the historical commentary, rather than passively absorb it. And it is the ironic void created centripetally by the tension between affectionate language and violent content, by the parody of *costumbrista* fiction, and by the absence of an interlocutor, with which Rulfo opens up the possibilities of the narrative within this centrifugally ironic framework.

Rural Unity: Internecine Rural Conflict in 'La Cuesta de las Comadres'

On the cover of the official publication of Cárdenas's 1936 speech 'La unificación campesina', peasants are depicted discussing and making decisions in an apparently democratic group while, in the background, neat, furrowed lines among the hills indicate a well-tended and prosperous countryside.[45] It was recommended in one school textbook that peasants become educated in aspects of the law which would help them defend themselves against the *hacendado*. The language of meetings, indeed, was highly polit-icised: 'reuniones generales' were held, 'comités' were formed, 'planes de trabajo' were presented, images depicted people in workers' overalls rather than peasant attire and those present were addressed as 'compañeros', echoing the Communist 'comrade'.[46] Beyond such language, Cárdenas's campaign for peasant unification had to be backed up by radical action in the countryside. As it turned out, the rhetoric was not entirely empty, for it is generally accepted that the most significant period of land reform, or 'reparto', occurred during Cárdenas's reign, with *ejidos* and private proper-ties being granted on a grand scale. The modernisation of the countryside in the form of communally-owned *ejidos* and tightly organised *campesino* groups was indeed a seemingly sincere vision and the statistics seemed to support the government's claims. Not only was land apparently being redistributed nationally, the constant referral to the days of the hacienda in the past tense suggested that the days of cruel landlords, *caciquismo* and exploitation were numbered, if not over.[47]

In 'La cuesta de las comadres', the success of the *reparto* is questioned through irony. There are enough centripetal situational ironies for an appre-ciation based solely on the fiction in itself: the narrator's comical kicking of the corpse to check that it is not alive; the fact that Remigio makes a murderer of the narrator by falsely accusing him of being a murderer; the absurdity of the narrator asking Remigio, the dead victim, to pardon him; finally, the fact that the only person in 'La cuesta de las comadres' who actually kills a Torrico is their only friend in the community. There is also centripetal verbal irony: Remigio's disingenuous understatement concerning the dead man just kicked by the narrator, 'No, no te creas, nomás está tantito atarantado ...' (49), and the narrator's use of the phrase 'Quisiera que te dieras cabal cuenta de que ...' (53–54) to a man who is dead. Despite the abundance of centrip-etal irony, there is no doubt also that an awareness of Cárdenas's peasant unity campaign can shed further light on the complex process of irony that lies within the text. In this story, a community is seen to wither away at the

---

[45] Lázaro Cárdenas, *La unificación campesina* (Mexico City: Partido Revolucionario Institucional, 1934).

[46] Rafael Ramírez, *El Porvenir, Plan Sexenal Infantil*, 4 (Mexico City: Secretaría de Educación Pública, Biblioteca Cuauhtémoc, 1937). Further images include neatly ploughed fields, hard-working peasants, teachers and smiling, well-behaved children making democratic decisions.

[47] For an example of this rhetorical tactic, see Emilio Portes Gil, *La escuela y el campesino* (Mexico City: Instituto de Estudios Sociales, Políticos y Económicos, 1936). This example is discussed at length in Chapter 5.

very time of the 'reparto', the agrarian reform which formed the basis of Cárdenas's national unity campaign in the countryside. The word 'reparto' is only mentioned once but it is key to the disappearance of the community and is a word that has a strong enough resonance in Mexico to evoke the story's historical context.

Many critics have commented on the theme of violence in Rulfo's works, a popular area of discussion being the detailed description of the killing of one of the tyrannical landlords of la Cuesta de las Comadres, Remigio Torrico. What has impressed many is the narrator's cold, clinical description as much as the violence itself. As Silvia Lorente-Murphy writes:

> El acto violento … lejos de ser interpretado con horror por parte de sus consumadores, aparece, por el contrario, como la reacción normal, casi trivial, y hasta inconsciente de estos seres habituados a concebir el absurdo de sus vidas, relegadas al abandono y miseria, como parte de una norma que les han impuesto.[48]

Lorente-Murphy's interpretation of the story's central act of violence stresses a symbolic subversiveness in the death of the landlord: '… el protagonista, al matar a Remigio Torrico, intenta acabar de alguna manera con los problemas creados por el *caciquismo* que sobrevivió a la Revolución'.[49] In this interpretation, I shall argue that the indifference of the narrator and his murder of Remigio, rather than representing an act of subversion, in fact betrays a certain *kinship* with his overseers that is evident throughout the story. This affinity, on an extra-textual level, suggests an acceptance of the imposed, patriarchal norm of violence.

Notwithstanding the domination of the Torricos, the narrator has immense respect for his landlords. In the very first line of the story, the narrator describes them as always having been 'buenos amigos' (46). He goes on to declare his satisfaction that his corn is enjoyed by them without salt and he then partakes with them in a robbery which results in a death. However, he says nothing in reproach of the murderers and, indeed, he even laments the fact that he is no longer of use in such activities. The narrator is therefore a character more likely to follow in the footsteps of the Torricos than challenge their authority. It is no surprise that his own killing of Remigio is chillingly reminiscent of the killing in the robbery committed by the brothers, at least in terms of the apparent indifference of the killer:

---

[48] Silvia Lorente-Murphy, *Realidad y mito de la Revolución Mexicana* (Madrid: Editorial Pliegos, 1988), p. 54.

[49] Lorente-Murphy, p. 54.

> Ya la luna se había metido del otro lado de los encinos cuando yo regresé
> a la Cuesta de las Comadres con la canasta pizcadora vacía. Antes de volv-
> erla a guardar, le di unas cuantas zambullidas en el arroyo para que se le
> enjuagara la sangre. Yo la iba a necesitar muy seguido y no me hubiera
> gustado ver la sangre de Remigio a cada rato. (54)

The narrator's unemotional attitude towards the blood of Remigio suggests
that he is little better than the victim of his crime, for the Torricos themselves
display a brash indifference to the murder they commit: 'Los oí que cantaban
durante largo rato, hasta que amaneció' (49). Indeed, the accompaniment of
murder with singing is indicative of a kind of 'dark harmony' at work in this
depiction of the countryside, where brutality is combined with an almost
pleasant sense of normality. For example, the sound of singing becomes the
sound of dogs barking as the morning arrives and, just after the act of murder,
the narrator recalls the festivities of Zapotlán, which themselves represent a
kind of 'civilised' backdrop to the murderous activities symbolised by the
almost ubiquitous birds-of-prey in Rulfo's fiction, *zopilotes*: '... en Zapotlán
estaban quemando cohetes, mientras que por el rumbo donde tiré a Remigio
se levantaba una gran parvada de zopilotes a cada tronido que daban los
cohetes' (54). This 'dark harmony', a fusion of violence with normality, is
noticeable after both murders and partly accounts for the curious absence of
psychological tension in the narrator's confession: he is completely satisfied
with the actions of both himself and the Torricos and, while it is clear that
the narrator acts in self-defence, it is equally clear from his description of
the action that the violence has not upset him. Though he feels compassion
for his dying victim, he also, somewhat grotesquely for the reader, seems to
consider himself benevolent for killing him off with a stab in the heart.

The narrator not only unconsciously buys into the normality of everyday
violence, he also receives uncritically the hierarchical structure of rural
society. Despite the violence, it seems that he has not lost his sense of where
he belongs and who he is in relation to Remigio. He has the presence of
mind to offer an explanation that he was incapable of giving in the time his
victim was alive. There is no need for an explanation if the narrator knows
he is innocent, yet he offers one in a tone of apology which suggests that
he has not been touched by the 'radical' spirit of the state's reforms: 'Mira,
Remigio, me has de dispensar pero yo no maté a Odilón ...' (53). If this is
in fact evidence of a latent spirit of Catholic confession on the part of the
narrator, it is interesting to note that he does not refer to God or religion
throughout his account and that the less loaded term 'dispensar' is preferred
to the more Catholic 'perdonar'. Indeed, is it the case that the role of the
absent state and the absent Church is assumed by the landlord? Does this
landlord exert as much power over his tenants when he is dead as when he

is alive? The narrator's manner here suggests that he feels somehow obliged to account for himself before his victim, notwithstanding the violence of the Torricos themselves and the fact that the victim is dead anyway. He repeats apologetically on a further two occasions that he did not kill Odilón, before finishing, 'Eso le dije al difunto Remigio' (54). The word 'difunto', used for the third time in the text, now seems to carry a centripetal verbal irony, for the peasant's natural subservience to the *hacendado* is far from 'difunto'. Neither is the colonial resort to violence which characterises the countryside and its hacienda-based culture. As we have seen in 'Acuérdate', as well as here, the spirit of the patriarchal system is, in fact, alive. How does this square with Cárdenas's 'socialist' peasant unification campaign?

Against the background of the historical context evoked by the word 'reparto', a feeling of unease is created by a situational irony in which patriarchal violence, rather than 'radical' reform backed by a united, 'revolutionary' country, seems to have achieved what that *reforma agraria* had intended but not managed: the death of the tyrannical landlord. On closer inspection, though, we see that in fact this death is merely physical and mechanical. The narrator demonstrates that, while the post-Revolutionary *reforma agraria* has taken place on a practical and mechanical basis, the *spirit* of the legislation – the extirpation of the hacienda along with the system of dependency and violence it represents – is alive and kicking and almost entirely responsible for the fragmentation of the rural community in 'La Cuesta de las Comadres'. It transpires, for example, that the tendency to violence is the real reason for Odilón's death too: a brawl in neighbouring Zapotlán results in the murder of Remigio's brother. In the very first paragraph of the story, the narrator describes the animosity between Zapotlán and la Cuesta de las Comadres:

> Ahora eso de que no los quisieran en Zapotlán no tenía ninguna importancia, porque tampoco a mí querían allí, y tengo entendido que a nadie de los que vivíamos en la Cuesta de las Comadres nos pudieron ver con buenos ojos los de Zapotlán. (45)

Lest we should think that this was a kind of tension that could be resolved with Cárdenas's concept of peasant unification, the narrator tells us that 'Esto era desde viejos tiempos' (45). In other words, this fragmented and hostile atmosphere is a constant of life in the countryside. Indeed, the frequent 'desavenencias' among the people of la Cuesta de las Comadres are as accepted as the Torricos's dominion, itself a kind of everlasting constant:

> Y si no es mucho decir, ellos eran allí los dueños de la tierra y de las casas que estaban encima de la tierra, con todo y que, cuando el reparto, la mayor parte de la Cuesta de las Comadres nos había tocado por igual a los sesenta

que allí vivíamos, y a ellos, a los Torricos, nada más un pedazo de monte, con una mezcalera nada más, pero donde estaban desperdigadas casi todas las casas. A pesar de eso la Cuesta de las Comadres era de los Torricos. El coamil que yo trabajaba era también de ellos: de Odilón y Remigio Torrico, y la docena y media de lomas verdes que se veían allá abajo eran juntamente de ellos. (45–46)

Peasant unification, socialist education and agrarian reform programmes are doomed to fail against such a resistant legacy of violence and division and, indeed, they have no effect on life in this part of the countryside: the *reparto* changes nothing in the patriarchal relationship between the *cacique*-land-lord and the *campesino*; nobody takes any notice of the legislation on land redistribution; there is an ongoing, violent and deep-seated rivalry between Zapotlán and la Cuesta de las Comadres whilst the state is completely absent from the scene, leaving colonial hierarchies in place. Furthermore, betraying his own attachment to semi-feudal patriarchal systems, the narrator expresses surprise, with the words 'sin embargo', at the community's rejection of the repressive set-up in la Cuesta de las Comadres:

Sin embargo, de aquellos días a esta parte, la Cuesta de las Comadres se había ido deshabitando. De tiempo en tiempo, alguien se iba; atravesaba el guardaganado donde está el palo alto, y desaparecía entre los encinos y no volvía a aparecer ya nunca. Se iban, eso era todo. (46)

The narrator's surprise reveals that he is at once a relic and an inadvertent flag-bearer of a patriarchal society based on violence. Thus, without specifically mentioning the anti-*hacendado* spirit of the *reparto*, Rulfo is undermining it by presenting to us – in a case of centrifugal situational irony with respect to the land reform programme – a character who is a sturdy, tenacious progeny of the *hacendado* mindset. Indeed, he is perhaps even hardened in this way of thinking by the fragmentation of the community brought about by the failure of the land reform programme: isolation (caused by urbanisation) seems to increase rather than diminish his loyalty to the Torricos.

Not surprisingly, then, the violent murder of a man the narrator respects is unexpected by the teller of the story: it is, as Rowe stresses, 'seen as normal, after the event, but at the time it comes from an unknown direction, outside awareness'.[50] I would suggest that this unconscious use of violence is a result of the narrator's uncritical assumption of violent patriarchal values which have been left unaltered by state intervention. Indeed, the state is seemingly unnecessary, for there had never been any need to dispute the fact that the

---

[50] Rowe, p. 37.

land had been and always would be the property of the Torricos: 'No había por qué averiguar nada. Todo mundo sabía que así era' (46). This was a far cry from Cárdenas's promise of state leadership for those who found themselves 'ajenos a toda civilización material y espiritual': 'La intervención del Estado', Cárdenas had promised in a speech in 1934, 'ha de ser cada vez mayor, cada vez más frecuente y cada vez más a fondo.'[51] Furthermore, not only has the state failed to deal with the power structures which make justice, peace and therefore unity in the countryside an impossibility, it has also ignored what it sees as the equally significant factor of fatalism among the peasantry. Despite Cárdenas's socialist education programme, the peasants are shackled by a sense of resignation rooted in a fatalistic attitude towards systems of power: 'Es seguro que les sobraban ganas de pelearse con los Torricos para desquitarse de todo el mal que les habían hecho; pero no tuvieron ánimos' (46). These failures have created, instead of a unified peasantry, a fragmented and finally 'disappeared' community, the remains of which are the relic of a violent and divisive *hacendado* mentality in the shape of a narrator seemingly unaware of the unacceptability of this mentality in the peaceful, democratic and unified countryside imagined by the state.

Within this pessimistic outlook, centripetal cosmic irony is utilised to portray a feeling of the impossibility of change in the countryside. One example of this is the fact that the Torricos's domination is linked, via the word 'calamidad', to climatic oppression in the form of freezes which destroy the crops:

> Creyeron seguramente que el año siguiente sería lo mismo y parece que ya no se sintieron con ganas de seguir soportando las calamidades del tiempo todos los años y la calamidad de los Torricos todo el tiempo. (50)

This is a form of centripetal cosmic irony: the submission to forces greater than the human is connected to the peasants' submission to the Torricos. The more centrifugal interpretation being invited here could be that the peasant unification and land reform campaigns are unlikely ever to dislodge the peasant–*hacendado* relationship which lies at the heart of the rural problem, for this divisive and hierarchical relationship is as permanent as the weather and the cycle of *heladas* which destroys the peasants' crops. This theme of permanence is a central feature, indeed, of Rulfo's photography. One good

[51] 'Mensaje al Congreso de la Unión al tomar posesión de la primera magistratura del país', in *Nuestra Historia, Manifiestos históricos de la lucha del pueblo de México por su independencia, libertad, justicia, dignidad y soberanía*, Tomo 1, Siglo XX (Mexico City: Comité Ejecutivo Nacional Democrático del Sindicato Nacional de Trabajadores de la Educación, 2009), pp. 97–98.

example is 'Erupción del Paricutín y templo de Parangaricutiro', which would have been taken not long after 1943, when a volcano 200 miles west of Mexico City violently erupted, burying the neighbouring villages of Paricutín and Parangaricutiro in volcanic ash.[52] What is telling is that Rulfo's middleground consists of the erupting volcano itself, the surrounding hills and a ruined church tower (another tower remains standing). In a carefully managed angle, Rulfo ensures that the upper, jagged outline of this destroyed tower follows that of the hills. Thus, the tower and the hills merge whilst the remaining, standing tower in the upper foreground looms higher than the volcano in the perspective provided, suggestively defying nature's attempt to crush both the church of Parangaricutiro and the colonial power structures it represents.[53] In this photograph, and in the story under discussion here, entrenched power structures, whether local or more extended, seem to remain as solid and permanent as cycles of weather as well as being resistant to potentially threatening events (a volcano in the photograph; the 'reparto' – or even the actual deaths of the Torricos – in this story). The result in 'La Cuesta de las Comadres' is the dispersal of the community.[54]

Meanwhile, and equally significantly, the rural community is deeply divided within itself and remote areas such as those that Rulfo knew in his childhood would be shut out from the world. This process is not only indicated thematically in the violent rivalry between la Cuesta de las Comadres and Zapotlán, it is also symbolically represented in the dense woods that separate the two places, ironically (in a cosmic sense) growing more dense at the time of Cárdenas's peasant unification campaign:

> Antes, desde aquí, sentado donde ahora estoy, se veía claramente Zapotlán. En cualquier hora del día y de la noche podía verse la manchita blanca de Zapotlán allá lejos. Pero ahora las jarillas han crecido muy tupido y por más que el aire las mueve de un lado para otro, no dejan ver nada de nada. (47)

The result of this process, for remote areas, is a picture of complete abandonment, by both man and nature:

> Los únicos que no dejaron de venir fueron los aguaceros de mediados de año, y esos ventarrones que soplan en febreros y que le vuelan a uno la

[52] Photograph in Carlos Fuentes et al., *Mexico: Juan Rulfo fotógrafo* (Mexico City: Lunwerg, 2001), p. 169.
[53] See Chapter 5 of the present study for more on the durability of Catholic power structures.
[54] Interestingly, the result of the volcano was also a dispersal occasioned by the evacuation of buried villages.

cobija a cada rato. De vez en cuando, también, venían los cuervos volando muy bajito y graznando fuerte como si creyeran estar en algún lugar deshabitado. (47)

Thus, just as the yearly freezes suggest the permanence of local oppression, natural phenomena such as the obstructing trees, the wind circling in a life-less area, the crows and the rain cycles suggest that abandonment is now a permanent feature of the countryside. These areas are remote and excluded from national processes in a way that runs against the grain of Cárdenas's rural propaganda, based as it was on a vision of a modern, integrated and unified peasantry. One explanation for the failure of this project would be that the desire for 'unity' in the countryside was not entirely sincere. It could be argued that it was merely a concept that Cárdenas fostered and manipulated in the 1930s to bolster the political unity that his regime required to maintain power, for it grounded his support in a mass following that would help him to stave off the type of political engineering and military uprisings that had constantly threatened the regimes of Obregón and Plutarco Elías Calles.

There is yet another explanation for the narrator's actions which takes us onto a more extreme form of centrifugal cosmic irony. If, centripetally, nature is seen to symbolise the permanence of all-pervasive and eternal local power structures within the story, is it possible that that same nature can be seen to symbolise the permanence of a discourse that is equally oppressive but not easy to pin down in Rulfo's narrative, i.e. the discourse of coloni-alism? Could this discourse, which creates a powerful sense of hierarchy and an attendant code of legitimised violence, be the real culprit for the type of peasant mentality which sees no contradiction between the act of killing a landlord in self-defence and retaining respect for him as a superior? There is no explicit mention of colonial history in Rulfo's work, whilst even the most historically contextualised criticism on Rulfo does not mention colonialist discourse as such. Nevertheless, as I hope the remaining chapters will show, there is plenty of evidence that the most centrifugal of targets in Rulfo's irony is a colonising discourse which can be read between the lines of post-Revolutionary rhetoric.

4

Ambivalence and the Crisis of the Mimic Man:
Irony and Context in 'Luvina'

In this chapter, I will consider the ways in which the narrative of a post-Revolutionary teacher, as related by Rulfo, represents ironically the remnants
of a colonial discourse.[1] As part of the context for this discussion, it is vital
to confront the wider implications of cultural studies in its relationship with
ethical considerations. Culture with a capital 'C', as Terry Eagleton warns
us, is dangerously exclusionary when dominant values become 'universal'
truths, and therefore exempt from political considerations: 'Culture in its
more mandarin sense, by disdainfully disowning the political as such,
can be criminally complicit with it.'[2] Any such interpretation of Mexican
culture, for example, might excuse the Mexican urban state of repression of
the Mexican rural population with the notion that 'universal' truths represented by an infallible Western civilisation must be absorbed by a 'backward' peasantry. On the other hand, there is also a danger of 'criminal
complicity' in culture with a small 'c', exemplified by 'blind particularism
… far too eager for a local habitation' where the glorification of individual
cultures can result in a 'pluralized nonconformism, in which the single
universe of Enlightenment, with its self-sameness and coercive logic, is
challenged by a whole series of mini-worlds displaying in miniature much
the same features'.[3] Thus, whilst acknowledging the peripheral viewpoint
of the Mexican peasantry, I do not wish to assume that they represent a
discrete world of fixed values of 'some pure essence of group identity'.[4]
On the other hand, if Eagleton's concerns have any validity, it is surely in
the suggestion that cultural studies ought not to ignore the political, and
therefore ethical, implications arising from any text that is read, validated
and circulated in a world of competing values.

---

[1]   Material from this chapter first appeared in an article in *The Journal of Iberian and
Latin American Studie*s (Cardiff), Vol. 11:1 (2005), 65–89. Its use here is by permission of the
publisher (Routledge, Taylor & Francis, http://www.informaworld.com).
[2]   Eagleton, p. 44.
[3]   Eagleton, pp. 42–44.
[4]   Eagleton, p. 44.

Therefore, there is, in Rulfo's (or anybody's) narratives, what I have called a political and ethical 'resonance' which is defined by its wider context. Luis Fernando Veas Mercado has suggested the importance of historical context in Rulfo's work, particularly the Cristero War of Rulfo's native Jalisco (1926–29), in which the state took military action to suppress a rural rebellion against anti-clerical measures.[5] More recently, Patrick Dove has invited politically-contextualised criticism 'of the relation between disillusionment with the complicit ideologies of revolutionary nationalism and modernization, the disastrous effects of which Rulfo's text never ceases to document, and the facets of Rulfian poetics that have borne repeated comparisons to the European avant-garde'.[6] The thoughts of Robin Fiddian, on the relative absence of contact between Latin American literary studies and postcolonial criticism, offer a possible avenue for exploration in the area identified by Dove: 'The apparent marginalization of these specialisms (Latin American and Luso-Brazilian Studies) within the relatively new subject of postcolonial studies … is unjustified and in need of interrogation.'[7]

In this chapter, I will attempt to meet the challenges issued by Eagleton, Veas Mercado, Dove and Fiddian by experimenting with postcolonial criticism as a tool for analysing Rulfo's work.[8] I will postulate that a specific text does not operate in an individual vacuum but as part of concomitant socio-historical and political processes which cannot easily be ignored unless political and ethical considerations are discarded too. This interpretative model will inform my exploration of the short story 'Luvina', in which the recollections of a state-employed teacher in rural, post-Revolutionary Mexico appear to either support or counter what I call the 'colonising discourse' of the urban, post-colonial Mexican state, depending largely on the extent of the reader's engagement with the historical, political and ethical implications of the story. Contextualisation, as John McLeod explains in *Beginning Postcolonialism*, can allow us to explore the position of a text in contemporary debates for, indeed, 'literary texts are always *mediations*: they do not passively reflect the world but actively interrogate

---

5   Luis Fernando Veas Mercado, *Los modos narrativos en los cuentos en primera persona de Juan Rulfo* (Mexico City: Universidad Nacional Autónoma de México, 1984), p. 76.

6   Patrick Dove, 'Reflections on the Origin, Transculturation and Tragedy in *Pedro Páramo*', *Angelaki, Journal of the Theoretical Humanities*, 6:1 (2001), 91–110 (p. 94).

7   Robin Fiddian, ed., *Postcolonial Perspectives on the Cultures of Latin America and Lusophone Africa* (Liverpool : Liverpool University Press, 2000), p. vii.

8   In this study, the hyphenated 'post-colonial' refers to the historical period following the colony up to the present, while the unhyphenated 'postcolonial' refers to the field of study pioneered and developed by authors such as Fanon, Said, Bhabha and Spivak in which the ethics of the discourse of colonialism is interrogated with reference to textual representations of that discourse.

it, take up various positions in relation to prevailing views, resist or critique dominant ways of seeing'.[9]

The 'prevailing views' under discussion here are those held by urban, state propagators of the colonising discourse referred to above. The use of the word 'colonising' in reference to the rhetoric of post-independence governments is intended to distinguish it from the 'colonial' discourse of the Spanish Empire. 'Colonial' indicates the perspectives and attitudes of the Crown and Church in relation to colonial society, while 'colonising' denotes the ever-evolving discourse of post-independence governments to the present day.[10] Rulfo's work is especially relevant to the colonising discourse of the pre-Revolutionary governments of Mexico (from Independence to 1910) and that of the post-Revolutionary government (1910 to 1940). The fusion of these two post-independence periods is justified by the lack of ground-breaking change in ideology and thinking after the Revolution. Although some 'revolutionary' changes may have taken place, as Alan Knight states, 'ideas and customs changed (if they changed at all) at a more glacial pace'.[11] Moreover, the use of the word 'colonising' itself refers to the quest for a coherent image of the Mexican nation on which both nineteenth-century governments and the post-Revolutionary regime were explicitly insistent.[12] However, I have argued in the previous chapter that the model of integration this produced was more apparently a post-colonial euphemism for engaging the countryside – the state's Other – in economic, political and social terms dictated by the urban state. Here, I would like to add that it had the effect of creating a modus operandi that was effectively a form of neo-colonial domination. As a result of

[9] John McLeod, *Beginning Postcolonialism* (Manchester: Manchester University Press, 2000), p. 144. I am indebted to McLeod for this work which demystifies many of the very useful theoretical models in the field of postcolonial criticism. Occasionally, for reasons of accessibility and clarity, I may quote his words rather those of the authors of the theories themselves.

[10] The issue of defining distinct temporalities within the field of postcolonial criticism is fraught with difficulties. The above distinction is suggested as a working model, which undoubtedly will be subject to ambiguities and imperfections. However, the advantage it allows us is the possibility of recognising that the period of the Spanish colony, at least in terms of the discourse it produces, is not a finite epoch but an ever-extant agent in the imagination of once-colonised peoples.

[11] Alan Knight, 'Popular Culture and the Revolutionary State in Mexico, 1910–1940', *Hispanic American Historical Review*, 74:3 (1994), 393–444 (p. 399).

[12] As Stanley R. Ross indicates, in his Introduction to *Is the Mexican Revolution Dead?* (New York: Alfred A. Knopf, 1966), p. 8: 'Ever since 1810 the Mexicans have been struggling to create an entity which could properly be called the Mexican nation. The Revolution sought to mold and to bind together the disparate elements that composed Mexico into a unified nation – one which would be economically as well as politically independent and which would be directed by Mexicans for the benefit of Mexicans.'

this colonising discourse, both the pre-Revolutionary and post-Revolutionary governments of Mexico failed to challenge the legacy of colonialism in the imagination of the country's people.

The two questions which now concern me, then, are the following: Firstly, what discursive strategies are employed in this colonising discourse? Secondly, if the teacher of 'Luvina' takes this discourse with him to the countryside, how specifically are these strategies countered in a postcolonial reading of Rulfo's story based on centrifugal irony?

The Colonising Discourse

In *Orientalism*, Edward Said posits the creation of an Orientalist discourse, a Western fantasy of the Orient rooted in institutions and literature, that legitimates the power relations between the West and the Orient: 'European culture gained in strength and identity by setting itself off against the Orient as a sort of surrogate and even underground self.'[13] In Latin America, the desperate quest for national identities in the nineteenth century created similar conflicts rooted in the post-colonial struggle between civilisation (Self) and barbarism (Other), most evidently in the terms laid out by Domingo Sarmiento in *Facundo* (1845), whose methodology was excruciatingly simplistic: '[he] reasoned that those factors missing in barbarism would be the factors that would cause civilization'.[14] His principal assault was therefore on regional *caudillismo*, the inverse of urban civilisation in Buenos Aires, whilst that of the Mexican post-Revolutionary state centred on the peasantry, seen as the inverse of urban civilisation in Mexico City. The education reformers of the Porfirian era 'consideraban que los campesinos eran una masa homogénea de parias enfermizos, aletargados y supersticiosos'.[15] Their response to this situation was to attempt the enforcement of its opposite: 'procuraron transformar a los hombres de campo en pequeños agricultores letrados, sobrios, limpios, "racionales", abiertos a los caminos en el mercado económico, y patrióticos.'[16] Thus, to some extent, both Sarmiento and the nineteenth-century Mexican reformers betrayed the same tendency towards the creation and use of binary oppo-

[13] Edward Said, *Orientalism: Western Conceptions of the Orient* [1978] (London: Penguin, 1995), p. 3.
[14] Allison W. Bunkley, *The Life of Sarmiento* (Princeton: Princeton University Press, 1952), pp. 211–12 quoted by C. A. Jones in *Facundo: Critical Guides to Spanish Texts* (London: Grant & Cutler, 1974), p. 33.
[15] Mary Kay Vaughan, 'Cambio ideológico en la política educativa de la SEP: programas y libros de texto, 1921-40', in *Escuela y sociedad en el periodo cardenista*, ed. by Susana Quintanilla and Mary Kay Vaughan (Mexico City: Fondo de Cultura Económica, 1997), p. 76.
[16] Vaughan,'Cambio ideológico', p. 76.

sites in constructing the urban Self 'by default', that is to say negatively from a vision of the rural Other.

In the state's attempt to impose urban 'civilisation' on that Other, the peasantry not only became the scapegoat for economic 'backwardness', but also represented the general 'recalcitrance' of the countryside in its resistance to modernity, accused as it was of hoarding capital through the Church, encouraging local boss rule in the form of *caciquismo*, harbouring religious fanatics, providing only a subsistence economy for 'lazy' peasants, and being the home of anti-social habits such as drinking, vagrancy and gambling (all Other). Meanwhile, the urban state sought to impose the positivistic values of 'orden y progreso' which would enshrine secularity, protestant work ethics and Western social norms (all Self). In 1890, Mary Kay Vaughan informs us, one of the foremost statesmen of the Porfirian era, Justo Sierra, 'wagered that the school would defanaticize Mexicans and teach a scientific understanding of the universe. It would nurture habits of work, punctuality and thrift. It would encourage abstinence from alcohol, gambling and tobacco.'[17] The elites of the nineteenth century therefore increasingly adhered to an urbanised Self of 'surrogate Protestantism' which, besides traditional ideas of thrift, hard work and hygiene, encouraged 'the rational pursuit of profit … and demanded a "hard frugality" and commitment to bitter competition'.[18] This capitalist work ethic inflicted a new world on peasants accustomed to communal village practices and subsistence farming, which were deemed to be against the very spirit of modernity.[19] Nevertheless, nineteenth-century ideas on education and secularisation would carry over into the next generation of education reformers. Their attack on peasant practices required a zeal and iconoclastic vigour similar to that of the long-absent missionaries of the colonial period. The irony here was that it was no longer the Church that sent out the missionaries, aiming to curb the excesses of state-sponsored *encomenderos*: it was now the colonising, post-Revolutionary state attempting to integrate the peasantry on modern, capitalist terms, with the Church now considered the cause of evil.

The ruined church in 'Luvina' stands, therefore, as a symbol of the post-colonial state's attack. The teacher attempts to fill the void left by the empty rural church with the Self of the state, replacing the colonial, Catholic 'Luz

---

[17] Mary Kay Vaughan, *Cultural Politics in Revolution: Teachers, Peasants and Schools in Mexico, 1930–1940* (Tucson, AZ: University of Arizona Press, 1997), p. 26.

[18] Alan Knight, discussing Max Weber's ideas in *The Protestant Ethic and the Spirit of Capitalism* (London: Unwin University Books, 1974), in *The Mexican Revolution* (Cambridge: Cambridge University Press, 1986), p. 84.

[19] Knight, *The Mexican Revolution*, p. 158.

Divina' with the secular 'Luz Divina' of the post-Revolutionary regime.[20] While the light of reason in the sixteenth century resided in the Kingdom of God and scripture, the light this time would emanate from the Nation and the Revolutionary Constitution, words that were capitalised in newspaper articles and printed versions of speeches. This secularising policy was reinforced in 1933 by President Plutarco Elías Calles when he gave his infamous *Grito de Guadalajara*, announcing the goal of 'psychological revolution' to be 'taking over the consciences of children and of young people' and the creation of a new 'national soul'.[21] Later, in Lázaro Cárdenas's amendment to Article 3 of the Constitution, a 'socialistic' education would demand a continued assault on rural 'fanaticism and prejudices' by creating in the youth 'an exact and rational concept of the Universe and of social life'.[22] During the term of Cárdenas, the Secretaría de Educación Pública (SEP) also attempted to present the state as the new patriarchal guardian of the oppressed underclass, replacing its old god(s) by mobilising Cultural Missions and local, *campesino* organisations in a national state project marketed as materially and spiritually benevolent.[23] Even in statues commissioned by the state one could sense the tone of paternalism, as we can see from this description of a homage to Zapata placed in Cuautla in 1932, containing the remains of the now-institutionalised 'state' figure: 'Atop the crypt stood a granite Zapata on horseback looking down to and placing a hand on the shoulder of a simple campesino, who looked up to him in admiration.'[24]

The language of enlightenment, or 'ilustración', was key to this strategy of leadership in the ways of modernity. The state murals of the 1920s, inspired by José Vasconcelos, the first minister of the new SEP (1920 to 1924), suggested universal themes, reflecting the new, high-flown emancipatory ideals for society, emphasised in works such as Orozco's *Maternidad*, Rivera's *La Creación* and Siqueiros's *Los Elementos*, where white or Europeanised figures symbolised these concepts. It is possible that these universal ideals are the 'ilusiones cabales' ('illusions intact') that drive the teacher to Luvina with such hope. What greater motivation for a romantic idealist than the redemption of a remote, neglected village through learning,

---

[20] The term 'Luz Divina' could possibly even be the inspiration for the title of 'Luvina': the light of 'reason' now ostensibly held solely by the state, and not by God.

[21] Knight, 'Popular Culture', p. 402.

[22] Revised article quoted from George C. Booth, *Mexico's School-Made Society* [1941] (New York: Greenwood, 1969) p. 2.

[23] For a description of SEP activity at this time, see Vaughan, *Cultural Politics*, pp. 27–36.

[24] Ilene O'Malley, *The Myth of the Revolution, Hero Cults and Institutionalisation of the Mexican State, 1920–1940* (Westport, CT: Greenwood Press, 1986), p. 60.

literacy and participation in the newly-forged, secular nation? In one of these murals, *La Creación*, religious imagery is appropriated by the state to form a picture of classical Enlightenment. The geometrical representations of the sun and the stars within it evoke a model of learning based on science. The figures beneath the benign gaze of the sun are robed in classical Roman or Greek costumes. Those sitting on the ground appear to be indigenous but they are also naked, suggesting passive reception of classical culture by a noble savage. In the cavity below the sun, meanwhile, there is an image of peasants in a fertile, productive corn field. The general impression in 'Creation' is one of a 'Luz Divina', that of the urban state, impregnating rural society with classical culture and economic vitality. In another manifestation of this discourse, Vasconcelos had 'Mexican schoolgirls dressed in Greek togas dancing in the style of Isadora Duncan'.[25] This type of cultural production was intended in no uncertain terms to conquer the imagination of the post-Revolutionary nation and to configure it in terms of European values, creating a discourse that was hierarchical, if not altogether racist. So, at last, we approach the second key question in our interpretation of the text under consideration: how does the state teacher's urbanised, hierarchical, Europeanised, Self–Other discourse prepare him for his experience in the town of Luvina?

Cosmic Irony: The Failure of the Revolution in 'Luvina'

The narrator of 'Luvina' discovers immediately upon his arrival in the eponymous town that the Revolution has not happened. Beyond the mournfully uttered words 'ilusiones cabales', the romantic narrative of conquest and 'redemption' is not even allowed to surface before we are confronted with Hayden White's 'diremption'. The rural characters, far from representing 'blank slates' primed for the reception of civilising practices, actually mock these practices and the elements of nature seem determined to ensure that the Revolution and its modernising plans will fail. The teacher's story immediately engages the reader, then, with an air of centripetal cosmic irony, by which I mean a sense of an individual's struggle for good – what he perceives as the Revolutionary cause or his 'ilusiones cabales' (122) – thwarted by the implacable stubbornness of his natural and human environment, which turns these ideals into a mere 'plasta', a shapeless lump of ideas (128).

Nowhere is this stubbornness more poetically portrayed by Rulfo than in the landscape, which seems resistant to any attempt at upheaval, its physical

[25] Mary Kay Vaughan, *The State, Education, and Social Class in Mexico, 1880–1928* (DeKalb: Northern Illinois University Press, 1982), p. 138.

sterility suggesting a symbolic resistance to cultural or economic 'fertilisation': the town sits on top of a hill where the dew settles in the air before it falls; which prevents the flimsiest of plants from growing and nearly all the others wither in the attempt; in contrast to the classical shades of colour in the mural *La Creación*, the air is black, the wind is 'pardo' (120), the horizon 'desteñido' (120). A resistant nature is implied in the first sentence with the alliteration of the sounds 'p' and 'd', connoting the hardness of the word 'piedra': 'De los cerros altos del sur, el de Luvina es el más alto y el más *pedregoso*. Está *plagado* de esa *piedra* gris con la que hacen el cal ...' (119, my italics). Nature is not just stubborn but hostile to the Revolution: the land is steep and treacherous ('... Y la tierra es empinada. Se desgaja por todos lados ...', 119), the only growing plant scratches the air like a knife on a flint ('uno lo oye rasguñando el aire con sus ramas espinosas, haciendo un ruido como el de un cuchillo sobre una piedra de afilar', 120), the infrequent rain merely lashes the earth and leaves it unusable ('llegan unas cuantas tormentas que azotan la tierra y la desgarran, dejando nada más el pedregal flotando encima del tepetate', 121), and the land can cut the human feet that dare to tread on it, 'como si allí hasta a la tierra le hubiera crecido espinas' (121).

Furthermore, the inhabitants of the town follow a patrilineal tradition that seems to exist outside the state's paternal influence: 'Los hijos se pasan la vida trabajando para los padres como ellos trabajaron para los suyos y como quién sabe cuántos atrás de ellos cumplieron con su ley' (126). The word 'ley' in this context reinforces the feeling that the peasants live outside the government's law, chronological timescale and logic. Indeed, the regularity of the visits of the returning sons and the summer rains gives the town an atmosphere of timeless untouchability, almost a caricature of the paradise represented in Rivera's *La Creación*: 'Los días comienzan y se acaban. Luego viene la noche. Solamente el día y la noche hasta el día de la muerte, que para ellos es una esperanza' (126). Consequently, the inhabitants refuse to leave the town because they cannot leave their dead, suggesting that their defence of this right has to do with a mystical attachment to land: a peripheral, unwritten law quite distinct from metropolitan, written state laws. The reader senses, therefore, that the teacher faces an impossible task in modernising Luvina in accordance with the wishes of the post-Revolutionary government.

However, the reader's sense of sympathy with the narrator, based on cosmic irony, is gradually undermined by a tone of condescension. With the children outside the shop where he tells his story, he is firm but not exactly overbearing: they may make a noise but not near *him*. With the inhabitants of Luvina, too, he seems to encourage movement to another area for their own benefit, without necessarily forcing the issue: 'Un día traté de convencerlos de que se fueran a otro lugar, donde la tierra fuera buena. '¡Vámonos de aquí! – les dije –. No faltará modo de acomodarnos en alguna parte. El gobierno nos ayudará' (126–27). Nevertheless, his description of the *reaction* of the peasants to this suggestion is revealing of a highly patronising attitude: in their eyes, there is only 'una lucecita allá muy adentro' (127). Light being a Western symbol of reason and knowledge in the discourse of Orientalism, this description indicates that the people are backward and not ready for 'Enlightenment', or the 'Luz Divina' of the state. This kind of paternalistic stance is concisely expressed by Joel Poinsett, the first US ambassador to post-colonial Mexico, who predicated that the labouring classes were 'laborious, patient and submissive, but [...] lamentably ignorant'. If they were to be integrated into 'public affairs', Poinsett went on, 'they must be educated and released from the gross superstition under which they now labour'.[26] Indeed, his conclusion is that the tight, colonial control by Spain 'prevented *the light of knowledge* from penetrating into this Country'.[27] Thus, according to Poinsett, it was the *failure* of colonial discourse to 'civilise' the peasantry that led to the latter's 'ignorance', not its condescending premise of the need to 'civilise' in the first place, evident in his assumption that the 'ignorant' wish to participate in 'public affairs' at all. A hundred years later, the need to 'civilise' (later, to 'develop') with 'the light of knowledge' is still taken as a given and the idea of reappraising this assumption does not occur to the teacher.

Thus, it appears that the teacher has a daunting task not only because of the resistance of the natural environment to modernisation, a centripetal cosmic irony *within the text*, but also because of the inability of the colonising discourse to treat the Other as human and civilised in its own right, a centrifugal cosmic irony requiring engagement with *context*. Any attempt to separate these two ironic motions, which, as I have argued throughout this book, are interdependent, would be to miss the point of Rulfo's irony. Once we perceive the teacher's patronising tone in the context of a wider colonising discourse, we return to the text and find that the language of the story reinforces this perception. For example, the word 'allá' onomatopoeically expresses the remoteness of 'Luvina', perhaps resonating with the connotation of 'lobos' in the original title of the story, 'Loobina'. It is mentioned fifteen times in the text, helping to create a sense of Self and Other, for the cumulative effect is to distance narrator, interlocutor and reader from Luvina. The use of 'allá' above ('una lucecita allá muy adentro', 127) associates this distance with a distance in light, or in intellect and capabilities. In

---

26 Joel Poinsett, 'The Mexican Character', in *The Mexico Reader:8 History, Culture, Politics*, ed. by Joseph and Henderson, p. 13.

27 Poinsett, p. 14. Emphasis added.

the following example, when the narrator is told of an apparently intransi-
gent belief in the law of the dead, the word 'allá' creates a tone that is both
resigned and disparaging: '*Y allá siguen.* Usted los verá ahora que vaya.
Mascando bagazos de mezquite seco y tragándose su propia saliva para
engañar el hambre' (127).[28]

The distancing effect is accentuated by the frequent use of another word,
'ellos', mentioned ten times as a subject pronoun in reference to the inhabitants of Luvina, at least three times as a *redundant* subject pronoun, emphasising their distance not only from 'Enlightenment' but from the teacher's
sense of Self:

> Allí no podrá probar sino un mezcal que *ellos* hacen con una yerba
> llamada hojasé, y que a los primeros tragos estará usted dando de volteretas
> como si lo chacamotearan. (122, italics added)

> *Ellos* me oyeron, sin parpadear, mirándome desde el fondo de sus ojos,
> de los que sólo se asomaba una lucecita allá muy adentro.' (127, italics
> added)

> *Yo* les dije que era la Patria. *Ellos* movieron la cabeza diciendo que no.
> Y se rieron. (127, italics added)

In the first quotation, there is the suggestion of an 'exotic' potion-like
substance associated with 'ellos'; in the second, we have the impresssion of
'ellos' as unblinking animals; in the third, the juxtaposition of the first and
third person creates distance. Combined, the words 'allá' and 'ellos' form
the dismissive term 'Allá ellos', almost as if the teacher might be saying: 'Si
así quieren vivir, allá ellos' or 'If that's how they want to live, that's *their*
lookout.' Thus, rather in the tradition of Sarmiento's thinking, the teacher is
trained to see in 'ellos' the aspects of Self he must suppress or distance in
order to form a secular identity, as though these elements were unacceptable
to both the personal and the national Self. He has, in short, internalised the
discourse of colonialism.

The centripetal cosmic irony implied in the teacher's struggle to convert
the peasantry to the Revolutionary cause, which might initially inspire
sympathy, or at least pity, is therefore weakened by the patronising tone of a
colonising discourse internalised by the teacher. Nevertheless, this reader at
least, finishes the story with his sympathy intact. Why should this be? For an
answer to this question, a far deeper exploration of the context of the story is

---

[28] Emphasis added.

required. The psychological complexity of the narrator, and any consequent sympathy for him, cannot be fully appreciated through a reading based on the centripetal cosmic irony described above, for this irony is arguably contained within the text itself. Indeed, we do not necessarily need to know about the Revolution or colonising discourses to understand that the teacher has arrived in an 'unsuitable' environment for Revolution. By exploring Rulfo's use of centrifugal verbal, situational and cosmic ironies in a more detailed postcolonial context, I hope to expose the ambivalence of the post-Revolutionary state's colonising discourse expressed in the figure of the teacher as a kind of tragic version of Bhabha's 'mimic man'. As a cultural missionary, this mimic man is rather more than a mere agent of a repressive state, and he invites a good deal of residual sympathy in the midst of a crisis we understand as not entirely of his own making. After all, as Eagleton puts it, 'Culture and crisis go together like Laurel and Hardy.'[29]

Context and Centrifugal Irony

In this chapter, I have so far prioritised local context in an effort to balance some of the predilections for 'universal', narrative concerns in the work of Rulfo. As indicated above, I will follow postcolonial methods with which the consideration of contingent historical and geographical specificities help to enable the 'empowerment' of a text as a subjective force which challenges the universalising norms propagated by the colonising state. After all, apart from objectifying the peasantry or other marginalised groups, colonial and colonising discourses can also define the ways in which we *read*. Seeing fiction in the context of liberal, humanist concerns for 'objective' or 'universal' truth, of which the holders are those (inevitably Westernised and bourgeois) minds who carry out the search, relegates local contexts to instances of 'local colour'. Indeed, critics have consistently viewed the work of Latin American authors in terms of 'universally-understood' concepts such as 'modernism' and 'postmodernism', which are essentially European and do not always sit well with Latin American texts, despite the insistence of some critics on citing authors such as Proust, Joyce, Faulkner and Kafka as the key influences on the literary output of that continent.[30] Such

---

[29] Eagleton, p. 37.

[30] Though he gives passing credit to Latin American poets such as Paz and Neruda, Carlos Fuentes is one critic who slightly overstates this influence from Europe. See, for example, this discussion of the breakdown of linear time in literature: 'William Faulker is an expression of it, James Joyce is a prime expression, as are Virgina Woolf, Marcel Proust and Kafka – they're all talking about a breakdown of linear time … And suddenly our novelists see themselves in this time which, by the way, [Latin American] poets had already seen.' See the interview with

influences do sometimes exist and have indeed been acknowledged by many Latin American writers. However, to propose such aesthetic frameworks as 'modernism' and 'postmodernism' as the most appropriate within the field of Latin American literary studies is arguably to confer a status of 'influencer' and 'influenced' on Latin American literature, with a bias towards Europe as the projector of 'influence'. On the other hand, postcolonial analyses of texts at least attempt, however imperfectly, to shift our understanding 'away from the abstract issue of a text's universal and timeless value and towards a more politicised approach which [analyses] texts primarily within historical and geographical contexts'.[31]

In the case of 'Luvina', I would argue that the key to unlocking the context of the story, and therefore a more complete understanding of the story's relationship with this context, is centrifugal irony. With a postcolonial reading of Rulfo's 'Luvina', I am attempting to disclose an extreme form of centrifugal irony in which the irony of a text may be said to engage profoundly with extra-textual referents, as opposed to centripetal irony which relies simply on the referents contained within the text itself. For example, the engagement with a possible postcolonial context in Jorge Luis Borges's short story 'Emma Zunz' is encouraged by his suggestively ironic description of the sailor and his purpose as instrument for the *porteña* who wishes to use him to fake a rape: 'El hombre, sueco o finlandés, no hablaba español; fue una herramienta para Emma como ésta lo fue para él, pero ella sirvió para el goce y él para la justicia.'[32] Thus, in a reversal of the colonial concept of Europe conquering the virgin territory of the 'new' continent peopled by a strange, dark race, it is the European man – vaguely and dismissively characterised as a Scandinavian, conjuring up images for the reader of somebody blond and blue-eyed – who has become the object of exploitation by the Latin American 'virgin'. This centrifugal situational irony is complemented by a centrifugal verbal irony in the word 'justicia', which now suggests a revenge rooted in history as well as in personal circumstances. Similarly, as discussed in the previous chapter, in 'El día del derrumbe', the peasant's cry of '¡Exacto!' during a speech which is far from clear or appropriate can be read as an ironic political gesture against the rhetoric of Revolution and its colonising discourse.[33] Returning to 'Luvina', if the teacher's patronising discourse threatens a sympathy on the part of

---

John King in *Modern Latin American Fiction: A Survey*, ed. by John King (London: Faber and Faber, 1987), p. 142.

[31] McLeod, p. 27.

[32] Jorge Luis Borges, 'Emma Zunz', from the collection *El Aleph* (Buenos Aires: Emecé, 1957), p. 63.

[33] The extent to which this is the irony of the writer as speaker, rather than that of the char-

the reader born of a sense of centripetal cosmic irony, we shall see that it is in centrifugal verbal, situational and cosmic irony that Rulfo creates an equally suggestive relationship with the political context of the story, allowing a *nuanced* sympathy to survive intact. This allows the story's cosmic irony to remain by creating an obstacle which is not fate, God or nature but the man-made colonising discourse in which the teacher is both trapped and participating.

The terms 'centripetal' and 'centrifugal' are borrowed from the reflections of Mikhail Bakhtin and, again, such terms are used for convenience only for they cannot be said to be independent of each other. Indeed, the extent to which one can draw a boundary between centripetal and centrifugal irony is highly uncertain, for 'every utterance participates in the "unitary language" (in its centripetal forces and tendencies) *and at the same time* partakes of social and historical heteroglossia'.[34] Just as helpful to this study, therefore, are Bakhtin's thoughts on this 'heteroglossia', which are most succinctly summarised by Raman Selden and Peter Widdowson:

> The term ['heteroglossia'] … asserts the way in which context defines the meaning of utterances, social voices and their individual expressions. A single voice is constantly (and to some extent unconsciously) producing a plenitude of meanings, which stem from social interaction (dialogue). Monologue is not really possible.[35]

In Rulfo's story, a 'monologic utterance' or 'speaking individuum' (centripetal) disguises a communication between urban and rural culture (centrifugal) in which the latter is given a rare voice.[36] Although this voice is ultimately that of the author who writes it, we could still argue, from a Bakhtinian point of view, that the act of writing it demonstrates 'the way language is made to disrupt authority and liberate alternative voices'.[37] For example, the story 'Luvina' contests urban discourse with an act of literary ventriloquism in which Rulfo voices the conflicting ideology and belief systems of rural Mexico, even though this is not immediately apparent, for it is the teacher's urban discourse, and the centripetal cosmic irony, which seem to dominate the story. This urban discourse itself is not necessarily one-dimensional in its

---

acter as speaker, is related to the notion of literary ventriloquism, which is considered towards the end of the chapter.

34 Mikhail Bakhtin, *The Dialogic Imagination* [1981] (Austin: University of Texas Press, 2000), p. 272. Emphasis added. Translation by Caryl Emerson and Michael Holquist.

35 Raman Selden and Peter Widdowson, *A Reader's Guide to Contemporary Literary Theory* (London: Harvester Wheatsheaf, 1993), p. 39.

36 These terms are discussed in Bakhtin, p. 270.

37 Selden and Widdowson, p. 39.

condescension towards the peasantry, and the teacher's status as 'mimic man' makes him an ideal expression of its ambivalence.

State and Mimic Man: Ambivalence in the Colonising Discourse

Before finishing 'Luvina', Rulfo wrote, in a report sent to the Centro Mexicano de Escritores, that the narrator of the story was to be a (presumably urban) state tax collector, with the key to the story being that the words of the teacher merely represent the *conscience* of the tax collector, rather than the utterings of a real human being.[38] However, the narrator in the final, published version of the story is a living former teacher and the interlocutor is almost certainly Luvina's *new* rural teacher, although the reason for the elimination of the urban tax collector was never made clear by Rulfo. On the one hand, we could say that the new rural teacher is almost certainly coached in urban ideology and therefore shares this facet of the tax collector's consciousness. However, the teacher also has a greater 'emancipatory' responsibility towards the peasants, making his position as mediator between the urban and rural sectors of Mexican society somewhat more likely to be 'ambivalent' than that of the tax collector.

To a greater extent than that of nineteenth-century governments, indeed, the discourse of the post-Revolutionary regime itself was also ambivalent in its relationship with the peasantry. As Homi K. Bhabha states, one of the aims of a colonial form of discourse is the creation of an inferior and dangerous Other: 'The objective of colonial discourse is to construe the colonised as a population of degenerate types on the basis of racial origin, in order to justify conquest and to establish systems of administration and instruction.'[39] However, this need to objectify an Other is contradicted in a modern, ostensibly egalitarian society by an equal need to *integrate* the colonised on terms with which the coloniser is familiar and comfortable. Thus, 'colonial discourse produces the colonised as a social reality which is at once an "other" and yet entirely knowable and visible'.[40] The cause for this ambivalence in Mexico is the survival of authoritarian colonialism and its consequent coexistence with 'emancipatory', post-Revolutionary rhetoric. These 'emancipatory' ideals were taken to heart by rural missionaries and quite reasonably, too, given that they were exemplified in the titles of articles written in the government's own *El maestro rural*: 'La ilustración de las masas', 'Las escuelas

---

[38] The report written by Rulfo for the Centro Mexicano de Escritores, which was sent on 15 January 1953, is quoted in Yvette Jiménez de Báez, *Juan Rulfo, del páramo a la esperanza, una lectura crítica de su obra* (Mexico City: El Colegio de México, 1990), p. 48.

[39] Homi K. Bhabha, *The Location of Culture* (London: Routledge, 1994), p. 70.

[40] Bhabha, pp. 70–71.

mexicanas educan a las masas' and 'Mexico quiere vivir en sociedad como pueblo civilizado'.[41] How does this ambivalence, between a distancing and integrative approach, manifest itself in the teacher of 'Luvina'?

In the report to the Centro Mexicano de Escritores quoted above, Rulfo proceeds to explore the causes of an imagined, ostensibly hostile countryside:

> ... va por primera vez a Loobina y, por consiguiente, obra como muchos hemos obrado en estos casos: imagina el lugar a su manera, ya que lo desconocido, en ocasiones, violenta la imaginación y crea figuras y situaciones que podrán no existir jamás.
>
> Espero haber logrado esta intención en el relato de Loobina ...[42]

Thus, what we have in the teacher's words is possibly the evocation not necessarily of a real village but of an imprecise Other in 'lo desconocido', creating rural 'figuras y situaciones' that exist only in his mind (originally in that of the urban state tax collector) in the form of a place strangely called 'Loobina', suggesting a 'wild' countryside in line with the type of one-dimensional colonialist discourse one might expect from an urban tax collector. In the same report, however, Rulfo also states that the story is 'enmarcado de un cuadro de desilusión'.[43] In fact, this disillusionment must have compelled Rulfo to find an alternative narrator exhibiting confusion, helplessness and a sense of being trapped by the falseness of the Self–Other dichotomy in which he is immersed, a cosmic irony in which the grand ironist is not an indomitable nature but, rather, a man-made discourse which is responsible for the narrator's disturbing 'figuras y situaciones que podrán no existir jamás'. The thoughts of an urban-trained rural teacher, rather than a more 'one-dimensional' urban tax collector, are a perfect and realistic vehicle for this interplay between objectifying, colonialist discourse and revolutionary, egalitarian rhetoric.

The teacher's role in the imposition of this discourse lies in the vulnerable interface between Self and Other, as a kind of go-between for state and countryside 'dialogue'. While there is no overt indication of his background, if we consider that the setting of the meeting with his interlocutor is apparently rural and that teachers are generally considered to be *petit-bourgeois* in this period of Mexican history, his position as go-between could be as geograph-

---

[41] Titles of articles written between 1922 and 1923 in *El Maestro*, reproduced in full in Valentina Cantón Arjona and Mario Aguirre Beltrán, *Revista 'El Maestro' 1921–1923. Raíces y vuelos de la propuesta educativa vasconcelista* (Morelia: Instituto Michoacano de Ciencias de la Educación, 1997), pp. 151–183.

[42] Jiménez de Báez, p. 48.

[43] Jiménez de Báez, p. 47.

ical and social as it is intellectual. This go-between may be described as a
'mimic man' for the urban colonisers, similar to one of T. B. Macauley's
famous class of Indians who, if we supplant the words 'Indian' and 'English'
with 'rural' and 'urban', would act as 'a class of interpreters between us and
the millions whom we govern – a class of persons Indian [*rural*] in blood and
colour, but English [*urban*] in tastes, in opinions, in morals and in intellect'.[44]
There is always the risk here of conflating different forms of colonial experience 'with an easy stroke of the "post"'.[45] But the psychological roots of
ambivalence may at least be surmised from the above description of the
mimic man, who, in the case of the post-Revolutionary rural missionary in
Mexico, would not only have the authoritarian attitude of one who is versed
in urban opinions, urban morals and urban intellect, but also a degree of
sympathy with the peasants' cause arising from socio-economic and possibly
ethnic proximity. Much more easily than could have been the case with a
state tax collector, then, the teacher's in-between status results ultimately in
the production of centrifugal verbal, situational and cosmic ironies which
generate the nuanced sympathy mentioned above.

Centrifugal Verbal Irony: 'Nation' and 'Reason'

The teacher twice asks his wife: '¿En qué país estamos?' (123–24). On both
occasions, the latter's response is to shrug her shoulders. The word 'país' is,
of course, loaded with the modern idea of nationhood. According to Timothy
Brennan, the word 'nation' refers 'both to the modern nation-state and to
something more ancient and nebulous – the "natio" – a local community,
domicile, family, condition of belonging', although the distinction is not
generally observed by nationalists.[46] The setting-up of boundaries in Latin
America was, indeed, a nationalist way of challenging anti-liberal imperi-
alism and joining the class of Europe by fostering imagined communities of
'deep horizontal comradeship' homologous to those of the mother continent.[47]
What was always uncertain, however, was the extent to which one could
call a group of communities in any given 'nation' a culturally-homogenous
group with a genuine 'condition of belonging'. As discussed in the previous

[44] T. B. Macauley, 'Minute on Education', in *Sources of Indian Tradition*, vol. II, ed. by
W. Theodore de Bary (New York: Columbia University Press, 1958), p. 49. Quoted by Bhabha,
p. 87.
[45] See Ella Shohat, 'Notes on the "Post-Colonial"', in *Social Text*, 31/32 (1992), 99–113
(p. 102).
[46] Timothy Brennan, 'The National Longing for Form', in *Nation and Narration*, ed. by
Homi K. Bhabha (London: Routledge, 1990), p. 45.
[47] Benedict Anderson, *Imagined Communities: Reflection on the Origins and Spread of
Nationalism* [1983] (London: Verso, 1987), p. 16.

chapter, for official organs such as the newspaper *El Nacional*, the task was to create just such a vision of belonging, as we see in a 1943 editorial that exploits the pull of the family metaphor: 'A través de la familia, esa primera forma de todos los amores, el hombre se eleva a un amor más amplio, más rico, al de la patria.'[48] The 'patria' is externally represented in the physical features of the country which are, in turn, part of the psychological makeup of its people, as one politician indicates, writing in *El Nacional*: 'Con la tierra se ha llegado a identificar a la patria, es un símbolo dentro de nuestra mística y el escenario de nuestra mexicanidad.'[49] With reference to sentimental appeals to the countryside, myths of the nation could be constructed through visual rhetoric, too, such as that propagated by the posters which were (and are) popularised by the state as a vision of the 'touristy' Mexico it wishes to portray.[50]

Despite these attempts to present a unified, modern Mexico, the narrator's experience of the peasants' relationship with the word 'patria' results in something of a minor trauma which threatens the very foundations of his status as a representative of the nation-state. The response of the peasants in this story suggests that the ideas of 'país' and 'patria' are alien to them, as we learn when the teacher tells the inhabitants of Luvina that the 'patria' is the mother of the government: 'Y se rieron. Fue la única vez que he visto reír a la gente de Luvina. Pelaron sus dientes molenques y me dijeron que no, que el gobierno no tenía madre' (127). On a literal level, the comment 'el gobierno no tiene madre' indicates that concepts of 'government' and 'nation' are based on nothing: Mexican family, togetherness or cultural homogeneity do not exist. This undermines the very purpose of the teacher's role in an ostensibly patriotic project. But the figurative meaning here is surely that the government's behaviour is 'descarado' or shameless. The narrator is most obviously referring to the non-literal meaning of the comment on the government: the idea that it is morally suspect because of its dubious parentage, the expression 'el gobierno no tiene madre' intimating that 'el gobierno es un hijo de la chingada'. Although the joke is on him, the narrator ultimately agrees with the peasants, his traumatic response to their non-acceptance of his role expressed in a resigned admission of intellectual defeat:

> Y tienen razón, ¿sabe usted? El señor ese sólo se acuerda de ellos cuando alguno de sus muchachos ha hecho alguna fechoría acá abajo. Entonces

48 *El Nacional*, 5 June 1943, p. 3.
49 José Pavia Crespo in *El Nacional*, 2 May 1955, p. 10.
50 For discussion of the process of selling a 'traditional' Mexico, see Alex Saragoza, 'The Selling of Mexico: Tourism and the State, 1929–1952', in Joseph, Rubenstein and Zolov, pp. 91–115.

manda por él hasta Luvina y se lo matan. De ahí en más no saben si existen. (127)

Here, 'tienen razón' literally means 'they are right'. The actions of the government ignite the teacher's latent or potential sympathy for his Other, the peasants, for he can see that they are treated either as criminals or as pupils of modernity. But the same phrase also implies that 'they have reason on their side': the project of Enlightenment, civilisation and reason is inverted by the discovery that 'reason' is not necessarily held by those holding material power. Suddenly, indeed, the narrator's own stance on the government has changed, for his *raison d'être* is challenged: the representative of reason, the urban state, is referred to disparagingly as '[el] señor ese'. The description of authoritarian marginalisation that follows could be interpreted therefore as a denunciation of the government's action as illogical, or at least 'unreasonable', and there is, indeed, a poignant situational irony in the process of travel from city to village, for this is a journey from the place of reason to the place of unreason but, upon departure, the reason the teacher has brought has been transformed into unreason and the unreason he expected to find is transformed into reason.

We could therefore say that the illogicality of his situation is keenly felt by the narrator in the sense that his belief in one side's version of the word 'patria' is being challenged by his experience of that of the Other. The situational irony that emerges from Rulfo's verbally ironising the words 'razón', 'patria' and 'país' is not only that the teacher's position as a representative of the 'nation' is destroyed by the simple assertion of an alternative viewpoint, but also that his position as a figure of authority is under threat too. Irony assumes that such a figure of authority is usually identified with superior intelligence for, as Barbe (sardonically) suggests: 'Only urbanites possess sophistication and irony ability', while most literature on the subject suggests that 'the most able person to detect an irony is a highly educated white male'.[51] This is surely borne out by Muecke's somewhat clumsily qualified assertion of the Western world's mastery of irony: 'If irony were largely confined to the Western world, as I have been led to believe (but I do not vouch for the fact) ... we should hardly think that [it] was of less importance for not being universal.'[52] Indeed, a major generator of the verbal irony of the story 'Luvina' is the fact that, here, it is the representative of the Western world, with supposedly superior intellect, who is the victim of the irony.

[51] Barbe, pp. 4–5.
[52] Muecke, p. 1.

Centrifugal Situational Irony: The Old and the New

The state's project of emancipation is impossible to implement if, as we
have just seen, the teacher sympathises with the peasants' rejection of the
government's iron hand. This iron hand is much more tangible than the velvet
glove held by the teacher, for, as we have seen, the teacher admits that the
government only acknowledges the peasantry when a 'fechoría' or crime has
been committed, whereupon the offender is normally killed. The teacher's
sympathy begins the process of the dissolution of the Self–Other dichotomy,
for it suggests the beginnings of a realisation that his task is to represent
a state which professes to redeem the countryside (making it part of the
national Self) yet only acknowledges its presence negatively (preserving it as
Other). This is partly why he describes his ideas as a 'plasta': he feels he is
an inadequately-informed agent of the state, armed with ideas that make no
sense in the reality in which he finds himself. His sense of Self is therefore
in deep crisis:

> Usted sabe que a todos nosotros nos infunden ideas. Y uno va con esa
> plasta encima para plasmarla en todas partes. Pero en Luvina no cuajó eso.
> Hice el experimento y se deshizo ... (128)

The Self, being the urban state and its agent the teacher, is represented in the
active 'hice', 'I did'. However, this 'active agent' is undone, for the experi-
ment 'se deshizo', broken by an *unknown* agent, hence the use of the passive
voice and the resonance with the verb 'cuajar' ('Pero en Luvina no cuajó
eso'), which is also used in the first paragraph to describe the arrested 'fall'
of mist. How are we to interpret this 'unknown' force? On a very superficial level, the 'unknown agent' is, just as in 'La Cuesta de las Comadres',
a particularly hostile nature which undermines state initiatives and to which
all inhabitants of rural areas seem to submit, hence the apparent (centripetal)
cosmic irony in the teacher's efforts. However, this view could be comman-
deered by Eagleton's 'criminally complicit' Culture (with a capital 'C') to
argue that the teacher's recollections prove the existence of an inferior Other,
subjugated by a hostile nature, steeped in barbarism, and incapable of reason
or civilisation. On the other hand, we could say instead that the nature that
the teacher describes is not at all as irrational and barbaric as he suggests
and is, in fact, entirely logical depending on one's perspective. Although it is
true that anthropomorphic images are used in the story to create a sense of an
unyielding, even hostile, nature, there is a sense in which this nature, warts
and all, is an integral and accepted part of peasant life.

The wind in 'Luvina' is examined by William Rowe, for example, as a
manifestation of a deity who, amongst other associations, was the god of

winds, Quetzalcóatl: a god who, menacingly for a modernising teacher but apparently not for the inhabitants of Luvina, is seen to be 'mixing animal and anthropomorphic qualities'.[53] This wind dismantles the Christian altar to reveal the pagan beliefs hiding beneath, making the church 'a mere shell (of Christian symbols and rituals) filled with a different content ... the animistic figure of the wind and the crosses which sound like skulls'.[54] The fact that the wind may represent an ancient, indigenous deity as deep-rooted in the indigenous psyche as Quetzalcóatl, rediscovered from under the rubble of the Catholic Church, indicates that this is an appropriate symbol for the reaction of nature itself to the presumptuous efforts of a civilising state: in a sense, this is 'the revenge of the Other'. After all, the wind here takes hold of things and rips off the roofs of houses: 'Se planta en Luvina prendiéndose de las cosas como si las mordiera. Y sobran días en que se lleva el techo de las casas como si se llevara un sombrero de petate, dejando los paredones lisos, descobijados' (120). This manifestation of the element of wind is contrasted, in a situational juxtaposition, with 'el rumor del aire moviendo suavemente las hojas de los almendros' (120) outside the bar where the teacher is talking, while the presence of children playing indicates the life and activity that are absent in Luvina. It is almost as if the gentle breeze is the disguising, civilising mask of the animistic, barbaric wind, again evoking Rowe's Christian 'shell' of a church.

The situational irony here rests in the fact that this 'uncivilised' Other defeats the presumptuous, civilising Self enshrined in the rural missionary representing the urban state. In a reversal of the Western fable in which the sun succeeds with warmth where the wind fails with force in making the traveller take off his coat, the wind here defeats the representative of the 'Luz Divina', who sheds his armour of Revolutionary values and eventually leaves. In Luvina, it seems that there is no place to hide from the wrath of the ancient gods, especially that of Quetzalcóatl. Thus, the wind scratches with its nails, scrapes the walls, tears off strips of earth, digs under doors with a sharp shovel, and, in a more culturally-specific metaphor that invokes images of *pulque* in the use of sacrificial rites, it appears to possess the individual: '... [bulle] dentro de uno como si se pusiera a remover los goznes de nuestros mismos huesos' (120). This image reinforces the contemporary suggestion by Octavio Paz that contact with Mexicans inevitably entails contact with a loaded past in which civilisation, rather than barbarism, resides:

> Cualquier contacto con el pueblo mexicano, así sea fugaz, muestra que bajo las formas occidentales laten todavía las antiguas creencias y costumbres.

[53] Rowe, p. 63.
[54] Rowe, p. 63.

> Esos despojos, vivos aún, son testimonio de la vitalidad de las culturas precortesianas. Y después de los descubrimientos de arqueólogos e historiadores ya no es posible referirse a esas sociedades como tribus bárbaras o primitivas. Por encima de la fascinación o del horror que nos produzcan, debe admitirse que los españoles al llegar a México encontraron civilizaciones complejas y refinadas.[55]

Thus, the wind appears to represent the re-emergence of Mexico's civilised, rather than barbaric, past. Although not consciously recognised, this must represent a huge surprise – or an unacknowledged trauma – for the teacher steeped in Western ideas of liberal emancipation.[56] As Fuentes suggests, the old is not necessarily defunct and the new is not perforce productive: 'Paradoja de México: las ruinas son eternas, la novedad es ruinosa.'[57]

Centrifugal Situational Irony: Self and Other

The penultimate paragraph of the story evokes, with sentences of roughly equal length, a barren monotony and lack of progress in the urban Revolution personified by the teacher, while nature in the form of a dark, 'otherly' night continues unaffected:

> Pero no dijo nada. Se quedó mirando un punto fijo sobre la mesa donde los comejenes ya sin alas rondaban como gusanitos desnudos …
>
>   Afuera seguía oyéndose cómo avanzaba la noche. El chapoteo del río contra los troncos de los camichines. El griterío muy lejano de los niños. Por el pequeño cielo de la puerta se asomaban las estrellas. (128)

Just as Demetrio Macías's elevated position in his initial 'revolutionary' attack is turned on its head at the end of Mariano Azuela's *Los de abajo* (1915), the teacher's lofty ideals have finally descended from the sky, not as the eagle and serpent of the Mexican flag but, in a less 'naïve' metaphor, as the pathetic bodies of flies, squirming like worms. Meanwhile, the secular paradise is receding fast as night encroaches on day and the hopeful sound of children playing grows ever more distant. In the most potent application of Rulfo's sense of centrifugal situational irony, the final act of the drunken narrator, lying back in his chair, invokes an image of passive, nonchalant surrender by the state's messenger, a surrender that is entirely, and ironically, in keeping with the state's image of a 'recalcitrant' peasantry unwilling to

---

[55] Octavio Paz, *El laberinto de la soledad* (Mexico City: Fondo de Cultura Económica, 1950), p. 98.

[56] Poinsett, pp. 11–14.

[57] Carlos Fuentes, in Fuentes et al., *Mexico: Juan Rulfo fotógrafo*, p. 16.

embrace modernity: 'El hombre que miraba a los comejenes se recostó sobre la mesa y se quedó dormido' (128). Thus, with the last line of the story, the civilising messenger has become his Other: the very lazy, drunken fatalist that he was supposed to eradicate!

This situational irony may, of course, be understood centripetally for this is the same teacher who encouraged the peasants to find land to work, earlier in the story. But an understanding of this centripetal irony also encourages the perception of centrifugal ironies, for the reader can now use the same interrogative process to look beyond the text to find a powerful contextual resonance in the irony, specifically in the post-Revolutionary state's cultural-economic programme. With this programme, it was hoped by the state that the peasantry would benefit not only from improved diets, better water and hygiene facilities, but also improved social behaviour, including the elimination of vulgarity and alcoholism, thus reducing its 'Otherness' to the urban elite. The battle against alcoholism, for example, was not limited to the comments of positivist educationalists like Justo Sierra in the nineteenth century. Francisco Madero's presidential campaign made a special point of eradicating this tendency among *campesinos*, suggesting that it was a liberal ideal that reflected middle-class anxiety over peasant unruliness. Indeed, Mariano Azuela's vision of 'la bola' in *Los de abajo* certainly reflects his own middle-class fears about the relationship between alcohol and violence.

There is, therefore, situational irony in the fact that the teacher, spearheading the civilising, and colonising, programme of the state, should himself fall prey to dipsomaniacal tendencies. As Rulfo states in the report quoted above, 'pues el profesor ha terminado por ser un borracho característico de los pueblos olvidados'.[58] This is the result of a combination of, on the one hand, the victory of the forces of nature, accepted by the rural Other as part of life, and, on the other, the teacher's burgeoning sympathy with the peasants, who are persecuted by the government. This creates, in turn, an almost complete breakdown in the teacher's Self–Other dichotomy, leading to his ironically *becoming* the Other which he was supposed to help destroy. As Eagleton indicates, this breakdown is almost inevitable: 'Industrial capitalism, with its rationalizing, secularizing bent, cannot help bringing its own metaphysical values into discredit, thus undermining the very foundation which that secular activity needs to legitimate itself.'[59]

---

[58] Jiménez de Báez, p. 49.
[59] Eagleton, p. 40.

Centrifugal Cosmic Irony: Colonising Discourse and the Search for Fixity

In 1936, *El Universal* published huge pictures of dams and canals built by the state near the coastal town of Mazatlán, selling it as evidence of 'la grandeza de México'.[60] Impressive numbers were quoted again in 1945 when presidential candidate Miguel Alemán spoke to the *Confederación Nacional de Campesinos* of his irrigation plans for the countryside.[61] The picture in 'Luvina', however, is of a rural population that has become a shadow, an ignored space, that has completely eluded this process, as the teacher seems to realise when he sees some women carrying jugs on their shoulders in search of water at an unearthly time of the morning. The verbally ironic response of the narrator to this memory is humorous and centripetal in that it plays the words 'trago' and 'sabor' against the teacher's increasing inebriation, all information contained within the text itself: '¿No cree usted que esto se merece otro trago? Aunque sea nomás para que se me quite el mal sabor del recuerdo' (125). More centrifugally, the lack of water is ironic because it represents a situational opposite to the government's desired creation of a well-irrigated, self-sufficient, surplus-exporting countryside. Furthermore, in contrast to the image of healthy, friendly natives in tourism posters, the peasants' teeth are 'molenques' (127), chewing 'bagazos de mezquite seco … tragándose su propia saliva para engañar el hambre' (127) and they cut poor, emaciated shadows of figures, 'repegados al muro de las casas, casi arrastrados por el viento' (127), with the women 'sin fuerzas, casi trabadas de tan flacas' (128).

Unfortunately, the above descriptions also accord with urban, stereotypical views of the peasantry as unhygienic and lazy. However, neither this apparent condescension nor the process of 'Othering' described above need affect our sympathy for the narrator if we accept that the teacher as mimic man has internalised the urban, colonising discourse and is unable to contest it as a free agent. We could then see the supposedly hostile nature that Rulfo creates, as well as the teacher's condescension towards the peasants, as the imaginative result of the teacher's own colonised mind which, as Rulfo seems to suggest in the report quoted above, is prone to the spontaneous creation of 'lo desconocido' from imagined 'figuras y situaciones'. The teacher is therefore trapped in hierarchical, colonial modes of thinking with which he manufactures an imagined, horrific Other which undermines any well-meant attempts at egalitarian 'redemption' with state education initiatives. These

---

60 *El Universal*, 1 November 1936, Photographic Supplement, p. 1.

61 Miguel Alemán, *Discursos de Alemán* (Mexico City: Partido Revolucionario Institucional, 1946), p. 103.

modes of thinking are here metaphorically represented by a stereotypically tenacious countryside and 'backward' peasantry created out of a yet-to-be-decolonised mind which associates the Other with just such qualities.

The teacher's struggle, the source of the story's cosmic irony, is therefore 'heteroglot' in that it is not only one of man against nature (centripetal) but at the same time that of man against his own colonising imagination (centrifugal). Within this greater struggle, his sense of agency is rendered impossible, for 'the mimic is created by the colonizing presence and as yet has no kind of intentional agency'.[62] In a sense, then, the teacher is caught in this very dilemma when attempting to relate to the Other: 'They are domesticated, harmless, knowable; but also *at the same time* wild, harmful, mysterious.'[63] Thus, the teacher's personal crisis resides in the feeling that the colonised subject is 'sliding ambivalently between the polarities of similarity and difference; he or she simply will not stand still'.[64] In such a situation, as McLeod proceeds to indicate, 'stereotypes are deployed as a means to arrest the ambivalence of the colonised subject by describing him or her in static terms'.[65] The stereotypes used here by the teacher are those that configure the town of Luvina as an 'otherly' Loobina: the wild and dangerous counterpart of the urban Self, where people are lazy, suspicious, superstitious and unyielding. But why does the silent interlocutor not contest these stereotypes?

The suppression of the voice of the interlocutor produces the possibility that the teacher is expressing his thoughts to a second-generation teacher coached in the same ideology in a *dialógo de sordos*. This raises the prospect of an 'anxious repetition' of the stereotypes which feed the colonising discourse:

> The *repetition* of the colonial stereotype is an attempt to secure the colonised in a fixed position, but also an acknowledgement that this can never be achieved ... the very fact that stereotypes *must* be endlessly repeated reveals that this fixity can never be achieved.[66]

Thus, both the narrator (through narrative) and the second-generation teacher (through complicit silence) cannot help but re-express stereotypes of lazy,

---

[62] Peter Childs and Patrick Williams, *An Introduction to Post-Colonial Theory* (Harlow: Pearson, 1997), p. 130.

[63] McLeod, p. 53. Emphasis by McLeod.

[64] McLeod, p. 53. It should be mentioned that McLeod is explicating the arguments of Homi K. Bhabha on ambivalence in colonial discourse.

[65] McLeod, p. 53.

[66] McLeod, p. 54, again paraphrasing the arguments of Homi K. Bhabha. Emphasis by McLeod.

superstitious, fatalistic peasants (and a hostile natural landscape) as these are the only tools with which the internalised colonising discourse can provide form to the countryside and the inhabitants of Luvina. They are also the only means the narrator has of stopping his own Self from sliding into a feared Other even though, as we have seen, this occurs anyway. This situational irony, coupled with the silence of the interlocutor in the face of the use of such stereotypes, indicates the psychological danger of an unobstructed repetition of the colonising discourse in which the teacher is trapped. In this context, the silence symbolises the teacher's encirclement by a cosmic, totalising force which is not only nature but the colonising discourse itself.

This kind of irony is, to some degree, quite volatile. To return to Linda Hutcheon's concept of 'irony's edge', to which I refer in the first chapter, is it possible that, as Clare Colebrook asks, 'such gestures of irony, far from avoiding the old myths of the West as the privileged viewpoint of reason, once again allow the West to speak in the absence of others?'[67] The problem arises most damagingly when irony is 'missed' but, as I see it, meaning – ironic or otherwise – is not so much to be missed or 'got' as *produced* by Rulfo's reader. My principal answer to Hutcheon and Colebrook, therefore, would be that the inadvertent enactment of the discourse being ironised is only a problem to the extent that centripetal irony has not prepared the recipient for the questioning of that discourse and, therefore, for the production of centrifugal irony. In this story, for instance, we have seen examples of all forms of centripetal irony: cosmic centripetal irony in the teacher's struggle against nature; situational centripetal irony in the teacher's falling asleep and being drunk; centripetal verbal irony in the use of the words 'trago' and 'sabor'. These centripetal forms of irony prevent the text from becoming an enactment of the discourse being ironised in the wider contexts of centrifugal irony because they train the reader's gaze to look between the lines and beyond the text itself. There is still, of course, the highly subjective task of weighing up the extent to which the centripetal irony is demonstrably potent enough to avoid the trap of 're-enacting' its object. In order to achieve this, there is no real alternative but the type of patient study of the work of individual artists that I attempt here except, perhaps, to undermine the right to interpret at all. If I make a value judgement in the process, and if that value judgement is Westernised, unintentionally colonialist or 'elitist in function', this may simply be one of the many dangers of all interpretation, whether it is based on irony or not.[68] Thus, the process of questioning and interpretation is never simple and, indeed, another important debate here is whether

[67] Colebrook, p. 159.
[68] Hutcheon, p. 94.

or not Rulfo's literary ventriloquism is a futile and presumptuous exercise in bourgeois imagination mirroring that of postcolonial studies itself.

Literary Ventriloquism

The teacher's stereotypes are an imitation of the stereotyping performed by Mexican leaders. Indeed, the peasants were somewhat despised by those who claimed to represent them: speaking of the peasants of Morelos in 1935, one politician suggested that 'the tendency towards progress, which is one of the characteristics of humankind is, in him [the peasant], highly atrophied'.[69] However, having read this story, we could easily replace his terms with the bracketed terms in italics, which might be utilised by the *peasantry* to criticise the *state*:

> The sad and naked truth of what we have seen in these people who personally knew Emilano Zapata is that the Morelos peasant [*the state official*] continues to possess the soul of a peon [*of an 'hijo de la chingada'*]: in religion a pagan-Christian [*an atheist*], he is fanatical and stupid [*pretentious and self-satisfied*], he blindly obeys the orders of the clergy [*the state and the president*], without perceiving whether they are good or bad; in civic [*spiritual*] terms he is a systematic enemy of all governments and social organizations [*other forms of thinking*], suspicious of any outside [*inside*] influence, apathetic [*self-righteous*] when it comes to any social organization or undertaking [*any attempt to consider alternative points of view*].[70]

The above exercise may seem contrived but we should perhaps heed the words of Bakhtin on the dialogic possibilities of a single word before passing judgement: '… every word is directed toward an answer and cannot escape the profound influence of the answering word that it anticipates'.[71] Colonising perceptions of a backward peasantry such as the one above, based on the civilisation/barbarism binary, pervaded the rhetoric of the post-Revolutionary government, but the answers they anticipated were absent from mainstream discourse, just as they are in the monologic structure of 'Luvina'. However, a contextual reading of 'Luvina' based on centrifugal irony can enable a kind of vicarious contestation, facilitated by centrifugal irony, which allows the reader to subjectivise the peasantry as real actors in intellectual history, rather than objectify them as passive receptacles, thus improving our chances of meeting Florencia E. Mallon's challenge of 'breaking down the artificial

---

[69] Donaciano Munguía, Cuernavaca, 20 August 1935, SEP 202/6. Quoted by Knight, 'Popular Culture', p. 404.

[70] Munguía, p. 404.

[71] Bakhtin, *The Dialogic Imagination*, p. 277.

division between analyst as intellectual and peasant as subject [and instead] understanding analysis as a dialogue among intellectuals'.[72]

Rulfo's story meets Mallon's challenge by ventriloquising the voice of the peasantry and empowering the reader to question the colonising discourse from the Other's perspective. The danger of this ventriloquism, as Eagleton puts it, is that it assumes a certain power that is universal in implication: 'Imagination, or colonialism, means that what other cultures know is themselves, whereas who you know is them.'[73] Furthermore, it is only the *bourgeoisie* (and the West) with its material advantage that can, through superior and increased leisure time, exercise enough 'imagination' to 'empathise' through literary ventriloquism. Indeed, one could argue that postcolonial criticism itself is merely the result of a form of universalising intellectual colonisation in which the process of manufacturing colonial texts in a Western postcolonial 'factory' is enabled by the privileged distance of trained readers.[74]

It must be misguided, however, to suggest that empathy is occasioned only by material advantage: the imagination required is surely not the product of wealth alone, or even a privileged education, any more than talent in a sport is the sole product of a fit, athletic body. Besides, art of Rulfo's kind, although inevitably a product of a *bourgeois* education, has a role nonetheless in facilitating every reader's imaginative search, similar to that of the teacher, for difference *within* her or his own context, and emerging with an improved ability to empathise with a local Other. This function of his art is surely enhanced for the reader who engages with its historical context using postcolonial criticism as a guide rather than a rulebook. As Eagleton puts it:

> You do not need to leap out of your skin to know what another is feeling – indeed there are times when you need rather to burrow more deeply into it ... And no cognitive form is more adroit at mapping the complexities of the heart than artistic culture.[75]

An experimental evaluation of 'local experience' as context, in the form of the postcolonial critique I have attempted here, is perhaps of some use in avoiding Eagleton's first sin of 'criminal complicity': the assumption of the

---

[72] Florencia E. Mallon, *Peasant and Nation, The Making of Postcolonial Mexico and Peru* (Los Angeles: University of California Press, 1995), p. 10.

[73] Eagleton, p. 46.

[74] See Arun P. Mukherjee, 'Interrogating Postcolonialism: Some Uneasy Conjunctures', in *Interrogating Post-Colonialism: Theory, Text and Context*, ed. by Harish Trivedi and Meenakshi Mukherjee (Shimla: Indian Institute of Advanced Study, 1996), pp. 13–20. For a concise summary of the arguments of critics of postcolonialism such as Mukherjee, as well as some answers to these critics, see McLeod, pp. 239–58.

[75] Eagleton, p. 50.

'universality' of a dominant Culture with a capital 'C'. We should perhaps consider that a colonialist, 'criminally complicit' interpretation of the story, such as that which Vasconcelos or Poinsett might have lent it, would rely on the civilisation–barbarism binary as sacrosanct and that the peasants' 'backwardness' in 'Luvina' would then be an example of the tenacious resistance to the Culture that they are supposed to need. To take the second peril of postmodernism described by Eagleton, the insistence on the truth of a single, oppressed culture with a small 'c', we can see from the above analysis that, when placed in the context of the official narrative and historiographical work, a story such as 'Luvina' can provide an alternative peasant voice, rather than a definitive 'history', allowing the reader to form a view of the past guided by multiple voices rather than one. Rulfo's skill, after all, is in enabling such voices to contest Culture without necessarily enshrining any single peasant culture as truth. As we shall see in the remaining chapters, he therefore provides us with more 'unfixed', constructively heteroglot and centrifugally ironic texts.

5

The Priest of *Pedro Páramo*:
Fetishistic Stereotyping and Positive Iconography

The most frequently analysed characters in *Pedro Páramo* are Juan Preciado, the eponymous *cacique*, and his unrequited love, Susana San Juan. These figures provoke debates on identity, power, patriarchy, violence and gender as well as opening doors to analyses of Rulfo's style and narrative structure. It is surprising, however, that so little has been written on one of the central characters of that novel: the priest, el padre Rentería. The characterisation of Rentería brings similar themes to the attention of the reader and, most importantly, provides a vehicle for Rulfo's multi-layered irony. Fragment 14 of the novel, the first in which we meet this character, is a densely dramatic introduction to Rentería's role as the priest of Comala, the ghost town that is the setting for *Pedro Páramo*. Verbal and situational irony in this fragment, in its (centrifugal) relationship with the rhetoric of Church and state in the post-Revolutionary era, is the focus of this chapter.[1]

One major exception to the dearth of critical analysis is José C. González Boixo's article 'El factor religioso en la obra de Juan Rulfo' which, in fact, acknowledges two situational ironies in the characterisation of the priest.[2] Firstly, the doubt-ridden priest in a community of souls desperate for salvation is a situational irony in itself: 'resulta intencionadamente paradójico que sea él, el pastor de almas, quien no tenga esa seguridad que debe infundir en los demás'. Secondly, the doubt which stems from Rentería's complicity with the *cacique* ('La iglesia aparece como cooperadora de las obras violentas, bien porque esté unida a los ricos, bien porque contribuya al mantenimiento de este tipo de sociedad') is expressed through *support* of the Church in the Church–state war of 1926–29 (the Cristero War) for, as González Boixo tells us, 'la antítesis de la duda es el fanatismo'.[3] There is a third situational irony,

---

[1]   Material from this chapter first appeared in an article in *The Bulletin of Hispanic Studies* (Liverpool), 83:3 (2006), 203–23. It is reproduced here by kind permission of the journal editors and the publishers, Liverpool University Press.

[2]   José C. González Boixo, 'El factor religioso en la obra de Juan Rulfo', *Cuadernos Hispanoamericanos*, July – September 1985, vol. 421–423, pp. 165–77.

[3]   González Boixo, pp. 169–71.

not mentioned by González Boixo: Rentería's intense, sincere and anguished efforts have entirely the least desired effect on Comala, leaving the *cacique* to reign over a spiritual desert in which souls are left abandoned, unabsolved, and in purgatory. A fourth and final paradox, alluded to but not explicitly expressed by González Boixo, stems from the fact that Rentería himself is in a state of sin, having colluded with the *cacique*, and this closes 'el círculo de condenación de Comala con su propia condenación'.[4] Thus, the sinning, unabsolved priest is incapable of saving his community, which explains his frustrations with Dorotea's pleas for absolution: '¿Qué quieres que haga contigo, Dorotea? Júzgate tú misma. Ve si tú puedes perdonarte' (143).

As useful as González Boixo's comments are, there is no specific mention of 'situational' or 'verbal' irony. This critic, more than any other, pays great attention to the ironies present in Rulfo's fiction but does not explore them in any systematic detail. Such ironies need to be excavated, although this does not make them over-elaborate or far-fetched for they can work on an unconscious level until they are brought to the surface through study; after all, many of the symbolic interpretations of Rulfo's work rely on much more oblique references to mythology. Irony can at least provide the solution to the critical dilemma which González Boixo repeatedly outlines, writing of the 'literary' and the 'non-literary' factors in the interpretation of Rulfo's work, arguing that 'ambos aspectos son perfectamente compatibles'.[5] For the purposes of this study, they are not just compatible but as good as identical. Rather than discrete 'aspects' of Rulfo's work such as 'literary, symbolic, universal' versus 'non-literary, regional, context-specific', I would suggest that there is a constant movement between centripetal text and centrifugal context. As we have already seen, though, these ironic movements intersect with such frequency that it is difficult to extricate them entirely from each other.

In relation to the above examples of situational irony, it could be argued that the first (the doubting priest) may be understood centripetally by a reader with no familiarity with Mexican history whatsoever, only with the knowledge that a Catholic priest should be sufficiently secure in his faith to deliver sacraments. Yet, Rentería's doubt is much more ironic when we consider the Church's martyrisation of the figure of the priest through the process of positive iconography described later in this chapter. In the second situational irony, the once doubt-ridden fanatic, we might say that we can spot the switch from Rentería's doubt to his fanaticism without extra-textual referents. Nevertheless, given that there is no reference to the actual politics of the Cristero

---

[4]   González Boixo, p. 171
[5]   González Boixo, p. 169.

War in the novel, much less any 'fanaticism' as such, a reader who has no awareness of the fanatical support of the Church by the majority of priests in Jalisco during this period cannot appreciate the full scale of Rentería's ironic turn-around. As far as the third irony is concerned (the futility of the priest's efforts), an awareness that thousands of lives were lost in the conflict and that the countryside itself was ravaged by war would surely add to the tragedy that it resulted in no change. Finally, the poignancy of the fourth irony (the sinful priest) is surely enhanced by a reader who appreciates the extent to which Catholic peasants in post-Revolutionary Mexico were almost always embroiled in a system of *cacicazgo* similar to that of Pedro Páramo, depending for their absolution on a colluding priest for the successful resolution of their own sinful lives. Most of these ironies therefore rely – for their *full* impact – on a social and political awareness of Mexican history which is all too often ignored by critics of Rulfo's work or, in the case of González Boixo and others, perceptively acknowledged without being fully explored.

To be more specific about my task here, I would like to discuss fragment 14 of *Pedro Páramo* with a view to arguing for the crucial importance of el padre Rentería as a political symbol which undermines – through centrifugal verbal and situational irony – the rhetorical, manicheistic portrayal of priests by both the Church and the state in the post-Revolutionary period of Mexican history. In the Comala discovered by Juan Preciado, the relationship between the priest (el padre Rentería), the *cacique* (Pedro Páramo) and the inhabitants of Comala has not changed significantly since the days of colony and *caciquismo*. In discussing *caciquismo*, we ought to make a distinction between this rural form of the phenomenon and the institutional or supra-local version. The *caciquismo* in Comala is almost a microcosm of the state-sponsored '*caciquismo*' of the Spanish Empire in the sense that it involves a 'mini-alliance' (*cacique*–priest) between a secular and a religious authority to ensure order. In *Pedro Páramo*, we see how, as a result of a post-Revolutionary struggle for power between Church and state on an institutional level, there is paradoxically a power vacuum in the local, rural areas where control is being contested. This allows local *caciquismo* – which the Church ostensibly rails against and the state wishes to extirpate – to flourish. However, whilst the *cacique* represents a figure of evil detested (if only officially) in both Church and state rhetoric, the priest becomes a rather more complex political pawn, which, in the case of the Church, is a martyr used to disguise the failings of this institution and, in the case of the state, an equally cynical 'fetishistic stereotype' within the terms set out by Homi K. Bhabha.[6]

---

6   Bhabha, 'The Other Question – Sterotype, discrimination and the discourse of colonialism', Chapter 3 in *The Location of Culture*, pp. 66–84.

State: The Priest as Fetishistic Stereotype

In the nineteenth and twentieth centuries, the state aimed to redeem the peasant with a 'civilising' programme of economic modernisation while the Church, in the face of capitalist excesses, continued to offer Christian salvation; but the common aim was patriarchal dominion over the soul of the peasant and of the countryside. This ideological conflict, and the battle over the rural domain, would manifest itself physically in the Cristero War. In 1926, the state passed the anti-clerical Calles Law, undermining the authority of the Church and provoking a rural conflagration which lasted for three years and cost thousands of lives.[7] The image of the priest became a political pawn in this period: stereotypical and iconic representations of the priest were used by state and Church respectively to maintain the fixity or rigidity of difference between Self and Other.[8] The key stereotype in the armoury of the post-Revolutionary state was the demonised priest as greedy and conniving, in lucrative league with the *cacique*, maintaining the 'superstitions' of parishioners in order to ensure their loyalty to the local boss and to improve his own financial situation. This type of local *caciquismo* was held by the state to be a relic of the colonial past, obstructing the 'progress' of the peasantry by preventing their integration into the market economy.

In a speech delivered by Emilio Portes Gil to a government convention on education in 1936, the former president presented this official view of the priest, to apparent 'risas y aplausos', repeating the phrase 'Ustedes saben que ...' to suggest the finality of the state's version of the past:

> Ustedes saben que en la hacienda existía siempre una capilla, a donde iban los campesinos con sus mujeres y sus niños a rezar, a oír la voz del cura que los amenazaba, si se comportaban mal en esta vida, con terribles castigos en la otra ... (Risas y aplausos) ... Ustedes saben que éste fue otro de los instrumentos usados por el patrón o amo, para corromper a los trabajadores y convencerlos de que pertenecían a la hacienda, y que, por ningún motivo, deberían de abandonarla.[9]

Portes Gil thus paints the countryside before the Revolution in a Marxist

---

[7] For accounts of the rebellion see David C. Bailey, *¡Viva Cristo Rey!: The Cristero Rebellion and Church–State Conflict in Mexico* (Austin: University of Texas Press, 1974), and Jean Meyer, *The Cristero Rebellion: Mexican People between Church and State* (Cambridge: Cambridge University Press, 1976).

[8] As Bhabha asserts in the opening sentence of Chapter 3 of his *The Location of Culture*: 'An important feature of colonial discourse is its dependence on the the concept of "fixity" in the ideological construction of otherness' (p. 66).

[9] Emilio Portes Gil, *La escuela y el campesino* (Mexico City: Instituto de Estudios Sociales, Políticos y Económicos, 1936), p. 15.

setting of feudalism, and the priest himself as a venal auxiliary to the evil *hacendado*: 'Como consecuencia de todo este mecanismo de presión autoritaria, el hacendado tenía la influencia suficiente para imponer su voluntad en toda la región.'[10] In the official publication of the speech, there is also an illustration, a woodcut, in which a hunched, portly priest walks towards a church. The principal marker of individual identity, the face, is hidden from view and the figure is seen to be moving away, giving the impression of a faceless or anonymous institution. In the absence of the face, a stereotype is constructed on a more abstract level from other, more simplistic visual indicators in the image: for example, the priest's personal bag of cash, which stands as an emblem of his collusive relationship with the *cacique*.[11]

In the 'socialist' rhetoric of the Cárdenas era, this collusive relationship ('este mecanismo de presión autoritaria') between the priest and the *hacendado* (*cacique*) was said to prevent the participation of the peasantry in politics and the economy. It represents fetishistically a pre-Revolutionary state, a 'barbaric' non- or anti-Revolution, the feared 'lack' in the revolutionary discourse, to be avoided at all costs:

> Fetishism is always a 'play' or vacillation between the archaic affirmation of wholeness/similarity – in Freud's terms: 'All men have penises'; in ours: 'All men have the same skin/race/culture' [In my reading, all men have revolution/nationalism/industrial capitalism] – and the anxiety associated with lack and difference – again, for Freud 'Some men do not have penises'; for us 'Some do not have the same skin/race/culture' [In my reading, some do not have revolution/nationalism/industrial capitalism].[12]

There was a transparent hypocrisy in this fear of 'non-Revolution': if the priest and the *cacique* exercised a local *contubernio* to subordinate the will of the peasantry, a parallel state–Church alliance for maintaining rural stability manifested itself, on a national level, in the détente that followed the reign of Cárdenas and, particularly, from the moment Ávila Camacho made the famous proclamation, 'Yo soy creyente': 'The state acknowledged the impossibility of extirpating the Church … and the Church legitimised the state and lent it its authority to domesticate the subject people.'[13]

Thus, the state's attack on local power structures is deliberately but unconsciously deceptive, for it masks a desire for the national form of the same

10 Portes Gil, p. 15. Emphasis added.
11 Woodcuts lent visual credence to state claims to represent the peasant. See David Craven, *Art and Revolution in Latin America 1910–1990* (New Haven and London: Yale University Press, 2002), pp. 25–75.
12 Bhabha, p. 75.
13 Meyer, p. 211.

system. In fact, the stereotype of the demonic priest has two aims: firstly to *mask* (metaphorically) the state's desire for the former colonialist relationship with the Church; secondly, to *reinforce* this mask (metonymically) with an exaggerated Other – 'evil' in the form of the demonic priest of local *caciquismo*. It is no wonder, then, that Portes Gil's audience both chuckles with delight in the narcissism of self-recognition ('risas') and, at the same time, reacts fearfully and defensively at a vision of its Other ('aplausos'). This understanding of the priest as fetishistic is clearer still if we refer to Bhabha's notion of a fetish as 'simultaneous play between metaphor as substitution (masking absence and difference) and metonymy (which contiguously registers the perceived lack)'.[14] We now understand the stereotype of the demonic priest as an 'arrested, fixated form' designed to steady or neutralise an unnerving and precarious vacillation between 'pleasure/unpleasure, mastery/ defence, knowledge/disavowal, absence/presence'.[15]

In Portes Gil's speech, for example, the state projects a stereotype of the greedy, conniving man of the Church in order to create a metaphorical, fetishistic mask for the same collusive qualities (which are 'non-' or 'anti-Revolution') within the state's *own* machinery. To allay the risk of self-recognition, the mask performs the second, equally important function of 'contiguously registering difference'. This inspires the applause, for the (metaphorical) process of masking is reinforced with a metonymic representation of these 'otherly', 'anti-Revolutionary' qualities within a priest representing the Church and therefore safely outside the domain of the state and the danger of self-revelation. Whether the mask represents desire or fear, the fetishistic stereotype that is the demonised post-Revolutionary priest is cast as negative and, in *Pedro Páramo*, this mask dissolves, losing its self-deluding function as well as its power to reinforce the image of an evil Other. Rentería is deeply disturbed by his position in the power structure of Comala and eventually rebels against it, despite the suggestiveness of venality in his name.[16] Furthermore, the senior priest whom Rentería visits in Contla, though hinting that he himself is not innocent, is appalled by Rentería's corrupt behaviour and implies that he must take action to redress it.[17] The complexity of the mental state of both Rentería and the Señor Cura is therefore at odds with any stere-

[14] Bhabha, p. 75.
[15] Bhabha, p. 75.
[16] Others have, of course, noted the significance of his name. For example, Jiménez de Báez, who relates it directly to 'la mercantilización de los sacramentos', p. 159.
[17] Rulfo, p. 60. Rentería's anguished state also jars with that of the priests of the indigenist novel: 'en la novela indigenista de las décadas anteriores aparecían esquematizados en su papel de opresores del pueblo, de común acuerdo con los caciques'. On the other hand, 'el padre Rentería mantiene una lucha interior entre su deber con el pueblo y la concesión de su favor a los ricos' (González Boixo, pp. 170–71).

otypically 'evil' tag given to priests, not only denting the image of a *feared* Other bent on corruption through local *caciquismo* but also pre-empting the *desired* Other of pre-colonial institutional *caciquismo*.

Church: The Priest as 'Positive' Icon

Before looking in more detail at Rentería, there is also a strong case for considering simpler, more 'positive', but equally official Church depictions of the priests involved in the Cristero Rebellion. Matthew Butler's comments give us cause for reflection on this point:

> Many Catholic writers ... seek to exalt the Church by describing a persecu-tion of mythical ferocity. While Calles is likened to Herod, Nero, or Diocle-tian, the clergy and laity comprise a uniform people of martyrs designate in revolt against a godless state. To achieve this instructive vision, however, a few exemplary martyrs – such as Father Pro and Anacleto González – are allowed to stand for the whole mass of priests and believers, in much the same way that Edmund Campion is revered as the protomartyr of the Elizabethan persecution in England.[18]

It seems, therefore, that a disingenuous positive iconography, rather than fetishistic stereotyping, is at work with regard to the Church's depiction of the priest. Here, the Church uses the martyred priest to mask its own Other-ness (sinfulness in collusion with a secular state) – an effective mask as it suggests heroic defiance of this collusion. At the same time, that mask is reinforced by the metonymic function of the icon that is the priest, the martyr representing the righteousness of the entire priesthood. Although there is both a metaphorical and a metonymic function to the Church's depiction of the priest, we should call this positive iconography rather than fetish-istic stereotyping because it creates a model based solely on *desire*, where the priest metonymically represents a desired projection of righteous Self, rather than an object of the state's simultaneous narcissistic desire *and* fear. Despite this relative simplicity, these Church views of the Cristero Rebellion are equally problematic. At the time of the publication of *Pedro Páramo*, the most famous priests in twentieth-century Mexico were still el padre Pro and Anacleto González, the martyred victims of the Cristero Rebellion. An active and elusive opponent of the state, el padre Pro was wrongly accused of the murder of Álvaro Obregón by a vengeful state possibly looking for an excuse

---

18 Matthew Butler, 'Keeping the Faith in Revolutionary Mexico: Clerical and Lay Resist-ance to Religious Persecution, East Michoacán, 1926–1929', *The Americas*, 59:1 (2002), 9–32 (p. 10).

to distract attention from rumours of an internal plot. When the real killer presented himself to save the respected father from death, Calles allegedly ordered the execution of el padre Pro regardless of the confession. The last words of the martyr were said to have been '¡Viva Cristo Rey!', the battle cry of the Cristero rebels.[19] The subsequent projection of his martyrdom was led by Antonio Dragón, who wrote the biography of the father under the title 'El martirio del padre Pro'.

The cover of the 1972 edition of the biography, the introduction of which I will examine in more detail below, exemplifies the kind of imagery which accompanies Catholic portrayals of the Cristero priest: in contrast to the government-sponsored woodcut, the priest is turned slightly towards the viewer. He is formally-dressed, his head bowed and hands turned out, with white lines running into the upper section of the body, representing the trail of bullets which follows from the photograph of a firing squad portrayed on the back cover of the book. The conversion of the bullets into more ambiguous white lines, perhaps suggesting long nails, enables the image to reverberate with echoes of crucifixion. The figure of Christ is overtly projected through the metaphor of the Mexican priest here, although the image is not without its political constraints in this respect. I would suggest that the reason that the priest is not facing the viewer directly, which would allow the viewer to engage with the representation with more empathy, is partly because the anonymous maker of the image is aware of a political necessity to avoid an over-direct and therefore potentially blasphemous identification with the Christ figure.[20] Nevertheless, as a strong metaphor for Christ, this image of the priest effectively disguises the lack of righteousness in the Church's collusion with the state. Furthermore, within this manoeuvre lies another hidden intention, I suggest, which is that of presenting the viewer with a marketable identity, a well-known priest, whose moment of martyrdom is presented to us as *metonymically* representative of that of the entire Mexican priesthood. This image of Pro as both metaphor for the righteousness of the Church and metonym for the Mexican priesthood underlies a Church narrative on the Cristero War which dates back to the 1930s and clearly still had currency in the 1970s. Its existence at this time is testament to the extent to which the Church felt able to sell its narrative as objective truth on the basis of such iconography. In the introduction (written in 1940), the Archbishop of Mexico was just as determined in his assertion that the book contained objec-

---

[19] For an account of the case of el padre Pro, see Rafael Ramírez Torres, *Miguel Agustín Pro* (Mexico City: Tradición, 1976).

[20] Although there is little space here to pursue such a study, there are interesting opportunities for comparison of this use of the crucifixion motif with those of Diego Rivera and José Clemente Orozco in, for example, *Salida de la mina* (1923) and *La trinchera* (1926).

tive proof of the innocent life of the man as the state had been in asserting his guilt. In fact, Church discourse was just as pretentious as the state's in its claims to universality and objectivity, or '*la verdad objetiva*' as Dragón puts it.[21] In the words of the Archbishop, the documents pertaining to the life of el padre Pro ('los escritos íntimos, cartas y apuntes') have been organised, 'harmonized' even, in order to 'reconstruct' the soul of Pro 'por la fidelidad fotográfica'.[22]

Whether their mechanisms were simple or complex, both Church and state projected the priest in ways that claimed to be objective and definitive. In el padre Rentería, on the other hand, Rulfo seems to present not 'la verdad objetiva', but subjective reaction; not real intimate writings, letters and notes, but fictional thoughts; not 'la fidelidad fotográfica' but figurative reality; not 'armonía' but discord; finally, he does not, as Portes Gil does, prefix any of his materials with the words, or a tone suggesting the words, 'Ustedes saben que'. Indeed, Rulfo challenges the narrative of the state as well as the counter-narrative of the Church by giving us a subjectivised, fictional, discordant and anti-manicheistic portrayal of a priest. Most importantly, Rentería's moral ambiguity challenges the moral certainty in the behaviour of the martyr Pro, whom the Archbishop describes as possessing 'el vivísimo deseo del martirio'.[23] Pro's desire for martyrdom is left un-nuanced in Dragón's account of his life for it is said by the Archbishop to emanate from 'la abundancia del corazón', 'el misterio de su intimidad con Jesús', and '[un] anhelo nobilísimo',[24] indicating a certainty of direction in the priest's assessment of his role as apparent as that of el padre Rentería is absent.[25] Nevertheless, as we shall see, Rentería appears to be seduced by martyrdom, perhaps finding solace in it as an 'easy' alternative to challenging the principal offender that is the *local* (rather than state) *cacique*.

Rulfo's carefully nuanced characterisation of Rentería suggests that the state's demonised stereotype of the priest and the Church's martyrisation of the same are based on manicheistic dualities. These dualities represent an ideological conflict where the only common aim between state and Church is

[21] Antonio Dragón, *El martirio del Padre Pro* [1940] (Mexico City, Populibros: 1972), Prólogo, p. x.

[22] Dragón, p. xi. One of the aims of the biography of el padre Pro was 'presentar a los demás la fisonomía espiritual de esa alma, disponer con arte los rayos de luz dispersos en esos documentos preciosos y coordinarlos *con tal armonía*, que surja en mágica visión la majestad de su alma'. Emphasis added.

[23] Dragón, p. xiv.

[24] Dragón, p. xiv.

[25] Certainly the biography of Pro itself is replete with suggestions of a man destined to become a martyr, from descriptions of his playing with armour as a child to the depiction of his selfless work administering sacraments at times of persecution and therefore great danger.

that of patriarchal domination. The fight for power between the two institutions therefore obscures the conflict over ideas, diluting moral boundaries set up by either, and setting up, paradoxically, a power vacuum on a local level. In this leaderless situation, the only dualities applied in the end are those that are lived each day by the peasantry and imposed not by the Church or the state but by local *caciquismo*: men and women; useful and useless; the 'haves' and the 'have-nots'. These binaries create a local system of 'law' which either overrides that of the state (legal and illegal) and the Church (righteous and sinful) or superimposes a *cacique* 'spirit' on the letter of state and Church law, rendering the official systems meaningless, and the fight between the state and the Church in the Cristero War almost a red herring for the emotionally-beleaguered priest. The pact between the Church and the state can no longer function in an environment in which only local boss rule, or the law of the jungle, reigns. Thus, a picture of the priest as victim is visible from under the pieces of the 'evil' mask imposed upon him by the post-Revolutionary state but, at the same time, a picture of a corrupted, colluding priest intervenes with the positive iconography of the Church. Rulfo's two-pronged attack on the discourse of Church and state is nowhere more apparent than in fragment 14, the first fragment in which the priest appears.

It should be noted here that, according to the time scales suggested by Peter Beardsell and Nilda Rosales, this fragment must occur *before* the Revolution itself.[26] Nevertheless, the priest's story continues through the Revolution and into the 1920s and, in any case, the depictions of the priest described above are not time-specific: the state's demonic priest was implied to have existed since the days of colony and the Church's image of the priest as martyr takes its cue from a long line of Mexican martyrs including the parish-priests-turned-independence-leaders Morelos and Hidalgo. Besides, we should consider that Rulfo's microcosmic Comala represents less a temporally-discrete reality than a metaphorical, fossilised countryside in which the *spirit* of *caciquismo* – its imaginative hold on the people, if not its physical manifestation in Pedro Páramo himself – is indestructible: the more obvious it is for the modern reader that little of this spirit has gone in present-day Mexico, the more acute the centrifugal irony. This interpretation may accord with Rulfo's wishes, for, indeed, he boasted of the lack of dates in his work:

> Es difícil saber en qué época sucede … En realidad no era tratar de involucrar ninguna época, ni revolución, ni nada. Ninguno de esos materiales.

[26] Beardsell, p. 80; Nilda Rosales, 'El tema del caudillismo en *Pedro Páramo* de Juan Rulfo', in *'Caudillos', 'Caciques' et Dictateurs dans le Roman Hispano-Américain*, ed. by Paul Verdevoye (Paris: Éditions Hispaniques, 1978), pp. 283–89.

Simplemente involucrar los hechos que habían pasado ahí. Y nunca se menciona una fecha.[27]

In a sense, in fact, Rulfo's novel appears to *subvert* chronology by disrupting cause and effect. Therefore, what we are looking for in a political reading of Rulfo's work is not the evocation of a specific, historical period but the less precise, more dramatic picture of an almost timeless power struggle.

Centripetal Verbal Irony: 'Hay esperanza, en suma'

After the sudden death of Pedro Páramo's son, Miguel, the priest opens fragment 14 with a consoling vision of heaven and hope: 'Hay aire y sol, hay nubes. Allá arriba un cielo azul y detrás de él tal vez haya canciones; tal vez mejores voces … Hay esperanza, en suma. Hay esperanza para nosotros, contra nuestro pesar.'[28] As we have no knowledge yet of the personal enmity between Rentería and Miguel, we may assume this to be the prelude to an intercession on behalf of the dead man to plead for his entry into the Kingdom of God after the sudden circumstances of a death which deprived him of the Last Rites. But we then learn that the priest has no intention of blessing Miguel Páramo, despite the protests of the congregation: 'Fue un mal hombre y no entrará al Reino de los Cielos. Dios me tomará a mal que interceda por él.' Instead of reciting mass for the purpose of absolution, Rentería has indulged in an act of confident vindictiveness which promises not hope but despair for the dead man. This takes us by surprise and forces us to refigure the words 'esperanza' and 'nosotros', which now appear to refer *not* to Miguel and mankind but to Rentería's flock, long oppressed by Miguel and his father. For this irony to work, the ironist (Rentería) must have a sense of authority and Rulfo has indeed (albeit temporarily) given the priest a fortified position from which he considers himself able to be, and justified in being, ironic, basing his confidence on the duality of righteousness and sin, the staple of Church discourse: Miguel is the 'bad', sinful 'other', while the priest is the 'good', righteous 'self'. Thus, the priest, knowing that Miguel was unable to show remorse for his sins, believes he controls the destiny of the dead, unabsolved man. It should be remembered too that he is also applying the letter of Catholic doctrine for his *own* ends, although we do not know at this stage that Miguel raped his niece. Whatever the motive, irony is intended by Rulfo in the priest's initial words of hope and it is based

[27] Juan Rulfo, *Autobiografía armada*, ed. by Reina Roffé (Buenos Aires: Corregidor, 1973), p. 29.

[28] Rulfo, pp. 90–91. Page numbers referring to this fragment will no longer be given, as all quotations may be found on these two pages.

on an illusory sense of control over Miguel's destiny governed by the legal concepts of sin and absolution.

Apart from Miguel, who are the victims of Rentería's verbal irony? If the first victim is the dead man, the second is the congregation, about to participate now in a futile ceremony in which the intention of the priest is the opposite of that which they expect and desire. Once this is openly acknowledged, in the failure to bless Miguel, the congregation protests. This is the first indication to the priest that, despite the necessity of the Last Rites, his desire to enforce this strict interpretation of Catholic law on Miguel – based on righteousness and sin – will not be accepted by a town increasingly under the capitalist control of the *cacique* Pedro Páramo and his wealth. His speech therefore turns into a less clear 'murmullo', a confused murmur, a symptom of the fact that Catholic doctrine and the priest himself are the third and most important victims of the irony of his words. For the recurring anxiety of the priest in the novel is rooted in a challenge to his public role with which he is unable to come to terms. As well as giving sacraments on the basis of 'righteousness' and 'sin' he must, at the same time, confront Pedro Páramo's corrupt exercise of power over the inhabitants of Comala, a process which complicates this duality, for the priest is ultimately caught between the demands of a Catholic law opposed to violent resistance and a local law implemented *with* violence. More centrifugally, his situation has its roots in the conflict between Spanish settlers, particularly *encomenderos*, and the pioneering missionaries of the colonial period who, as well as

> [shielding] the Indians from the corruption and immorality of the European settlers and the labor demands of an encroaching colonial economy … imposed Christian beliefs, social practices … and political organization through a mission system that undermined the Indians' potential for resistance and rebellion.[29]

Rentería attempts therefore to negotiate a morally acceptable course through a 'grey area', a process which, for Bhabha, is an inevitable result of colonialism.[30] However, as we shall see, the priest's non-violent attempt to resist colonial discourse by applying the *letter* of Catholic law and condemning Miguel to purgatory is defeated by a local *spirit* of the law that is defined by the *cacique*'s own moral code, based principally on money, and imposed

---

[29] Mark A. Burkholder and Lyman L. Johnson, *Colonial Latin America* [1990] (New York: Oxford University Press, 1998), p. 92.

[30] Bhabha, p. 52: '… the common, conversational distinction between the letter and spirit of the Law displays the otherness of Law itself; the ambiguous grey area between Justice and judicial procedure is, quite literally, a conflict of judgement'.

with violence on a congregation whose power to resist has been squashed
by Rentería's own collusion. This 'law of the jungle' that is *caciquismo* also
negates the law of the (national) state, as Miguel goes unpunished for his rape
by state law too, creating the conditions for a 'stateless' as well as 'godless'
society in which the *cacique* can take, or rather keep, control. In fact, it is
local patriarchy based on capitalistic individualism (itself an adequate definition of *caciquismo*) rather than the patriarchy of the Church or the state, that
defines the binaries on which society is governed in Comala. Thus the words
'Hay esperanza en suma' rebound ironically on the priest, for whom there is
little hope against the local *caciquismo* which rules Comala.

Centrifugal Verbal Irony: 'Padre'

There is a pivotal line in the middle of fragment 14, just before the priest
sprinkles holy water on the body of Miguel, which illustrates the importance
of Miguel to the community: 'Aquel cadáver pesaba mucho en el ánimo de
todos.' Here, we sense what is meant by González Boixo when he talks of the
'sentimiento comunitario de pecado, de culpabilidad' in Comala.[31] As well
as the fact that the corpse represents the sin of the community, there is also a
sense of a void – Comala's lack of an heir – and, in the next line, an oblique
sense of the struggle of two fathers *over* this void, a kind of premonition of
the Cristero War: 'Estaba sobre una tarima, en medio de la iglesia, rodeado de
cirios nuevos, de flores, de *un padre que estaba detrás de él, solo, esperando
que terminara la velación.*'[32] The use of the indefinite article with the word
'padre' creates ambiguity, for there is a biological father (Pedro Páramo),
perhaps waiting for the Mass to end before he makes his personal protest;
but there is also a spiritual father (Rentería), who is also waiting for the end
of the service so that he may be free of his personal torment. Underlining the
centrality of the theme of patriarchy, there are in fact three figurative fathers
at work in *Pedro Páramo*: the Church, the state and the *cacique*. This use of
the word 'padre' is therefore a form of verbal irony because its significance is
extended beyond its immediate, biological denotation to include also its non-
physical dimensions. The purpose of Rulfo's irony is indeed to encourage
the reader to go beyond the literal and ask questions of the invisible *context*
of the novel, in a 'centrifugal' direction. Just as the teacher is seemingly
confused by the word 'país' in Rulfo's short story 'Luvina', the priest here is
confronted with the nature of 'fatherhood', and the reader, in turn, is invited

31 González Boixo, p. 170.
32 Emphasis added.

to question this word and its underlying connotations of authority, power, and control.

An ironic, or at least interrogative, understanding of the word 'padre' reveals the significance of the state's attempt to monopolise patriarchal values in the Mexican psyche, to replace the Church as the chief patriarchal institution after the Revolution. This attempt was apparent in the manner in which, for example, 'heroes' from the Revolution were 'officially' beatified in ceremonies which resembled religious occasions in their attention to formality and ritual. These figures were then manufactured to look as masculine and fatherly as possible so that real, 'physical' people of the Revolution, imbued with a spiritual aura, were transformed into something akin to saints, 'Fathers of the Revolution'.[33] The government's attempt to monopolise respect for the mediatory power of the father figure was thus based on a combination of physical and spiritual values. However, the *cacique*, a rival to state and Church patriarchy in rural areas, is just as clever, for this is why Pedro Páramo, as we shall see, expects and desires absolution for his dead son: in the Catholic world of Comala, his material authority also depends on spiritual legitimacy. Just as clever as the appropriation of Church rituals is the way in which the *cacique* undermines Rentería by applying the state's technique of monetary reward for loyalty.

Spiritual and Material Authority

Returning to fragment 14, the priest has now spoken and the congregation's sheep-like obedience is empty of genuine expectation, suggesting that the patriarchy represented by the priest is already losing currency: 'Después se arrodilló y todo el mundo se arrodilló con él.' Then they repeat after the priest: 'Ten piedad de tu siervo, Señor,' and 'Que descanse en paz, amén.'[34] The latter is described simply as a reply from 'las voces' and, indeed, we wonder whether the parishioners' loyalty to the priest is not based simply on habit: if, at this stage, everyone is aware that Miguel Páramo has effectively been condemned according to Catholic law, why else would they continue with the ceremony? In the next sentence, indeed, there appears to be an allegorical transference of loyalty and obedience from one institution to another: 'Y cuando empezaba a llenarse nuevamente de cólera, vio que *todos abandonaban la iglesia llevándose el cadáver de Miguel Páramo*.'[35] The abandonment is physical but the implication is of a spiritual abandonment of the

---

[33] O'Malley, p. 140.

[34] There is, of course, a familiar verbal irony in these phrases too, for the characters have not been shown mercy and they live/die in anything but peace.

[35] Emphasis added.

institution of the Church in favour of a local, temporal *caciquismo*. There is here a danger that the righteousness/sin duality will become inexorably tainted by the influence of money, thus dissolving the barrier between the two. In such a situation, the priest's role as mediator between his parishioners and God is crucial, and resistance to *caciquismo* will be the only effective option. Ultimately, the priest will fail to take on this challenge, preferring, as we shall see, to resort to a futile martyrdom.

When Pedro Páramo himself approaches the priest and kneels by his side, the *hacendado* hijacks the notion of humbleness invested within the act of kneeling in order to assume its power, in what is almost a reflection of the brazen attempts of the government to possess the same sacred aura by adopting Catholic rhetoric. This attempt to engineer a dominant discourse is therefore a tool employed not only by the state but by *caciques* to subjugate other discourses, feeding as it does on the pool of spiritual legitimacy described above. After Pedro Páramo kneels, the reader at last receives 'clarification' of the priest's situation: Pedro Páramo's son had allegedly murdered Rentería's brother and raped his niece, Ana. But the *hacendado* mischievously uses the phrases 'según rumores' and 'según el juicio de usted' when listing his son's misdemeanours, suggesting that these crimes have not been proven according to the (private) system of law he controls, a system which creates a spirit rather than a letter of the law, thus undermining the institutional righteousness/sin moral code of the priest, as well as the legal/illegal code of the secular state, with a largely arbitrary version of objectivity and truth that challenges both. In doing so, he also stealthily acquires the tone and vocabulary of a priest: 'Considérelo y perdónelo como quizá Dios lo haya perdonado.'

His plea is a comparatively long piece of speech in the novel, reinforcing his control over history: the self-proclaimed subject of history – the *cacique*, rather than the state – enforcing his view of the past on the 'de-voiced' object, the priest, successfully creating a hierarchy of truth or perhaps only one version of it. In order to achieve this, the appropriation of the latter's tools of rhetoric is vital and the crimes of the past are therefore laundered by the stolen symbols of the Church – the holy water, the kneeling, the vocabulary and the tone – just as the crimes of the 'heroes' of the past are laundered through their beatification in the state's 'Fathers of the Revolution' ceremonies. However, just as Pedro Páramo adopts the rhetoric and aura of the Church for his own purposes, he also utilises the material authority on which the state relies: he lays money on the *prie-dieu* and self-assuredly stands, asking/ordering the priest to accept the gift. He then leaves as though the forgiveness of his son were now a *fait accompli*, certain as he is, of course, that the real mediator of social relationships is money. Of course, the use of gifts and money to buy loyalty was a policy of the post-Revolutionary government spearheaded by the union leader Luis Morones during the 1920s in his struggle against rival Catholic unions.[36] Here, however, we see how the *cacique* is the ultimate winner for he uses the techniques of both Church (spiritual legitimacy) and state (material legitimacy) to establish control over law and order in his realm. Indeed, the fact that the fragment occurs before the Revolution is here not a hindrance to the irony but an enhancer, for the *cacique*'s complete mastery over rural power systems suggests that the bellicose efforts of priests, peasants and federal soldiers alike would always be in vain. The pre-Cristero years, seen from a distance, seem to underline all the more damningly the futility of an institutional, almost internecine war which failed to address an all-powerful local *caciquismo*.

The Challenge: Resistance and Martyrdom

The empty church, like the empty church of Luvina, now signifies the empty mission of the institution and the burden of responsibility falls heavily on the priest to revive the moral project of the Church by refusing the *cacique*'s money and defying the connotations of venality in his own name. However, Rentería, like any rural Mexican priest in this period, cannot live on his salary and seems to defer this responsibility to his own 'father', God. He finds the latter's judgement – apparently an instruction to accept the *cacique*'s money – unpalatable, though the priest weepingly does accept it. Given the nature of the injuries Miguel has caused him (the murder of his brother and the rape of his niece), this is for the reader a surprising and perhaps disappointing result, for, initially in this fragment, the priest is the ironist: his outwardly superior posture, refusing to bless Miguel Páramo, and his ironic use of the words normally used in a Mass for the dead, place him in a position of authority in the eyes of the reader. By the end, the reader can see that the tables have turned, for the father, it transpires, is not the priest, but the *hacendado*, and the moral code which prevails is not the spiritual one of the Church, or even the 'legal' one of the state, but that of *caciquismo*. Thus, Rentería's final acceptance of Pedro Páramo's bribe represents an ironic inversion of the advice of Jesus: 'Render to Caesar the things that are Caesar's and to God the things that are God's' (Mark 12. 17). Here, Rentería respects the rule of money, performing the exact opposite of the meaning intended by Jesus.

This picture of hopeless surrender we have seen here is not equivalent to the state's vision of a priesthood in deceitful, reckless collusion. Similarly, the priest's eventual joining of the Cristero Rebellion does not symbolise the priesthood's heroic defiance of the *cacique*. While his discomfort at the

---

[36] Meyer, *The Cristero Rebellion*, pp. 22–23.

dilemma arising from Miguel's death has been registered and the opposition to the fetishistic 'evil' stereotype of the state has accordingly been counter-pointed with a more nuanced, subjective depiction of sensitivity, it is equally inescapable – notwithstanding the priest's reluctance to collude – that his acceptance of the *cacique*'s will undermines the Church's narrative of the morally spotless, martyred priest. In fact, as we have seen, his situation is far more complex and ambivalent than state and Church representations of the role of the priest imply, based as it is on a feeling of being trapped between representing the discourse of (local) *caciquismo*, on the one hand, and confronting it, on the other. By the end of the fragment, indeed, Rentería is cornered, a situation echoed in his physical position ('Se echó en un rincón'), for his own strict, binary interpretation of justice ('Por mí, condénalo'), based on righteousness and sin, is reduced to insignificance. The superior posture he adopts at the beginning of the fragment proves to be chimerical: despite his nominal position as 'padre', he is in fact as much a pawn of the *hacendado* as he is of God. Visually, this centripetal cosmic irony is mirrored in the imagery of the fragment: his position in front of the congregation holding forth is transformed into one of kneeling alone with his tormentors – Pedro Páramo and God – and, by the end, into one of abject misery as he weeps in the corner of the sacristy.

The critical position of the Mexican priest is also represented in Rulfo's photographic portrait of the actor who plays the priest in the film *El despojo* (1960), taken during a break in the shooting of the film.[37] The metaphor of performance is crucial, of course, to Rulfo's photograph but its physical composition is even more powerful. The gnarled and convoluted tree 'behind' the priest suggests an inner turmoil which stands in opposition to the crisp outline of the priest himself, suggestive of a misleadingly two-dimensional figure. The tree is initially observed to be behind the priest but this perspective is only available to the viewer: the subject is blissfully unaware of the juxtaposition. There is also a disturbing contradiction in movement as the wind pushes the priest's cloth (his public role) forward while the angle of the land seems to point to his inevitably falling backwards (towards the inner complexities represented by the tree). The photographic space allotted to the sky, as well as the sheer size of the tree, indicate that the private angst of the priest will triumph over the public performance, despite the resistance indicated by the folded arms. The tension in this photograph, like the tension in this fragment, challenges the manicheistic use of the priest as icon and stereotype in the images and words produced by the Church and

---

[37] The photograph is reproduced in Carlos Fuentes et al., *México: Juan Rulfo fotógrafo*, p. 130.

state.[38] Indeed, the remaining fragments of the novel concerning Rentería chart this burgeoning moral tension, undermining the state's fetishistic stereotype of the evil, conniving accomplice to the *cacique* at the same time as questioning the martyrological images projected by the Church. In the most tragic situational irony of the novel, the state as a target for the priest's rage is a red herring: his involvement in a manufactured conflict between Church and state, in which the figure of the priest is a manicheistic pawn of political rhetoric, leaves the real culprit on a local level – *caciquismo* – firmly intact, the inhabitants of Comala unblessed and the town itself abandoned to ghosts in purgatory.

Irony in Martyrdom: A Long and Winding Path

In fragment 15, with the priest's sense of righteousness already corrupted by money, we begin to see how he internalises the discourse of *caciquismo*. Perhaps in order to assuage his conscience, the priest seems to instil some doubt in his niece as to whether it was really Miguel Páramo who committed the rape, eventually putting her in the position of having to recall the crime. Rentería has therefore internalised the capitalistic moral code of Pedro Páramo, tacitly accepting the latter's version of events and therefore his binary of 'haves' and 'have-nots'. Burdened with guilt, he struggles to sleep, in fragment 17, in which he acknowledges to himself that, while he takes money from the rich for his 'mantenimiento' in return for absolution, he delivers no pardon for the poor because they have nothing to give him but prayers. This centripetal situational irony can be placed (centrifugally) in sharp contrast to the morally forthright behaviour of el padre Pro, who is said to be conscientiously direct and almost clinical in his dealings with his flock, helping to feed the poor and having, even while on the run, 'el sosiego para sondear como admirable sicólogo los senos profundos de las almas y, como maestro de espíritu, para la palabra oportuna, señalar el remedio eficaz, mover los corazones, y caldearlos con el fuego divino'.[39] On the other hand, Rentería's private acknowledgement of his venal behaviour leads to an admission of treachery: 'He traicionado a aquellos que me quieren y que me han dado su fe y me buscan para que yo interceda por ellos para con Dios' (95).

There is also a centripetal dramatic irony in his last-ditch efforts to save the souls of Comala after this fragment. This is supplied by the reader's knowledge, from the structure of the novel, that his dawning martyrdom is to prove fruitless. Indeed, fragment 18, returning to the first thread of the

---

[38] I am indebted to the director of the Fundación Juan Rulfo, Víctor Jiménez, for the initial reading of the tree as representative of the mental state of the priest.

[39] Dragón, p. xvi.

novel concerning Juan Preciado, picks up on the imagery of a town that has long been condemned to darkness: 'Ya estaba alta la noche. La lámpara que ardía en un rincón comenzó a languidecer; luego parpadeó y terminó apagándose' (97). This is Juan Preciado's first night in the Comala created by its absentee fathers: a lightless town, full of the 'murmullos' of those condemned to live there for eternity. In the next eleven fragments, we read, as he hears, the cries of Toribio Aldrete, the small landowner hanged for his attempt to resist Pedro Páramo's encroachment; later, the excited cries of delight of his mother Dolores, hoodwinked into marrying the *hacendado*; the sycophantic machinations of Fulgor Sedano; Chona's voice pleading with her boyfriend to allow her to wait for her father's death before leaving town. Then Juan Preciado hears how his father marginalises those nameless inhabitants of the town who feel in some way wronged by him: 'Esa gente no existe' (134). He also hears of the death of his grandfather as a result of a cycle of vengeful violence. In short, the voices heard between fragments 17 and 41 tell the story of Comala's ironic descent into *caciquismo* as post-colonial discourses (of both Church and state) attempt and fail to tighten their grip on light and darkness, right and wrong, truth and untruth, legality and illegality. When the narrative brings us back to Rentería, we have a deeper understanding of the burden he carries if he is to be a responsible priest and save the souls whose voices we have heard. The centripetal dramatic irony in his thoughts, words and actions is created by the structure of a novel which informs us *a priori* that any martyrdom is doomed.

The path to martyrdom is nevertheless the real substance of the priest's story and his significance in the novel, for it is loaded with dramatic irony. This path is long and tortuous, even if it begins inconspicuously in fragment 41, where we find Rentería in reflective mood. In an effort to understand how he has reached a stage of such anxiety, he recalls the baptism of Miguel Páramo. At the death of Miguel's mother, the priest handed the baby to Pedro Páramo but the latter suggested he take care of him himself and make him a priest. Rentería's reply is telling: 'Con la sangre que lleva dentro no quiero tener esa responsabilidad' (138). This refusal to take on a task that would perhaps have saved the child from the claws of his father seems to be at the root of the priest's anguish, for the rest of the novel demonstrates a certain shirking of responsibility until the very end. His memory of the scene has configured it in terms deeply resonant of original sin: 'El muchachito se retorcía, pequeño como era, *como una víbora*' (139).[40] The *hacendado* thus accepts the task of raising the child, but what does this mean to him? There is

---

[40] Emphasis added.

an almost comical answer to this question in the manner in which he suggests
a toast in honour of the occasion:

> – Por la difunta y por usted beberé este trago.
> – ¿Y por él?
> – Por él también, ¿por qué no?
> (139)

Clearly, for the *hacendado*, raising children is something of an insignificant
pastime, an attitude which must alarm the priest, who, indeed, seems to regret
having done nothing about the situation. With the memory of this shirking of
responsibility still swimming around his mind, he attempts now to hide from
his parishioners when they travel to the *Media Luna*, a neglectful attitude, the
irony of which is not lost on the priest himself: 'El se agachó, escondiéndose
en el galápago que bordeaba el río. "De quién te escondes?", se preguntó a sí
mismo' (139). The situation becomes almost ludicrous as, despite the priest's
attempts to hide, people can still see him:

> – ¡Adiós, padre! – oyó que le decían.
> Se alzó de la tierra y contestó:
> – ¡Adiós! Que el Señor te bendiga. (139)

This humorous exchange shows that Rentería cannot escape his responsi-
bilities any longer: he is forever committed to his public role as a priest,
re-emerging from the bush in an image which recalls Rulfo's photograph ('se
alzó de la tierra y contestó'), and in a psychological process that will eventually lead to his participation in the Cristero War.

In desperation, however, el padre Rentería tries an easy way out just one
more time. He now goes to a priest in Contla to obtain absolution for his
corrupt behaviour. However, he fails and the rebuke of his fellow priest
amounts to an instruction to become responsible for his sins, to act rather than
simply to settle for absolution. The reason Rentería must act is that Pedro
Páramo has destroyed his Church while Rentería himself has been complicit
and has refused to use the potential for resistance invested within him as a
priest. '¿Qué has hecho de la fuerza de Dios?' (140), Rentería is asked by
his colleague, who laments the fact that Comala has now become a town
governed by superstition and fear rather than faith.[41] In order to change this
condition, the senior priest suggests that it is not enough to be good, long-
suffering and hard-working. Additionally, one must refuse to operate on the

---

[41] This situation, incidentally, suits the local boss, of course, as superstition is not as strong
a motive for rebellion as faith, while fear, in turn, helps to keep people humble.

same terms which the local boss uses to manipulate relationships with others, based on money and violence. Indeed, this would simply mean sinking to their *moral* level in order to benefit from their superior *social* status, as the priest suggests in his pun on the word 'mejor': 'con tu alma en manos de ellos ¿que podrás hacer para ser mejor que aquellos que son mejores que tú?' (140). With this, the priest refuses to give Rentería absolution, thus effectively closing the door on this avenue of spiritual redemption.

Now the task of self-redemption is in the hands of Rentería himself and on it depends not only his own future but that of Comala. This is symbolically portrayed by Rentería's tale of the seeds he had once bought to grow in Comala only to see them die. This tale, of course, is reminiscent of Jesus's parable of the mustard seed and the kingdom of heaven, implying the priest's recognition of his individual responsibility in the future of Comala. Rentería's colleague, however, also connects it to the dominance of Pedro Páramo, and the priest of Comala agrees:

> – A veces lo he dudado; pero allí lo reconocen.
> – ¿Y entre ésos estás tú?
> – Yo soy un pobre hombre dispuesto a humillarse; mientras
> sienta el impulso. (141)

The line which ends this dialogue seems to suggest that Rentería is now preparing to take the gamble of physical rebellion: he is prepared to be humiliated only up to a point, 'mientras sienta el impulso'. Henceforth, the characterisation of Rentería centres on his struggle to accept *spiritually* his responsibility, choosing instead to join the Cristeros in a *physical* battle that will leave the *cacique* to do as he wishes.

War is by no means an easy option either, as Catholic discourse runs counter to this impulse, especially when we consider the gospel of Matthew: '*But if any one strikes you on the right cheek, turn to him the other one also*' (Matthew 5. 39). We can only assume, therefore, that Rentería's decision will be a complex one, not subject to easy interpretation either by the state as that of a raving priest defending a colonial discourse or by the Church as that of a determined, heroic last stand against a godless government. Instead, the novel appears to suggest that Rentería's ultimate conversion to the Cristero cause is misguided as it is based on a physical rather than a spiritual impulse. To say this, is not to state that the author is opposed to resistance, for, in the first place, the novel advocates nothing. Nevertheless, there were known alternatives to the type of resistance which merely continued the cycle of violence in the history of the countryside, the most effective of which was not martyrdom but passive resistance led by priests who remained in their towns and villages to allow the clandestine continuation of sacramental rites: 'Indeed, much passive resistance had no greater aim than maintaining the devotional health of the community, protecting what might be termed the "spiritual economy", the ritual and spiritual exchanges which governed relations between the laity and the Church.'[42] Thus, it is this specifically communal spirituality that is in danger of being ignored for the much more self-centred struggle of a priest to follow the Church's martyrological line and do what he believes is 'righteous'. The personal nature of this struggle is made apparent when, just before leaving the house, he tells Ana that he considers himself 'un hombre malo'. Although he dutifully returns to the confession box after his meeting with Pedro Páramo, the dishevelled-looking priest sitting down to take confession imagines himself 'lleno de polvo y de miseria' (142). There is a degree of sympathy for the character on the part of both the reader and the author. Rulfo's juxtaposition of the carefree and unrepentant *hacendado* with the deep-thinking, angst-ridden priest is situationally ironic in its depiction of two sinners for it is, in fact, the morally-concerned, well-meaning man who considers himself evil while the corrupt *cacique* believes in his own immunity, glibly expounding the same 'disculpas' as ever.

As a result of Rentería's guilt, there is a moment of almost existential angst in which the priest's moral tension seems to be suffocating him:

> Y mientras oía el Yo pecador su cabeza se dobló como si no pudiera sostenerse en alto. Luego vino aquel mareo, aquella confusión, el irse diluyendo como en agua espesa, y el girar de luces; la luz entera del día que se desbarataba haciéndose añicos; y ese sabor a sangre en la lengua. El Yo pecador se oía más fuerte, repetido, y después terminaban: '"por los siglos de los siglos, amén", "por los siglos de los siglos, amén", "por los siglos …"' (144)

The image of the blinding light suggests both confusion and a type of enlightenment for which he may not yet be ready. The taste of blood, meanwhile, hints that some form of self-sacrifice is necessary if he is to escape his routine inaction. However, the cursory manner in which he dismisses the queue of confessors at the end of fragment 41 suggests that he has not yet resolved the complexities of his commitment to the community and, perhaps, that his action may be too little, too late. As the priest walks to the sacristy in search of rest, he leaves behind a dissatisfied group, producing the sound which is the leitmotiv of the novel: 'Detrás de él, sólo se oyó el murmullo' (144). This is a haunting sound, echoing the 'gnashing of teeth' that Jesus promises to those who fail to reach the kingdom of heaven and which we are reminded of in Revelations (Revelations 16. 10–11).

---

[42] Butler, p. 13.

The fact that this 'murmullo' is 'all' he hears reminds us of the homogenised 'montón de mujeres' (142) he refers to in an earlier exchange with Pedro Páramo, suggesting that he has failed to take account of the *individual* tragedies hiding behind the 'murmullos', engrossed merely in his own need for martyrdom. Indeed he considers the final confessor to be surrounded by an indecipherable 'desventura': he keeps returning to confess but the priest, wrapped up in his personal mission, does not seem to see the uniqueness of each visit. The desire for martyrdom seems to be diluting his sense of responsibility to his parishioners on an individual basis. The danger seems to be that becoming a martyr entails a certain ignoring or, at best, objectification of one's parishioners as a homogenous 'flock'. The reader is left pondering several questions at the end of this fragment: Is the priest as guilty as Pedro Páramo of an undiscerning attitude towards those for whom he is responsible ('Esa gente no existe')? Is this attitude going to change? Will the priest confront the *hacendado*? In what way, and is it too late anyway? However, through the ironic structure of the novel, Rulfo scuppers any sense of suspense, for, in this novel, we know the answers before the questions: the town is full of souls in purgatory. Thus, it seems that the priest's metamorphosis really must be in vain, underlining the centripetal cosmic irony of his situation and the centripetal dramatic irony in our reading of his actions and words. Such a nuanced picture of the priest, meanwhile, rooted in an inability to fathom the good/bad duality, lies in stark (centrifugal) contrast to either that of the morally certain el padre Pro or that of the evil accomplice to the *cacique*.

To some extent, Susana San Juan inadvertently encourages Rentería in his rebellion. In fragment 64, Rentería's explanation that he has come to prepare Susana for death is met by Susana with a familiar ironic refrain: '¿por qué entonces no me deja en paz?' (183). The tables have truly been turned: the ironist in fragment 14 was the priest, and the victim was Miguel Páramo; now, the ironist is a dying member of his 'flock' and the victim is the priest and everything he is supposed to believe in. When Rentería replies, indeed, he himself betrays a hint of the absurdity of a faith which promises salvation only by the impersonal repetition of words, denying people the creativity of expression to externalise their pain, preferring instead not to listen but to lull the pain to sleep: 'Te dejaré en paz, Susana. *Conforme vayas repitiendo las palabras que yo digo, te irás quedando dormida.* Sentirás como si tú misma te arrullaras' (143).[43] Susana does not buy this suggestion: she pretends to do what the priest says only to throw his words back in his face, converting spiritual imagery into physical revelling, with a sexual glint in her eye:

----

43 Emphasis added.

'Tengo la boca llena de tí, de tu boca. Tus labios apretados, duros como si mordieran oprimidos mis labios …' Se detuvo también. Miró de reojo al padre Rentería y lo vio lejos, como si estuviera detrás de un vidrio empañado. (143)

Such is her disaffection with patriarchy, it seems, she no longer identifies with any of its manifestations, be it the domineering father, the well-meaning priest or the concerned lover. Her hallucinatory fixation on her fantasy relationship with 'Florencio' is based on a physical indulgence resulting from spiritual abandonment. It suggests a rebellion against the love of all these 'padres': the paternal love of San Bartolomé, the pastoral love of Rentería and the nostalgic/sexual love of Pedro Páramo. Susana's rejection of all forms of patriarchy informs a position that denies the function of stereotypes created by patriarchal authority. She is neither naïve, nor a whore, nor quite entirely 'insane'. One wonders, then, whether this is the turning point for Rentería, when he finally takes on a similar challenge to patriarchal authority. After Susana's death, indeed, the next and last we hear of him is that he has joined the Cristeros in a war that cost thousands of lives. However, it is misguidedly against the patriarchal discourse of the state, rather than the more powerful *caciquismo*, that Rentería takes up arms. This recourse to physicality, as Susana's death and 'madness' should have warned him, is no answer to oppression but, for a colluding priest like Rentería, martyrdom at least guarantees his soul.

The result is that local *caciquismo* is left to triumph unchallenged as we see in at least three situational ironies in the novel's presentation of the war. Firstly, although, when el Tilcuate asks which side to join, Pedro Páramo is unequivocal ('Eso ni se discute. Ponte al lado del gobierno,' 187), the army sponsored by the *cacique* ultimately joins the men of Rentería, an outcome which seems to accord with Meyer's view of the conduct of armed bands in the Cristero Rebellion: '… bands would be organised, or would fall apart, in accordance with the vicissitudes of the military operations undertaken and the military and economic opportunities that presented themselves'.[44] The second, more centrifugal situational irony therefore is that the fate of the war is in the hands not of the powerful state but of the local *cacique* to whom local bands of fighters will answer. The most potent situational irony is the third: that the motivation driving el Tilcuate's men seems to be a superstition which Rentería's own spiritual neglect has helped to engender: 'Me iré a reforzar al padrecito. Me gusta como gritan. Además lleva uno ganada la salvación' (188). The use of the diminutive 'padrecito' may be affectionate but it is also somewhat belittling and, in the context of the dialogue with Pedro Páramo,

[44] Meyer, pp. 6–7.

it places the priest on an inferior social plane. Despite the priest's efforts, it seems there is little chance of his unsettling the landowner's grip on Comala. What is worse and more ironic still, is that his adversary now no longer seems to care: 'Haz lo que quieras,' Pedro Páramo eventually tells el Tilcuate (188). The abandonment of Comala is therefore total: the priest is physically absent and the *hacendado* is not capable of or interested in restoring to the people the faith which validates their existence. Furthermore, the priest's moral dilemmas result simply in his signing up to one manicheistic discourse (martyrological – Church) to contest another (the demonic priest – state), reinforcing both stereotypes in the process. Despite his good intentions, the man who is the thorn in his life and that of his community remains unpunished and stronger than ever.

6

Pedro Páramo: Irony and *Caciquismo*

Pedro Páramo dies thus in the final pages of Rulfo's novel: 'Dio un golpe seco contra la tierra y se fue desmoronando como si fuera un montón de piedras' (195). The physical death of a *cacique*, I contend here, is an illusion, both of the death of this *cacique* and of the death of *caciquismo*, a colonial discourse. In the major irony of the novel, we find that the protagonist's 'desmoronamiento' does not categorically signify his death, either on a centripetal level (as the character of a novel) or on a centrifugal level (as a representative of *caciquismo*). In the novel, *caciquismo* persists in spite of the death of the *cacique* because the attachment between the protagonist and the inhabitants of his community is so strong that they – and he – are forever trapped by the destiny he commands for them, both before and after they die. On a *centrifugal* level, *caciquismo* itself survives beyond the death of individual *caciques* because it is an institution so firmly entrenched in the Mexican psyche that, rather than die, it merely transforms and renews itself, be it through neo-, urban or national forms of the same system. The end of *Pedro Páramo* can thus be considered an ironic commentary on the post-Revolutionary rhetoric which boasts of the termination of the ancient, unofficial system of rural relations that is *caciquismo*.

This reading is based on an analysis of social and economic relationships within the countryside. As Raúl Benítez Zenteno tells us, the subject of *caciquismo* is key to any such work: 'No es posible explicar algunas de las relaciones entre las clases sociales rurales … desconociendo la participación en lo político, en lo económico y en lo social, del cacique.'[1] For our purposes, therefore, the figure of Pedro Páramo as a *cacique* is a vital object of study in any politicised analysis of Rulfo's work. His status as a *cacique* has often been taken for granted: although some critics explain the term with common adjectives associated with the Latin American *cacique* (for example, 'pudiente, violento, vicioso, materialista, implacable'[2]), most choose simply to use

---

[1] Raúl Benítez Zenteno, in *Caciquismo y poder político en el México rural*, ed. by Roger Bartra (Mexico City: Siglo Veintiuno, 1975), p. vii.
[2] Mirjana Polic Bobic, 'La recepción del personaje Pedro Páramo', *Cuadernos Hispanoamericanos*, 421–23 (1985), 399–403 (p. 399).

the term as an accepted description of the protagonist. Nilda Rosales and, more recently, José C. González Boixo explore the meaning of the term with a greater degree of scrutiny and their work will be considered here. But it has not yet been acknowledged by these or any other critics that an acceptance of the fact that Pedro Páramo is a *cacique* is itself a contextually-charged interpretation which necessitates a thorough assessment of the definitions of the word in historical and contemporary contexts.[3]

According to the rhetoric of Revolution (e.g. '¡Mueran los caciques!'), the *cacique* had had his day but, as Luisa Paré's work showed in 1975, reports of the death of *caciquismo* had been exaggerated: 'la Revolución, aunque haya matado, exiliado o momentáneamente vencido a los caciques … no ha destruido el caciquismo'.[4] Writing around the same time, Karl H. Schwerin agreed, arguing that colonial forms of *caciquismo* would 'lay the origins of social and political attitudes and practices that still have a residual effect in some aspects of Latin American society today'.[5] Indeed, the survival of *caciquismo* was a fact in the second half of the twentieth century to the extent that the figure had again become a political pawn:

> The revolutionary regime has from time to time seized upon the cacique as a kind of scapegoat, foisting upon him most of the outstanding sins of omission and commission which the revolution has accumulated over the course of its first half century. Thus could Presidential candidate José López Portillo, while on the campaign trail [in 1975], candidly admit that the nation still had not succeeded in dispelling 'los mismos fantasmas' which oppressed the countryside in 1910, chief among them the spectre of *caciquismo*.[6]

The 'fantasmas' of Rulfo's *Pedro Páramo* seem to resonate with López Portillo's phrase, especially after the discovery of an ultimately unsent reply by Rulfo to a question put by the Argentine journalist Máximo Simpson. The latter asks Rulfo whether *Pedro Páramo* is principally 'la historia de un cacique' or, more generally, 'una gran metáfora sobre el destino del hombre,

---

[3] The only serious attempt to combine historical evidence on *caciquismo* with a look at fiction is Robert Kern, ed., *The Caciques, Oligarchical Politics and the System of Caciquismo in the Luso-Hispanic World* (Albuquerque: University of New Mexico Press, 1973). Although *Pedro Páramo* is curiously omitted, Kern's book will form much of the basis for reflections on *caciquismo* here.

[4] Luisa Paré, in Bartra, *Caciquismo y estructura de poder en la Sierra Norte de Puebla*, p. 31. See also Gilbert M. Joseph, 'Caciquismo and the Revolution: Carrillo Puerto in Yucatán', in *Caudillo and Peasant in the Mexican Revolution*, ed. by David Brading (Cambridge: Cambridge University Press, 1980), pp. 193–221.

[5] Karl H. Schwerin, 'The Anthropological Antecedents: Caciques, Cacicazgos and Caciquismo', in Kern, *The Caciques*, p. 5.

[6] Joseph, 'Caciquismo and the Revolution', p. 194.

como el relato de un sueño dentro de un sueño'. According to the reply, it appears that – for Rulfo, at least – an understanding of *caciquismo* and its ancestry is vital to anyone seeking to interpret the novel. The 'mala yerba' of *caciquismo* has historical roots dating back to the time of the conquest of the Americas, with branches extending into the twentieth century:

> Pedro Páramo es un cacique. Eso ni quien se lo quite. Estos sujetos aparecieron en nuestro continente desde la época de la conquista con el nombre de encomenderos, y ni las Leyes de Indias, ni el fin del coloniaje, ni aún las revoluciones, lograron extirpar esa mala yerba.[7]

Thus, colonial *caciquismo* survived Mexican independence and pre-revolutionary *caciquismo* survived a rhetorical assault by post-Revolutionary government to emerge alive and kicking today. Even now, in the twenty-first century, as any Mexican newspaper website search on the word 'cacique' will reveal, these figures are living and relevant political actors. In the character of Pedro Páramo, Rulfo therefore presents us with a tool for an exploration of the psyche and capacity for endurance of an emblematic Mexican patriarch.

Critical overview

The subject of *caciquismo* in Rulfo's fiction, like many other political aspects of Rulfo's work, remains under-explored. On the other hand, the more general topic of *caciquismo* in Latin American fiction has been given excellent, 'historicised' treatment by Marshall R. Nason in the 1975 collection of historical and literary essays edited by Robert Kern, *The Caciques*.[8] Nason discusses literary representations of *caciques* by Latin Americans, including the Mexican authors Mariano Azuela (*Los de abajo*, 1915, and *Los caciques*, 1917) and Emilio Rabassa (*La bola*, 1887, *La gran ciencia*, 1887, *El cuarto poder*, 1888, *Moneda falsa*, 1888). Rabassa attacks *caciquismo* most directly, treating those characters who are servile to the *cacique* with 'heavy satire ... [attesting] to [his] skepticism concerning rural bossism'.[9] In Azuela's *Los de abajo*, Nason perceives Azuela's opposition to *caciquismo* as 'a major social ill of the Mexican nation and as one which must be cured by extirpation'.[10] Nason proceeds to give an excellent account of

---

7   The original question and Rulfo's entire response can be found in *Los murmullos, Boletín de la Fundación Juan Rulfo* (Mexico City: Quadrata), 1 (1999), pp. 47–49.

8   Marshall R. Nason, 'The Literary Evidence, Part I: The Term *Caciquismo*, its Variants and its Literary Scope', in Kern, *The Caciques*, pp. 27–42 and pp. 99–117.

9   Nason, p. 101.

10   Nason, p. 102.

the treatment of *caciquismo* in the works of Rómulo Gallegos, Eduardo Caballero Calderón and Roberto J. Payró. In conclusion, he says that these accounts of the phenomenon range 'from tongue in cheek satire to high moral indignation'.[11] He then argues for the relevance of literary accounts to social science-based investigation, thereby opening a door for the particular relevance of *Pedro Páramo*: 'The mutually reinforcing interpretations seem, at the very least, to attest to the accuracy of analysis achieved by serious students of the problem, both scholarly and literary, despite the propensity for emotional overlay in the literary approach.'[12]

In fact, it is precisely in the area of 'emotional overlay', or 'mapping the complexities of the heart', as Eagleton puts it, where literature can help to form a picture of the past and, through irony, its relevance to the present.[13] This is particularly the case in *Pedro Páramo*, in which a reduced tendency to manicheism and demonisation in the treatment of the *cacique* helps the author to avoid the trap of empty satire, unbounded vitriol and over-optimism.[14] Nason argues that such objectivising of the *cacique* in most novels which deal with this figure obstructs more considered appraisals:

> The cacique figure is almost always treated 'from the outside', which is to say that the viewpoint employed tends to be that of the omniscient author. Such treatment has the effect of inhibiting spiritual or sentimental identification between the reader and the fictional character.[15]

It is all the more surprising in that case that Nason does not cast his perceptive eye on Rulfo's *Pedro Páramo*. Like Azuela and Rabassa, Rulfo attacks the institution of *caciquismo*; unlike them, he does so not with 'high indignation' or 'satire' but with *irony*. It is through irony that Rulfo's *Pedro Páramo* subverts nineteenth-century narratives which contain what González Boixo terms 'personal testimonial, a direct means of denouncing reality, with visible signs of Manichaeism, and very much in the tradition of what is known as "thesis" literature'.[16] González Boixo himself puts forward the case for

---

[11] Nason, p. 117.

[12] Nason, p. 117.

[13] Eagleton, p. 50.

[14] For example, Nason describes Azuela's wartime optimism in the novel *Los caciques* thus: '[the novel] underscores a certain surging intuition about what the people must attack, as well as the fact that the Revolution, though a shapeless burst of resentment, was fortunate enough in many cases to single out appropriate targets. Caciquismo, as represented in *Los caciques*, was such a target, and the inference is that only revolution could bring an end to bossism, even though no explicit alternatives are postulated.' Nason, p. 103.

[15] Nason, pp. 117–18.

[16] José C. González Boixo, 'The Underlying Currents of "Caciquismo" in the Narratives

Rulfo's more sympathetic, less manicheistic portrayal of the *cacique*, based on his love for Susana:

> [This love] brings the image of the heartless 'cacique' up against one of a human being whose suffering equals that of his victims ... Unlike the traditional model of the 'cacique', Pedro Páramo acts out of motives other than the simple exercise of power, or the accumulation of wealth. The novel clearly enunciates what seems to be his fundamental motivation: by being powerful he hopes to win the love of Susana San Juan.[17]

Despite this subjectivisation of the *cacique* with 'emotional overlay', González Boixo contends that Rulfo still employs manicheism by simultaneously creating a demon, for the *cacique* operates as a counterpart to God the Father by condemning the souls of Comala to a kind of paradise lost.[18] Thus, he concludes:

> God the Father is the Creator; Pedro Páramo is the evil destroyer ... In using the figure of the 'cacique' Rulfo created a meditation on his immediate reality, but it is also a meditation on good and evil, on the duality that dominates human reality: truth and falsehood, or life and death.[19]

However, González Boixo does not suggest an interpretation which explains how this manicheism can work in *conjunction* with the sympathetic portrayal of the *cacique* he himself presents. Pedro Páramo's existence as a symbol of evil seems to contradict his potential for tender love: how is this possible? For Nilda Rosales, on the other hand, the reader's sympathy with the *cacique* remains very strong and there is no suggestion of categorical 'evil' at all, for 'los recuerdos de Pedro Páramo son tales que lo eximen de culpa, lo presentan bajo el mejor aspecto, borran, desdibujan el caudillo'.[20] As a result, she concludes, 'Pedro Páramo supera toda etiqueta, su psicología compleja,

of Juan Rulfo', in *Structures of Power, Essays on Twentieth-Century Spanish-American Fiction*, ed. by Terry J. Peavler and Peter Standish (New York: State University of New York Press, 1996), p. 109. According to González Boixo, the indigenist narratives of Alcides Arguedas, Jorge Icaza and Ciro Alegría continued with this 'thesis' tendency in the twentieth century, as did Doña Bárbara. The latter may have been at the beginning of the process and it is only with works such as *Yo el Supremo* (Augusto Roa Bastos), *El recurso del método* (Alejo Carpentier) and *El otoño del patriarca* (Gabriel García Márquez) that we see 'interior projections' which are less manicheistic.

17 González Boixo, pp. 114–15.
18 González-Boixo, p. 116.
19 González-Boixo, p. 118.
20 Rosales, p. 290.

como la de cualquier ser humano, se niega al encasillamiento, exige un análisis, merece la comprensión, suscita la piedad.'[21]

This notion of the impossibility of assigning Pedro Páramo a category based on good or evil accords with my own reading. So far, I have argued that Rulfo manages the complexities of the good–evil duality through a deft use of irony whereby characters cannot be categorised morally without contradicting some aspect of their behaviour. The *cacique* is no exception for he is not a cast of negativity but he is nonetheless a *cacique*, itself an 'encasillamiento' which seems universal among critics of Rulfo's work (including Rosales), although the term itself is rarely explored. González Boixo's interpretation of the word 'cacique' is at least a perceptive start:

> For them [the peasants], the Government is 'el señor ése' who remembers them only to persecute them. The personification of such an abstract entity as the government allows its identification with the 'cacique' … Without question, the 'cacique' as well as the government are depicted by Rulfo as agents of violence, exercised from a position of power against helpless peasants.[22]

The point that the government and the *cacique* operate in these very similar ways is indisputable but González Boixo does not rigorously ground the argument in history and context, as I try to do here. Meanwhile, Rosales acknowledges the different meanings behind the terms 'caudillo' and 'cacique' but fails to alight on a preferred term and justify it:

> Pedro Páramo es un señor rural, cacique si se quiere, caudillo local en todo caso, sin dejar de notar que dichas expresiones son etiquetas comunes para realidades a veces muy diferentes. En efecto, tales denominaciones se aplican a menudo a fenómenos sociales que si se parecen en cuanto a una cierta manera de ejercer el poder, difieren en lo que respecta a su origen.[23]

Given that neither Rosales nor González Boixo seem to tackle the theme of *caciquismo* in *Pedro Páramo* 'head-on', the very term at least needs interrogation if only so we can be sure that we are indeed talking about the type of cacique to which Rulfo refers above: a relic of the *encomendero*. Having explored the characterisation of Pedro Páramo and his *cacicazgo*, I will chart the development of the system over the years to the present day with a view to examining the different historical and contemporary dimensions of Pedro Páramo's *caciquismo*. I will then argue that Rulfo's work shows us not the

---

[21] Rosales, p. 295.
[22] González Boixo, p. 120.
[23] Rosales, p. 283.

death of this *caciquismo* but, through a process of centrifugal irony alluding to the rhetoric of Revolution, its actual rebirth.

Characteristics of the Cacicazgo According to Alfredo Espinosa Tamayo

In his *Psicología y sociología del pueblo ecuatoriano* (1918), Alfredo Espinosa Tamayo provides us with a highly astute characterisation of Latin American *caciquismo*, which he describes as 'un hongo parásito', a Spanish import related to the *latifundia*.[24] Nason conveniently lists the characteristics of Espinosa Tamayo's *caciquismo* in his summary of the book: remote rural setting; the exercise of power by individuals of low station; unbridled self-interest; cruelty and indifference; extra-legality; hypocrisy; sexual abuse; manipulation of the electoral process; resistance to progress.[25] Our *cacique* can be identified with these traits in the following ways.

Remote Rural Setting

The word 'remote' in Nason's summary refers to the 'pequeñas poblaciones' mentioned by Espinosa Tamayo, in which *caciques* 'no tienen competidores o le es fácil deshacerse de los que se presentan'.[26] Geographical remoteness is key here but it is related to temporal remoteness: distance from political centres enables the *cacique* to bypass any historical processes which may threaten his realm. So when the *cacique*'s messenger scours the depths of the sierra to find the father of Susana, San Bartolomé, 'en una covacha hecha de troncos, en el mero lugar donde están las minas abandonadas de Andrómeda' (45), one would think this hiding-place to be already very secluded; yet it is here that the effects of an erupting Revolution are felt, forcing San Bartolomé to find a safer, yet more isolated location in Comala, as Pedro Páramo explains to Susana:

> Ya para entonces soplaban vientos raros. Se decía que había gente levantada en armas. Nos llegaban rumores. Eso fue lo que aventó a tu padre por aquí. No por él, según me dijo en su carta, sino por tu seguridad, quería traerte a algún lugar viviente. (45)

Thus, we have here an echo of Abundio's joke that Comala is hotter than hell: it is also even more 'remote' than an abandoned mine town, and therefore safe from revolution. Within such a safe, remote domain, the *cacique* can

---

[24] Nason, p. 36.
[25] Nason, p. 36.
[26] Alfredo Espinosa Tamayo, *Psicología y sociología del pueblo ecuatoriano* [1918] (Quito: Banco Central del Ecuador, Corporación Editora Central, 1979), p. 276.

impose his will with impunity and his mini-state easily spirals downwards into a cycle of death, violence and poverty. It is (verbally) ironic, then, that Pedro Páramo should call Comala a 'lugar viviente' but this could be seen as typical of the delusion of a *cacique* for whom life barely extends beyond the boundaries of his landholdings.[27] Indeed, as San Bartolomé tells Susana in the fragment which follows the above extract, Comala is anything but 'viviente': 'Hay pueblos que saben a desdicha. Se les conoce con sorber un poco de aire viejo y entumido, pobre y flaco como todo lo viejo. Este es uno de esos pueblos, Susana' (152).

Within this 'safe', 'remote', 'dead' environment, it is easy for the *cacique* to do away with potential competitors. Speaking of the Colombian variety of *caciquismo*, the writer Eduardo Caballero Calderón gives us the following insight on such behaviour:

> The cacique knows that it's better to be a mouse's head in a village than a lion's tail in the big city [...] Power, to be absolute, must be bounded by a river, a mountain, a high plateau, i.e. *things that can be encompassed by one's gaze*, and nearby so that they can be measured and roamed over on horseback.[28]

This notion of absolute power within defined, local boundaries is reminiscent of Abundio's description of the Media Luna for the benefit of Juan Preciado in the second fragment:

> Mire usted ... ¿Ve aquella loma que parece vejiga de puerco? Pues detrasito de ella está la Media Luna. Ahora voltié para allá. ¿ve la ceja de aquel cerro? Véala. Y ahora voltié para este otro rumbo. ¿Ve la otra ceja que casi no se ve de lo lejos que está? Bueno, pues eso es la Media Luna de punta a cabo. Como quien dice, *toda la tierra que se puede abarcar con la mirada.* Y es de él todo ese terrenal. (69, emphasis added)

Juan Preciado has entered a different country, less built-up, less 'civilised' but just as real as his own. Here, the rules are different for they are made by a single man: there is not even any pretence of nineteenth-century liberal democracy or post-Revolutionary statism. The remoteness of the setting prepares the reader for a world in which values considered extraordinary and

---

[27] According to Espinosa Tamayo, the *cacique* is indeed naturally xenophobic: 'todo elemento extraño autóctono es para él un enemigo que trae ideas subversivas y ni aun siquiera gusta de que transitoriamente vayan forasteros a pasar algunos días en sus dominios'. Espinosa Tamayo, p. 276.
[28] Nason's translation in *The Caciques*, p. 39. Emphasis added.

'backward' in the liberal rhetoric of Revolution are made to appear unbearably ordinary.

The Violent Exercise of Power

The arbitrary exercise of power by a *cacique* is the subject of this chapter but we should not forget the top-down effect of the *cacique*'s violent use of authority. For Espinosa Tamayo, an individual who carries out the *cacique*'s 'dirty work' is of lower social status, tied-in with favours and capable of committing 'toda clase de abusos'.[29] A clear example in *Pedro Páramo* is the *cacique*'s administrator, Fulgor Sedano, who is properly introduced to us in the nineteenth fragment of the novel. In an example of verbal irony, he appropriates official legal language only to apply a veneer of credibility to a largely arbitrary application of law against the small landholder, Toribio Aldrete: '"Fulgor Sedano, hombre de 54 años, soltero, de oficio administrador, apto para entablar y seguir pleitos, por poder y por mi propio derecho, reclamo y alego lo siguiente …" … Y terminó: "Que conste mi acusación por usufruto"' (99). The protests of Aldrete against 'ese hijo de la rechintola de su patrón' (Pedro Páramo) are verbally ironic in that they seem to be offset against the elevated language of the legal declaration. But they are ignored by Fulgor Sedano, who employs – in turn – a vicious verbal irony himself when asked by Doña Eduviges if any of his men will be staying the night: 'No, nada más uno' (99) replies the administrator, knowing that he is about to leave Aldrete for dead. He knows also that he has deliberately softened the resistance of the man by bantering in macho fashion and making him drunk, 'dizque para celebrar el acta' (99). Fulgor acts with impunity here, and with a certain air of confidence.

However, just like the priest in fragment 14, Fulgor is reminded of his relatively inferior station in the next fragment, in which he is told to address the *cacique* correctly: 'No se te olvide el "don"' (101). Despite this, the administrator remains faithful, to the end of the novel, seeming to enjoy being under Pedro Páramo's thumb, as he twice tells the *cacique*: 'Palabra que me está gustando tratar con usted' (103) and 'Me vuelve a gustar como acciona usted, patrón, como que se le están rejuveneciendo los ánimos' (154). For all this, when he is killed while defending his boss's interests, the latter displays no emotion at all when told of his passing (163). As Nason states in his summary, such characters are also marked by a certain political naivety, though this trait is even more clearly evident in the man who seems to replace the administrator, el Tilcuate, particularly when he allies the men entrusted to

[29] Espinosa Tamayo, p. 277.

him by Pedro Páramo with the Cristeros because, as we noted in the previous chapter, he likes what they shout and the promise of salvation (188).

Unbridled Self-Interest

Espinosa Tamayo describes the *cacique* as 'amoral y sin conciencia ni escrúpulo', all characteristics which are certainly evident in the behaviour of Pedro Páramo.[30] We have just seen how the *cacique* uses his henchman to manipulate the law and procure documentation produced under duress. He is also seen to perform the following unscrupulous actions: clearing his debts by hoodwinking Dolores into marriage (104–06); usurping land with the threat of violence (111); allowing his lawyer to fake the suicide of Rentería's brother in order to protect Miguel Páramo from murder charges (174); killing all the men who attended a wedding at which his father was accidentally killed by a deflected bullet (148–49). He also urges el Tilcuate to ransack a neighbouring town in order to feed his men (178), an action which conjures up the image of a scene in *Moneda Falsa* by Rabassa, who – in Nason's reading – describes the effects of a pillaging in the following way:

> Work comes to a standstill; the ox-goad is needed for combat and the ox himself serves as fodder for that ferocious beast; fields are laid waste, the forests are burned, homes are looted without any justification other than the whims of a brutal cacique; the end results are tears, desperation, and hunger.[31]

This picture of havoc is suggested but not described in Pedro Páramo's instruction to el Tilcuate to ransack Contla. The glibness of the instruction contrasts with the picture of ruin that the reader imagines, thus creating another instance of Rulfo's irony. Rather than providing his readers with the scene, as would be the case in a more direct condemnation, Rulfo expects them to imagine it and they are thus able to come to the conclusion them-selves that Pedro Páramo's self-interest is 'unbridled'.

Cruelty and Indifference to Human Need

The Latin American *cacique* is 'duro y cruel con sus jornaleros o trabajadores del campo con los cuales extrema sus abusos, castigándoles duramente por la menor falta con penas de azote y prisión en el aparato de tortura denomi-nado cepo'.[32] Torture as such is not evident but there is violent cruelty in Pedro Páramo's maiming of a man who attended the wedding in which his

---

[30] Espinosa Tamayo, p. 278.
[31] Nason, p. 101.
[32] Espinosa Tamayo, pp. 277–78.

father was killed, even after being told by the man that he was not there (148). Generally, however, Rulfo's characterisation is much more subtle than this, for there is much more in Pedro Páramo of what Nason terms 'indifference to human need', in which the *cacique* is 'impasible ante la desgracia ajena',[33] as suggested in his response upon hearing of a woman whose son has been murdered by Miguel: 'Esa gente no existe' (134). Such indifference is most poignantly brought home to the reader in fragments 58 and 59 where we discover that his most loyal servant, Gerardo Trujillo, having performed some of his least salubrious legal evasions, is allowed to leave Comala unrewarded for his efforts. In fragment 58, we learn of his desire to quit Comala for Sayula as *villistas* roam through the north of Mexico during the first half of the Mexican Revolution. It is difficult to say whether we should admire the lawyer's loyalty or cry in pity when he tells the *cacique* that he will miss him and 'las deferencias' that he pays him (172). When asked by his former boss to continue his role for him in Sayula, the lawyer refuses and the language he uses to explain himself is verbally ironic, an understatement now understood by the reader: 'Ciertas irregularidades [...] Digamos [...] Testimonios que nadie sino usted debe conocer. Pueden prestarse a malos manejos en caso de llegar a caer en otras manos. Lo más seguro es que estén con usted' (172). Pedro Páramo agrees and promises to burn the relevant documents but he also asks for the lawyer's reassurance that his property is safe from appropriation, a centrifugal allusion to the threat of land usurpation in Zapata's 'Plan de Ayala'.

Having given his reassurance that there is nothing to fear, the lawyer uses the Mexican term of polite departure, 'Con su permiso' (172). The description of his departure reflects the cosmic irony of the lawyer's lifetime efforts, the short steps accentuated poetically by the one- and two-syllable words: 'El licenciado Gerardo Trujillo salió despacio. Estaba ya viejo; *pero no para dar esos pasos tan cortos, tan sin ganas*. La verdad es que esperaba una recompensa' (172–73, emphasis added). We then learn that he had served three generations of the Páramo family – Lucas, Pedro and Miguel – and that he had clearly hoped for a payment that would secure his future retirement, 'una retribución grande y valiosa' (173). For the reader, who has observed the behaviour of the *cacique* throughout the novel, there is almost humorous irony in Gerardo's incredible hope that Pedro Páramo, the *cacique*, would suddenly be overcome with generosity: 'Siguió andando hacia la puerta, atento a cualquier llamado: "¡Ey, Gerardo! Lo preocupado que estoy no me ha permitido pensar en ti. Pero yo te debo favores que no se pagan con dinero. Recibe esto: es un regalo insignificante"' (173).

---

[33] Espinosa Tamayo, p. 276.

Just as he does with Fulgor Sedano, without so much as a crack of the whip, the *cacique* has in fact reduced Gerardo to the lowly status of a beggar. Even when he returns to request a payoff, he offers to take care of any offending papers in return and his manner is even more deferential: 'Algo extra, por si usted lo tiene a bien' (174). After bargaining, he manages only to obtain a thousand of the five thousand he had hoped for and it is here, as Pedro Páramo counts out the money, that we obtain some measure of the 'rencor vivo' with which Abundio describes the dead protagonist at the beginning of the novel. Espinosa Tamayo refers to the 'rencor vengativo de todos aquellos a quienes [el cacique] ha ultrajado y ofendido', optimistically arguing for land appropriation and education towards the end of his chapter.[34] But this 'rencor vivo' is, as Blanco Aguinaga indicates, the result of a *permanent* sense of marginalisation, a reality which is immune to change: 'Realidad en que unos pocos mandan, hacen y deshacen, viven hacia fuera, mientras a los demás se les niega su existencia como individuos para la historia.'[35] This feeling of marginalisation can be associated with Leopoldo Zea's (otherwise optimistic) view of the effects of the Revolution in increasing dependency on the *cacique* so that 'personal loyalty led to abuses and deceptions, which in turn caused resentment, suspicion, timidity and unreliability'.[36] For Gerardo, this feeling of dependence on the *cacique* is particularly galling as he recalls the sacrifices and dangers to which he has subjected himself in order to save the family from legal complications, and even jail, particularly with Miguel:

> Lo libró de la cárcel cuando menos unas quince veces, cuando no hayan sido más. Y el asesinato que cometió con aquel hombre, ¿cómo se apellidaba? Rentería, eso es. El muerto llamado Rentería, al que le pusieron una pistola en la mano. Lo asustado que estaba el Miguelito, aunque después le diera risa … Y lo de las violaciones, ¿qué? Cuántas veces él tuvo que sacar de su misma bolsa el dinero para que ellas le echaran tierra al asunto: 'Date de buenas que vas a tener un hijo güerito!', les decía. (174)

Gerardo's cynical complicity is clearly just as despicable as the behaviour of Miguel but it is an indication of Rulfo's skill in producing a non-manicheistic vision of a *cacicazgo* that the reader can feel confused here as to whether or not to feel sympathy for the needy, old lawyer who acts as its agent. This is especially so when the bitterness of the *cacique*'s legacy is made clear when he finally hands Gerardo a paltry thousand pesos:

---

34 Espinosa Tamayo, p. 279.
35 Blanco Aguinaga, 'Realidad y estilo', p. 200.
36 Doremus, p. 162.

Aquí tienes, Gerardo. Cuídalos muy bien, porque no retoñan.
Y él, que todavía estaba en sus cavilaciones, respondió:
– Sí, tampoco los muertos retoñan – y agregó –: Desgraciadamente. (174)

There is centripetal verbal irony in this comment by Gerardo for, in fact, the dead do return in this novel, but not to gain revenge. They return to suffer in the same suffocating, oppressive *caciquismo*, even after their deaths. In other words, the revenge promised by the distant rumours of Revolution will merely turn into a continuation and reinforcement (a vengeance of its own) of the old order, which, as we shall see in the centrifugal reading, is physically dead but alive in spirit.

Extra-legality Sustained by Nepotism
According to Espinosa Tamayo, nepotism is inevitable in a *cacicazgo*: '[si] el cacique tiene descendencia, ésta pesa sobre la población como una dinastía de pequeñas despotas que de generación en generación se van heredando el feudo que violencias y artimañas del padre de familia supieron conquistar'.[37] The story of Miguel Páramo exemplifies this: a recognised association with the *cacique* by blood allows him to act with total impunity. Apart from the misdemeanours listed above by Gerardo Trujillo, namely the killing of Rentería's brother and several rapes, he is apparently guilty of the rape of the daughter of the priest's brother. As we have seen in the previous chapter, Pedro Páramo is able to brush the accusations away with the word 'según': 'según rumores' and 'según el juicio de [Rentería]' (91). The extra-legality is not only applied to state law but also to Catholic law as the *cacique* instructs the priests to forgive and forget 'como quizá Dios lo haya perdonado' (91). Even though the *cacique* respects the need for the priest to give absolution, he does so only in the Weberian sense of a 'sort of insurance against the uncertainties of what might come after death, or because … an external obedience to the commands of the Church was sufficient to ensure salvation.'[38] Despite such extra-legal behaviour, there is a feeling that the welfare of Comala depends on the spiritual and physical well-being of the *cacique*. Certainly, the congregation attending Miguel's funeral desire and expect him to be absolved. Why should the fate of the people of Comala be so completely wrapped up with that of their oppressors? The answer may lie in the history of community formation in Mexico and, more specifically, the issue of land itself.

At the heart of the conflict between the priest and the *cacique*, for example, is the struggle to establish patriarchal jurisdiction, within which the issue of

---

37 Espinosa Tamayo, p. 280.
38 Max Weber, in *Max Weber, Essays in Economic Sociology*, ed. by Richard Swedberg (Princeton, NJ, and Chichester, Sussex: Princeton University Press, 1999), p. 72.

origin of the land is as important as the identity of its heir. Before the Spanish colony, land had belonged to *calpulli* in Mesoamerica, kinship groups who allotted territories to families for the benefit of those families, although the leaders of these groups, *calpulleque*, would take care that it was also adequately used in the community's interests for the upkeep of the local temple, schools and food for the poor.[39] Land was then used in systems of intensive agricultural production by the colonising Spaniards, who (in Rulfo's own interpretation above) are here represented by Pedro Páramo in an echo of the colonial, state-sponsored *encomendero*. The European interpretation of fallow land as vacant or surplus favoured the individual farmer and did not sit well with the *calpulleque*, who viewed this land as still belonging to the community even if a member of that community who 'owned' that land had died.[40] With the rise of *hacendados* and their patrilineal laws of entailment, Spanish coercion tactics during the colonial era led to encroachment on this communal land and this, in turn, encouraged the creation of powerful local *caciques* similar to Pedro Páramo in their influence and authority over a territory.

Despite the colonial and post-colonial individualist accumulation of territory, ancient communal attachments to land and familes attached to that land seem not to have disappeared in *Pedro Páramo*. The displeasure of the congregation at the non-absolution of Miguel in fragment 14 may be explained therefore, in terms of *syncretic* spiritual needs based on the fusion of individualist 'settlers' law' with communal, pre-Columbian traditions. The syncretism is created by the combination of a spiritual attachment to the land of Comala as a site of *communal* belonging, with, on the other hand, a secular, patrilineal law emphasising *individual* land ownership and entailment. This syncretic combination results for the people of Comala in the association of the spiritually-condemned Miguel with the spiritual condemnation of the entire town. In its powerful parochialism, this thinking is a legacy of pre-Columbian times as well as colonialism and thus represents an obstacle to Church and state discourse. It helps to strengthen *caciquismo* which is both corrosive in its corrupt influence on Catholic practice, and obstructive to the operation of liberal, metropolitan, state law. Thus, in *Pedro Páramo*, extra-legality is itself sustained by a powerful local patriarchy in which the

---

[39] While some land was private, this was seen as somehow beneficial to the cause of the greater community, or the Empire, as communal possession was the rule. See Chapter 2 of Jacques Soustelle, *Daily Life of the Aztecs on the Eve of the Spanish Conquest*; translated from the French by Patrick O'Brian (Harmondsworth: Penguin, 1961), pp. 36–94.

[40] For more on the subject of land and law in this period, see 'The Spanish and Indian Law: New Spain', in *The Inca and Aztec States, 1400–1800: Anthropology and History*, ed. by George. A. Collier, Renato I. Rosaldo and John D. Wirth (New York: Academic Press, 1982).

heir to the Media Luna must be allowed to act with impunity if the community supported by Pedro Páramo's business is to survive. The local, spiritual dimensions of this relationship between community and 'father' therefore militate, and win, against those of the Church and state.

Hypocrisy

Pedro Páramo's hypocrisy in his dealings with other characters is based on deliberate misapplication of state and Catholic laws. To exemplify the former, a few fragments after Fulgor Sedano brings the charge of 'usufructo' or 'falsifying boundaries' against Aldrete, we witness a scene in which the invisible presence of *caciquismo* is at its most terrifying. In what he still considers his private property, a man – Galileo – protests when he is told by his own brother-in-law that he must have sold it to Pedro Páramo. No reason is given for this information ('Pues son de Pedro Páramo', 111) and Galileo is warned that he is due a visit from Fulgor Sedano on charges of land squatting, the implication being that he will meet the same fate as Aldrete. Such monopolistic, bullying behaviour certainly accords with Espinosa Tamayo's characterisation of the *cacique*: 'procura acaparar todas las fuentes de riqueza y de produccion desde el cultivo de la tierra hasta la venta de mercaderías'.[41] In so doing, the *cacique* in this novel uses the law to create a local rhetoric of piety and legality while he himself breaches it at every opportunity. Thus, he is able to create a mini-nation independent of state law: 'No te preocupen los lienzos,' he tells Fulgor, 'No habrá lienzos. La tierra no tiene divisiones. Piénsalo, Fulgor, aunque no se lo des a entender' (103). The law regarding division of territory is therefore used only when it serves the *cacique*'s interests, a fact which centrifugally refers us to the *reforma agraria* and the immense difficulty of any radical plans to redistribute land.

In the characterisation of the *cacique*, the hypocritical use and abuse of state law is coupled with a disingenuous appropriation of Catholic law. Indeed, the hypocrisy which Espinosa Tamayo specifically refers to concerns the *cacique*'s relationship with religion for, despite being amoral, he is a 'creyente fervoroso' to the point of superstition:

> Tiene por lo general como patrono algún santo o santa al cual profesa grande veneración y que es para él más bien una especie de fetiche o amuleto y un intercesor o abogado que le haga perdonar sus pecados y lo libre de las penas de la vida eterna.[42]

This kind of hypocrisy has been discussed in the previous chapter, in which I

---

[41] Espinosa Tamayo, p. 277.
[42] Espinosa Tamayo, p. 278.

argued that – as well as hypocrisy – there is in fact a good deal of ingenuity in Pedro Páramo's appropriation of Catholic discourse, especially with regard to the power struggle between the *cacique* and the priest. As we have seen in the previous chapter, Pedro Páramo is capable of manipulating the discourse of the Church in order to further his own ends, for example when he kneels beside the priest and asks him to forgive Miguel. At the same time, his own actions as described above display a marked disregard for the word of God with respect to others.

These examples of hypocrisy are easy to find and cast into the pot marked 'caciquismo' without further elaboration. The harder question concerns why the *cacique* should need to be so adept at hypocrisy at all and what this hypocrisy with regard to Church and state discourse means in a specifically political and ironic reading of the novel. One possible answer is that a talent for hypocrisy is key for the *cacique*, for it enables him to manipulate the discourse of Church and state in order to disguise his own, local, private objectives of total dominion. In turn, this implies a weakening of the principles of external, national institutions, such as those involved in the Revolution and the Cristero Rebellion, and a corresponding strengthening of the *cacicazgo*. Thus, for the reader who is aware of the efforts of the Church and state to dominate the 'conscience' of the countryside, it is centrifugally ironic that the *cacique* should be so easily capable of twisting their discourse to create his own, a 'private conscience' and a 'private judiciary' with its own logic independent of the interference of either of these institutions.

Constant Sexual Abuse of Women of Lower Station

Espinosa Tamayo characterises the typical hacienda as a 'harem disperso' in which the *cacique* possesses a certain *droit de seigneur*, 'igual a los antiguos señores feudales'.[43] This is certainly borne out in fragment 26, where we learn that a certain Filotea Aréchiga procures girls to work for the *cacique* and that the women whose conversation reveals this information do not wish to have anything to do with 'ese viejo' (110). It is clear that 'working for' Pedro Páramo entails more than just cleaning and cooking duties and that the women who work for him are 'of lower station'. In fragment 60, Pedro Páramo's 'seigneurial' visits to the servants' quarters are poetically associated with the roar of a bull: 'Esos animales nunca duermen,' says Damiana. 'Nunca duermen. Son como el diablo, que siempre anda buscando almas para llevárselas al infierno' (175). Yet, his sexual abuse is taken as a welcome given by Damiana, who laments not being able to help:

43 Espinosa Tamayo, p. 278.

¡Ah qué don Pedro! – dijo Damiana –. No se le quita lo gatero. Lo que no entiendo es por qué le gusta hacer las cosas tan escondidas; con habérmelo avisado, yo le hubiera dicho a la Margarita que el patrón la necesitaba para esta noche, y él no hubiera tenido ni la molestia de levantarse de su cama. (175)

With another roar of the distant bulls, she shuts the window, covers herself up to the ears in her blanket and considers how happy Margarita must be (176). In the following fragment, however, Margarita is described as a 'puñadito de carne' (179) by Pedro Páramo, who had tried to turn her into Susana in his mind, 'una mujer que no era de este mundo'. His encounters with women 'of low social station' are therefore over-physical and unsatisfying and it seems that he is unable to change this colonial, 'seigneurial' mode of interaction with the opposite sex to create a fulfilling relationship with Susana.

During her tempestuous dreams, indeed, it is revealing that Pedro Páramo fails to engage with Susana on a spiritual level: 'Mientras Susana San Juan se revolvía inquieta, de pie, junto a la puerta, Pedro Páramo la miraba y contaba los segundos de aquel nuevo sueño que ya duraba mucho' (171). Indeed, his discomfort with this type of inexplicable pain is made clear: 'Si al menos fuera dolor lo que sintiera ella, y no esos sueños sin sosiego, esos interminables y agotadores sueños, él podría buscarle algún consuelo' (171). Even his gaze is fixed on her physical movements rather than her psychological torment: 'Así pensaba Pedro Páramo, fija la vista en Susana San Juan, siguiendo cada uno de sus movimientos' (171). The *hacendado*'s inability to see beyond the physical manifestations of her torture is underlined in fragment 62 where, finding her again in a state of convulsion, he can only cover her nude body with the sheets. Thus, there is an extent to which Pedro Páramo's ineffectual relationship with Susana could be said to be the result of an attitude towards women formed by an internalised, over-physical and 'seigneurial' discourse of *caciquismo*, which includes the sexual abuse of women 'of lower social station'.

Why, in that case, is there such room for sympathy for the *cacique* in his relationship with Susana, as González Boixo asserts when he argues that his suffering 'equals that of his victims' (see p. 129)? In Pedro Páramo's relationship with women we have one of the major situational ironies of the novel in his position as *cacique*: the many women he abuses mean nothing to him whilst the one woman he loves is not available to him. This is precisely because the physicality of his role as *cacique* does not prepare him for a love that is more than lust. This further begs a 'centrifugal' question: is he to blame for this spiritual impotence or is it that, like the teacher in 'Luvina' with regard to the objectified peasant, he is trapped in a colonial discourse which allows him no other basis on which to interact with the opposite sex?

The ground here is shaky for there is a certain, erroneous logic that could lead to a reasoning-away of what could accurately be termed multiple rape. Yet, in the sensitive portrayal of his love for Susana, Rulfo implies there is a kind of cosmic irony in the *cacique*'s relationship with women, for, just like the teacher, he is grappling with a colonial discourse which is more powerful than he is. The reader therefore at least partly identifies with the *cacique* because of a natural sympathy for any character whose tragic flaws prevent her or him from fulfilling a laudable destiny, which, in this case, is love. In most tragedies, such flaws would be the result of fate, God or nature but here, it appears to be an oppressive discourse which the *cacique* has been born into. Does this make his seigneurial visits to the servants' quarters understandable, even if they are not justifiable? This is a question that Rulfo does not answer and we are left to consider a response which at least takes into account any modicum of sympathy we have for Pedro Páramo, based on his seemingly genuine love for his childhood sweetheart.

Unabashed Manipulation of the Electoral Process

There is no electoral process in *Pedro Páramo* but this should not disturb our reading of the protagonist as a *cacique*. According to Espinosa Tamayo, the *cacique*'s political behaviour is in fact defined by an absence of politics. He avoids 'autorida política' but governs instead by working in 'la sombra por medio de sus allegados y amigos'. In this way, he is able to create a sub-system of favours in which modern democractic politics is irrelevant: 'procura que todos le deban la situación que ocupan y se hallen bajo su dependencia ... El que mantenga siquiera relaciones amistosas con sus enemigos se le hace sospechoso y pronto procura hacerlo destituir.'[44] There is indeed a network of dependency in *Pedro Páramo* and certainly no electoral process to speak of, a fact which is significant in the creation of the 'government-within-a-government' that is Comala. In this town, what could be decided by votes in a free and liberal society is in fact decided by contacts, wealth, violence, luck and, ultimately, one man whose control of resources is such that free elections are almost unthinkable.

Democracy and revolution barely touch the town: sheltered from these processes by its seclusion, it seems to survive any potential threat to its power structure by the sheer self-perpetuating logic of *cacicazgo*. As Pedro Páramo tells Fulgor Sedano when he protests that his actions against Aldrete may be against the law: '¿Cuáles leyes, Fulgor? La ley de ahora en adelante la vamos a hacer nosotros' (107). The attempt to create laws on a national scale, which is implicitly that of the government itself, is the butt of Pedro Páramo's

---

[44] Espinosa Tamayo, p. 277.

mockery. As Antonio Ugalde suggests, 'The cacique is the lord and chief of his territory, and of the life and destiny of its inhabitants ... [who] has total or near total political, economic and social control of a geographic area.'[45] Thus, the absence of an electoral process is yet another example of Rulfo's centrifugal irony, particularly for those Mexican readers schooled in democracy, because it evokes instead a world of favours which is beyond the reach of modernity. In this reality, democratic Revolution is but a distant whisper which, as we shall see now, is blown away with ease.

Unyielding Resistance to Anything Resembling Political/Social Progress
As we have noted in previous chapters, the government's legitimacy is based on the sanctity of a social Revolution. Rulfo incisively satirises one of the myths which feed this self-righteousness: that of the local band of revolutionaries seeking social justice. In fragment 54, the commanders of a local revolutionary army are invited to dine at Pedro Páramo's table. When they have finished eating, the *cacique* asks if he can help in any other way. '¿Usted es el dueño de esto?', asks one of the revolutionaries (Perseverancio), 'abanicando la mano' (166). Before Pedro Páramo can answer, however, he witnesses a leadership dispute. '¡Aquí yo soy él que hablo!' declares another member of the group (166). The question of leadership is later thrown into doubt again by Pedro Páramo's henchman, Damasio or 'el Tilcuate', who suggests that the real leader was the one who had said nothing throughout the discussion. Whoever the leader is, the *cacique* ignores the dispute and coolly repeats his offer and, this time, the 'second leader' replies, dropping the 'd' in *usted*, unlike the marginally more 'cultured' Perseverancio:

> Como usté ve, nos hemos levantado en armas.
> – ¿Y?
> – Y pos eso es todo. ¿Le parece poco? (167)

Here, with the single-letter word 'Y', uttered by Pedro Páramo, Rulfo undermines not only the ideas of those revolutionaries at the *cacique*'s fictional table (centripetally) but also, more centrifugally, the idea of a Mexican Revolution itself. The civil war between 1910 and 1920 is reduced here to Eduardo Ramón Ruíz's notion of nothing more than a 'great rebellion', in which a great deal of rhetoric was pronounced, thousands of lives were lost but, ultimately, to no avail for there was no structural change in society and no prospect of it.[46]

More specifically, in this passage, Rulfo ironises the complexities of lead-

---

[45] Antonio Ugalde, 'Contemporary Mexico: From Hacienda to PRI', in Kern, *The Caciques*, p. 124.

[46] Eduardo Ramón Ruíz, *The Great Rebellion* (New York: W. W. Norton, 1980).

ership during the years of Revolution: the constant wrestling between generals of differing classes for command, whether at local or national level. Who, in any case, was the real leader? In the absence of a clear answer, the strength of political leadership in Pedro Páramo grows in inverse proportion to the uncertainty in the 'revolutionary' camp. The question of political leadership in general is thus relativised, as we see again in this paraphrased exchange over thirteen years (1913–26) between el Tilcuate and Pedro Páramo:

> El Tilcuate siguió viniendo:
> – Ahora somos carrancistas.
> – Está bien.
> – Andamos con mi general Obregón.
> – Está bien.
> ...
> – Se ha levantado en armas el padre Rentería. ¿Nos vamos con él, o contra él?
> – Eso ni se discute. Ponte al lado del gobierno.
> – Pero si somos irregulares. Nos consideran rebeldes.
> – Entonces vete a descansar.
> – ¿Con el vuelo que llevo?
> – Haz lo que quieras entonces.
> – Me iré a reforzar al padrecito. Me gusta cómo gritan. Además lleva uno ganado la salvación.
> – Haz lo que quieras. (187)

Over the thirteen years between the signing of Venustiano Carranza's Plan de Guadelupe in 1913 and the outbreak of the Cristero War in 1926, *hacendados* become commanders though they care little for any cause that may be espoused. Yet they control the fate of a region; and soldiers, for their part, decide to join one group or another on the basis of whether a certain chant rolls off the tongue nicely or on the odds of getting to heaven if they happen to be led by a priest. Furthermore, the *cacique* acts as he wishes and the 'remoteness' of the ignored rural world of Comala is counterpointed, from a rural perspective, with the remoteness of the urban world, urban laws and urban wars. We could say that this is a renewal of the relationships in the colony, where metropolitan wars, laws and bureaucracy were seen in a negative spectrum ranging from irrelevant to highly irritating top-down impediments to the individual domains of *encomenderos* and *hacendados*.

Indeed, the point made most vehemently by Espinosa Tamayo is that the *cacique* is also an 'enemigo del progreso': 'mira con desdén o con prevención todo intento de introducir alguna novedad o algún adelanto en su pueblo'. The rhetoric of Revolution ought to be one that is feared by the *cacique*, for his preferred 'ambiente' is 'el letal y admormilado de las poblaciones de poco movimiento'.[47] Returning to the revolutionaries at the *cacique*'s table in fragment 54, we can see that Pedro Páramo reacts not with fear but with an indifference based on a knowledge of the untouchable permanence of his own power. The simplicity of the second (nameless) leader's statement, 'nos hemos levantado en armas', is supposed to impress but the *cacique*'s immediate '¿Y?' indicates he is untroubled by the revelation that they have risen in arms, particularly with a peasant leader who probably has little idea of political issues. By asking why they have risen in arms, indeed, he disingenuously trumps the unfortunate man:

> – Pos porque otros lo han hecho también. ¿No lo sabe usté? Aguárdenos tantito a que nos lleguen instrucciones y entonces le averiguamos la causa. Por lo pronto ya estamos aquí. (167)

At this point, the more politically-sharpened Perseverancio intervenes again:

> Nos hemos rebelado contra el gobierno y contra ustedes porque ya estamos aburridos de soportarlos. Al gobierno por rastrero y a ustedes porque no son más que unos móndrigos bandidos y mantecosos ladrones. Y del señor gobierno ya no digo nada porque le vamos a decir a balazos lo que le queremos decir. (167)

Perseverancio's outburst is reflective of the socio-economic concerns which spawned the local revolts that made up the Revolution and his use of the term 'el señor gobierno' suggests an unclear equation between the *cacique*'s local power and the government's national power. Indeed, in the final sentence in the quotation above, according to Nilda Rosales, there is an echo of the Plan de Ayala, in which local issues are inextricably linked to a 'national' and even global cause: 'Que el Sr. Madero, y con él el mundo entero, sepa que no depondremos las armas hasta que los ejidos de nuestros pueblos nos hayan sido restaurados.'[48] But if the reader now believes there may be some genuine belief in social justice in this small army, the exchange that follows adds a strong note of suspicion, through a more centripetal situational irony: the 'revolutionaries' sell their soul in order to acquire the *hacendado*'s money for crucial resources (167). The movement here is reduced to what it truly was in many local areas – a protection racket. Casildo requests a moderate fifty thousand and Pedro Páramo offers a hundred thousand plus three hundred

---

[47] Espinosa Tamayo, p. 277.
[48] Oscar Delgado et al., *Reformas Agrarias en América Latina* (1965). Quoted in Rosales, p. 287.

men. The offer is accepted but Perseverancio, the last to leave, threateningly reminds the *cacique* to fulfil his promise even though the *cacique*'s commitment to the revolutionary cause is suspiciously unpolitical, as indicated by the dismissive use of the possessive pronoun in 'su revolución' (167). Meanwhile, 'Perseverancio' is clearly a verbally-ironic name, for the perseverance with his cause appears to be unlikely to bear fruit. In the following fragment, indeed, Pedro Páramo is seen to reaffirm his authority when he orders Damasio to take charge of the 300 extra men he has donated and take over the leadership of the group in exchange for a small farm and some cattle. The *hacendado*'s lawyer, Gerardo, later informs him that Damasio has been defeated by 'unos que se dicen *villistas*' (171), again suggesting the protean nature of revolutionary causes and categories. Clearly, nobody knows how to tell a real *villista* from a bandwagon-hopper.

Thus, we see in this episode not so much a 'resistance' to change as an indifference to it, which suggests that any social or political change is doomed in the face of the stranglehold on local power and resources which the *cacique* confidently possesses. It is true that Pedro Páramo has to exercise his brain in order to manoeuvre the debate and the terms in his favour – there is some skill in the deceptive coolness – but this is not so much 'unyielding resistance' as canny indifference, suggesting that social and political progress quite simply do not apply in his domain. Caballero Calderón gives an appropriate explanation for such indifference in a *cacique*:

> For him, there are no laws or circumstances, and he doesn't die until he is killed, the latter occurring only when there is a total change of regime and he has not taken the precaution of doing a flip-flop to prevent his falling out of the papaya tree … Caciques are like the Kikuyu grass, there's no one who can uproot them.[49]

Thus, the reason for this indifference, as we shall see now, is that *caciquismo* was never going to be vanquished. At the time the first readers of Rulfo's work purchased their copy of *Pedro Páramo*, *caciquismo* was alive and any suggestion of its death would have rung hollow.

The 'Death' of the Cacique

Our *cacique* allows himself to die almost voluntarily and he takes his dependent community with him. What Juan Preciado finds is a town still living in the suffocating oppression of *caciquismo*, which implies not the

---

[49] Eduardo Caballero Calderón, *Obras* (Medellín: Editorial Bedout, 1963), Chapter 5. Quoted and translated by Nason, p. 40.

death of this institution but the enduring *strength* of identification between a *cacique* and his community, rooted in a colonial past. Indeed, what will kill the bright new hope, the son Juan Preciado, who appears to have escaped Comala, are the fragments of a colonial discourse, 'los murmullos', no less powerful for being decimated: 'Me mataron los murmullos. Aunque ya traía retrasado el miedo. Se me había venido juntando, hasta que ya no pude soportarlo. Y cuando me encontré con los murmullos se me reventaron las cuerdas' (127). The metaphor of strings snapping appropriately suggests a resistance that fails, for the murmurs seep out of the colonial brickwork and surround him: 'Y de las paredes parecían destilar los murmullos como si se filtraron de entre las grietas y las descarapeladuras' (127). As the Director of the Juan Rulfo Institute in Mexico, Víctor Jiménez, tells us, there is a keenly felt identification between colonial ruins and history in Rulfo's world-view in his writings on architecture:

> Abundan aquellos que servirían a la perfección para documentar una historia del período colonial muy poco piadoso con los encomenderos y el clero de la época: se trata a menudo de escritos sobre construcciones de poco valor artístico ... pero muy reveladoras de la violencia que entrañó la sujeción del país en aquel momento de su historia.[50] (70)

Jiménez also suggests to us that Rulfo's writings on the crumbling of architecture echo with the words used to describe the *cacique*'s death in the novel: 'Incluso la mención del "desmoronamiento de algunas ruinas, como la doble Capilla Abierta" de Meztitlán puede evocar en el lector las palabras finales de la novela (recordando también las imágenes de muchas de sus fotografías de arquitectura).'[51] The edifice of colony may be in ruins but, for Rulfo, the buildings are very much spiritually alive, as we see most clearly in the photograph 'Muro en ruinas', in which the bare face of a ruined colonial church wall is made to resemble a terrifying mask through Rulfo's perceptive lens. The 'eyes' are indicated by two oval holes either side of a supporting wall which serves as a nose, whilst the mouth is a long, horizontal hole that cuts across the 'nose'. The low angle of the camera and the relatively condensed space apportioned to the sky give the image an overbearing aspect. The haunting quality is enhanced by a lower foreground of dead grassland and idle rocks and by the off-centre angle, which gives the wall/mask the appearance of 'gazing' into the distance. By catching the angle of the sun at a precise moment, Rulfo divides the mask into a light and a dark side, capturing the detail of decay in the former and the more symbolic resonance

---

[50] Jiménez, *Los murmullos*, p. 70.
[51] Jiménez, *Los murmullos*, p. 71.

of death in the latter.[52] Many of Rulfo's photographs focus on the ruins of churches to the level of obsessive detail and it is no coincidence that the murmurs in the novel are also associated with the unsatisfied rumblings of Rentería's unabsolved parishioners, on whom he turns his back in fragment 41: 'Detrás de él sólo se oyó el murmullo' (144). As we have seen in the previous chapter, the flight of the priest and the resultant murmurs of his parishioners are indirectly a result of the power of *caciquismo*. The murmurs of the novel represent the legacy of misery of a colonial discourse which allows the spirit of a community to be strangled by an individual.

Above, we have argued that *caciquismo* developed syncretically over the colonial period to tie a communal spiritual destiny attached to land with the life of a single individual and his heirs. Here, we shall assert that the enduring power of *caciquismo* in Mexico is a result not only of syncretism but also of its political vitality and adaptability, as suggested in Espinoso Tamayo's conclusion, described as 'irate' by Nason:

> El caciquismo viene a constituir una institución, un poder arbitrario y despótico que sustituye al poder político, que viola todas las leyes, las cuales sólo le sirven de red con la cual enreda a sus contrarios saliéndose él [...] amparado de la impunidad que su influjo político, social y económico le proporciona; bajo su férrea garra los pueblos viven oprimidos, inquieta la sociedad, cohibidos los campesinos y pequeños propietarios: rencorosos todos, atemorizados los más; estancados el comercio, la agricultura y la industria; absorbidas todas las energías y las iniciativas; despilfarrados y pillados los caudales públicos.[53]

Therefore, the *cacique* can, through his extra-legal dominance, destroy a whole area economically, socially and politically. As Peter Beardsell tells us, not only is Pedro Páramo 'autocractic, self-interested, ruthless, above the law and capable of murder' but 'the economic dependency of a region on one individual is shown to be potentially disastrous'.[54]

The banal catalyst for this disaster in Comala is the failure of the inhabitants accurately to interpret the ringing of bells which marks the death of the *cacique*'s unrequited love, Susana San Juan, resulting in a farcical festival recalling that of Rulfo's short story 'El día del derrumbe'. Apart from the rubble in which the government official's visit takes place, the farce in that story rests on the discord between the upbeat rhythm of the national anthem and the riotous public reaction to the official's speech, the former being inappropriately triumphant and

52 Photograph in Carlos Fuentes et al., *Mexico: Juan Rulfo fotógrafo*, p. 175.
53 Espinosa Tamayo, p. 280.
54 Beardsell, p. 85.

the latter empty of understanding. *Pedro Páramo* approaches its end with a similarly inappropriate public reaction to what is supposed to be a sombre occasion. The death of Pedro Páramo's childhood love, Susana, like the governor's speech in 'El día del derrumbe', is marked by music intended as meaningful, this time the incessant ringing of bells: 'Y de día y de noche las campanas siguieron tocando, todas por igual, cada vez con más fuerza, hasta que aquello se convirtió en un lamento rumoroso de sonidos' (186). But despite the news of Susana's death and the eventual end of the bell-ringing, a party ensues: 'No hubo modo de hacerles comprender que se trataba de un duelo, de días de duelo. No hubo modo de que se fueran; antes, por el contrario, siguieron llegando más' (186). The distance between the community that is celebrating and the individual who controls their lives is marked by the location signifiers 'allá' and 'acá': '*Allá había feria*. Se jugaba a los gallos, se oía la música; los gritos de los borrachos y de loterías. *Hasta acá llegaba la luz* del pueblo, que parecía una aureola sobre el cielo gris. Porque fueron días grises, tristes para la Media Luna' (186–87).[55] This is a period of festivity in which the people seem to have become free of oppression, for they have temporarily let go of their leader and are almost literally deaf to the ringing of bells, a sound that is suggestive of conquest and subsequent colonial domination, one of the main aims of invading *conquistadores* having been to build churches upon ancient ceremonial sites. As such, it is a kind of rebellion but the implacable will of the *cacique* will overcome not only that of the people but also that of the Church and state, the two institutions at the heart of colonial domination. For, although there is a distance between community and *cacique*, there is not to be a break-up of this relationship but a renewal of it on harsh, vengeful terms.

This renewal of the relationship is signalled when the *cacique* takes offence and swears revenge on his town:

Don Pedro no hablaba. No salía de su cuarto. Juró vengarse de Comala.
– Me cruzaré de brazos y Comala se morirá de hambre.
Y así lo hizo. (187)

The biblical tone of these last words has the resonance of divine authority and there follows a period of destruction and hunger of which we have already been made aware by Dorotea; the proximity of 'allá' and 'acá' here contrasting with the earlier distancing and therefore indicating the *cacique*'s resumption of control:

Desde entonces la tierra se quedó baldía y como en ruinas ... *De allá para acá* se consumió la gente; se desbandaron los hombres en busca de

---

55 Emphasis added.

otros bebederos. Recuerdo días en que Comala se llenó de adioses y hasta nos parecía cosa alegre ir a despedir a los que se iban ... Luego algunos mandaban por la familia aunque no por sus cosas, y después parecieron olvidarse del pueblo y de nosotros, y hasta de sus cosas. (149, emphasis added)

Thus, for poorer characters like Dorotea who, unlike Gerardo the lawyer, are unable to pack up and leave, the situation becomes the suffocating aftermath of the decision of a single man, while others cling to the hope of receiving inheritance much as some cling to the hope of heaven:

Otros se quedaron esperando que Pedro Páramo muriera, pues según decían les había prometido heredarles sus bienes, y con esa esperanza vivieron todavía algunos. Pero pasaron años y años y él seguía vivo, siempre allí, como un espantapájaros frente a las tierras de la Media Luna. (150)

The result of this tenacious will to live/die is the death of others. In Dorotea's account of her own death and that of the *cacique* there is no mention of any political reaction despite the arrival of the Cristero War, which is seen only in terms of its 'draining off' of the few men that were left in Comala:

Y ya cuando le faltaba poco para morir vinieron las guerras esas de los cristeros y la tropa echó rialada con los pocos hombres que quedaban. Fue cuando yo comencé a morirme de hambre y desde entonces nunca me volví a emparejar. Y todo por las ideas de don Pedro, por sus pleitos de alma. Nada más porque se le murió su mujer, la tal Susanita. Ya te has de imaginar si la quería. (150)

Indeed, the very fact that Dorotea sees Pedro's death, will-to-live/die and murder of Comala in terms of his tragic love for Susana suggests a relationship with the *cacique* which is more forgiving and spiritual than economic, social or political.

The lack of resistance to Pedro Páramo in the novel is thus indicative of a relationship forged on powerful spiritual bonds and colonial patriarchal traditions associated with the power of the *cacique*. The overwhelming impression throughout is of the characters' deference to the man in political, social and economic terms: Dolores allows herself to be fooled by the *cacique*'s offer of marriage; Fulgor Sedano succumbs to his direct approach and his aura of authority; Rentería accepts the *cacique*'s money; Gerardo walks away from the *cacique* with no more than a sarcastic remark; Perseverancio's tough stance evaporates, for he disappears after fragment 54; el Tilcuate follows orders long after Pedro Páramo is incapable of giving them; Damiana the maid stays with him to the death. There are certainly instances of resentment such as that demonstrated by Gerardo above. Added to that, we could interpret the words of Ángeles on the death of Susana in fragment 63 ('El se lo merece. Eso y más,' 181), as well as those of Perseverancio, as suggestive of the 'rencor vivo' of which Abundio speaks at the beginning of the novel. Indeed, the latter's murder of Pedro Páramo at the end has been interpreted by many as an act of both vengeance and resistance. Moreover, Rentería devotes his life to the cause of the Cristeros in an effort to salvage some social justice. Yet, surely the situational irony of the efforts of both Abundio and Rentería is that Pedro *survives*. Not only does he survive, in fact, but his influence continues to such an extent that even his son, returning long after the *cacique*'s own death, is suffocated by the 'murmullos', the oppression or 'rencor vivo' which his rule has created.

Despite this legacy, the reader still has sympathy for the *cacique* based on the tragedy and cosmic irony of a man losing his childhood love, as we have seen above. There is further sympathy to be drawn in the grim example of centripetal situational irony where Pedro Páramo, on the verge of death, hopes that he is not heading for another night of ghosts:

> 'Con tal de que no sea una nueva noche', pensaba él.
> Porque tenía miedo de las noches que le llenaban de fantasmas la oscuridad. De encerrarse con sus fantasmas. De eso tenía miedo. (194)

This, of course, is exactly what he *is* heading for: Comala will continue to exist but only as a ghost town. Both the reader and the character know also that the after-life awaiting him will be as hellish for him as it will be for those he has victimised:

> Sé que dentro de pocas horas vendrá Abundio con sus manos ensangrentadas a pedirme la ayuda que le negué. Y yo no tendré manos para taparme los ojos y no verlo. Tendré que oírlo; hasta que su voz se apague con el día, hasta que se le muera su voz. (194)

Thus, the depiction of his death does not leave any note of triumph for the reader, who knows that both Pedro Páramo and his victims will suffer, as they have done throughout the novel. To some extent, then, we can return to the beginning of the novel and find that nothing has interrupted its basic essence, despite Juan Preciado's ill-fated journey. The grimness of the irony at the end indicates that the mood of the novel has not changed, and underlines the absence of moral progression which is evident in the plot. It is this very 'timelessness', the *centripetal* sense that nothing has changed or ever will change, that makes the *centrifugally* ironic political statement of the book: that the Revolution did not happen and that, in any case, laws do not change, because the *cacique* obeys only his own. However, as we have seen above, even the *cacique* himself can suffer from this discourse, which is much stronger than he is. This may be a pessimistic conclusion but, with a brief look at the history of the word 'cacique', we see that the spiritual survival of the discourse of the *cacique*, in the form of fragments and 'murmurs', is an interpretation of Pedro Páramo's death that is entirely in keeping not only with Rulfo's views but with the historical evidence too.

A thorough contextualisation of the *cacicazgo* in *Pedro Páramo* appears to lead us to the conclusion that the system as we see it in the novel occupies a critical place in the history of the institution, which makes it both a relic of an old, localised, indigenous form and a warning of a modern, insidious, and national form. The origin of the word 'cacique' is the Arawak word 'kassiquan', which means 'to have or to keep a house'.[56] In the original chiefdoms or *cacicazgo*s, principally in the Caribbean, indigenous *caciques* acted as priests, judges, warlords and guardians of 'common tribal descent'.[57] Although *cacicazgo*s were also rigidly hierarchical in the indigenous world, in this communal society, reciprocity was also a key aspect in the function of relationships, for tribute was used by *caciques* to fund fiestas, public works and craftwork, making the *cacique*'s authority and legitimacy '[depend] wholly on the common consent of the other members of the society'.[58] After the conquest of the Caribbean, the word 'cacique' was used by the conquering Spaniards in the Spanish Empire to refer to local chieftains throughout Spanish America. Thereafter, the word came to take on the association of a mediatory power between the colonisers and the colonised and there was an evident ambivalence in the attitude of the Crown towards indigenous *caciques*. To some degree, indeed, their function approached that of Bhabha's 'mimic men' in the sense that they were used to impose colonial discourse on the subject people.[59] However, the original function of the indigenous *cacique* was not so blatantly that of a mimic man or enforcer for, as Karl Schwerin informs us,

---

[56] Paré, p. 36.

[57] Schwerin, in Kern, *The Caciques*, pp. 5–6. The phrase 'common tribal descent' is quoted by Schwerin on page 6 and taken from Kalervo Oberg, 'Types of Social Structure among the Lowland Tribes of South and Central America', *American Anthropologist*, 47 (June 1955), 472–87 (p. 484).

[58] Schwerin, p. 6.

[59] Schwerin, p. 15: 'After all, native leaders were becoming an essential if minor cog in the colonial administrative system, which stressed indirect rule as a consequence of the lack of sufficient Spaniards to administer the empire. The linguistic problem was another administrative obstacle, and in any case official policy, encouraged by the missionaries, sought to keep the Spaniards and Indians apart. Native rulers thus were important as a liaison between the two.' See also Paré, p. 16, on the intermediary role of the *cacique*.

They were cultural brokers who represented Indian interests before the
larger society by serving as spokesmen in complaints or requests directed
to higher functionaries, or in assuming leadership in some legal dispute. At
the same time, due to their Spanish associations, they were a channel for
the introduction of new ideas and concepts.[60]

At this stage, therefore, there appears to be a strong communal initiative
among indigenous *caciques*. Nevertheless, the transition to the position of
state *enforcer* was already under way: 'They also exploited the people they
governed for tribute, sexual services or labor assessments. In this sense they
were petty local bosses exercising their prerogatives of office.'[61] In this position of power between two cultures, then, the institution of *caciquismo* – in
an adapted version of its original indigenous form – was uniquely able to
survive the traumas of conquest: 'The cacique found a settled, functional and
remunerative position in society and so made the transition from preconquest
to postconquest life.'[62] However, very few genuinely powerful 'caciques'
were in fact indigenous by the time of Independence. From the very beginning of the conquest, a process of replacement of ancient systems of control
occurs which, as Rulfo indicates himself, never seems to end:

> El *cacicazgo* existía como forma de gobierno siglos antes del descubrim-
> iento de América, de tal suerte que los conquistadores españoles sólo
> 'echaron raspa', es decir, les fue fácil desplazar el cacique indio para tomar
> ellos su lugar. Así nació la encomienda y más tarde la hacienda con su
> secuela de latifundismo o monopolio de la tierra. Esa es la realidad, sin
> tapujos ni metáforas ni nada de sueños.[63]

Indeed, very soon after the conquest, *caciques* began to be replaced by 'mestizo
or mulatto personnel or non-noble Indian hirelings' more closely associated
with the Crown's interests, creating 'pseudo-*caciques*' in Mexico and Peru.[64]
By the end of the colonial period, Charles Gibson asserts that *caciques* were
likely to be *mestizos* as long as they 'managed their lands, rents, agricultural
production, and mode of life in approximation of the generalised norms of
hacendados and rancheros'. Thus, any success as a *cacique* was in the form
of *latifundismo* rather than indigenous *cacicazgo*, although this 'circum-
stantially overlapped with *cacicazgo*'.[65] Therefore, by the early nineteenth

---

60 Schwerin, pp. 16–17.
61 Schwerin, p. 17.
62 Schwerin, p. 17.
63 Rulfo, in *Los murmullos*, pp. 48–49.
64 Charles Gibson, in Kern, *Caciques in Postconquest and Colonial Mexico*, pp. 22–24.
65 Gibson, p. 26.

century community-oriented 'indigenous *cacicazgo*' had little meaning: 'Neither the urban economy of Mexico City nor the hacienda economy of the countryside favored the preservation of the old cacique status.'[66] It was in that century, then, that the word began to form a meaning which, whilst retaining elements of the original definition of 'cultural broker', erred towards individual tyranny or surrogate tyranny on behalf of the state:

> The term cacique was vulgarised and lost hereditary significance – the process was already under way in colonial times – and acquired the meaning of political boss or local tyrant ... It is symptomatic of these later transformations that Emiliano Zapata's *Plan de Ayala* (1911) could classify caciques with hacendados and científicos as the greatest enemies of reform. [Yet these latter-day caciques took much from the cacique patterns of the colonial period.][67] (Gibson's parentheses)

The colonial *cacique* was essentially an individualist, a local tyrant, whereas 'the authority of the [indigenous] cacique rested upon mutual consent of the governed far more than upon the exercise of arbitrary political power'.[68] Indeed, for this very reason, genuine indigenous *cacicazgo*s would disappear 'within a few short decades of the arrival of the Spanish': 'This was due in great part to the weakness of chiefdom organization, which depended less upon force than on mutual agreement as to what constituted the common good.'[69] The colonial and post-independence *cacique*, meanwhile, was devoted to personal gain and the imposition of his individual will on others, like one of the many men in Mexico who, for Rulfo, acquire status and power through wealth: 'hombres que adquieren poder mediante la acumulación de bienes y éstos, a su vez, les otorgan un grado muy alto de impunidad para someter al prójimo e imponer sus propias leyes'.[70]

In *Pedro Páramo*, it could be argued that the transition from indigenous *caciquismo* to post-colonial *caciquismo* is not complete and that elements of communality persist. On the one hand, the communal legacy of indigenous *cacicazgo* places the spiritual and material destiny of an entire town within the confines of the reciprocal system of *caciquismo* while, on the other, the individualism of European capitalism means that this destiny is controlled by one man, rather than communally controlled. Thus, when Pedro Páramo decides to fold his arms and preside over the death of Comala, he is able to command the end of an entire community, as a legacy not only of indigenous

---

66 Gibson, p. 26.
67 Gibson, p. 26.
68 Schwerin, p. 11.
69 Schwerin, p. 14.
70 Rulfo, *Los Murmullos*, p. 49.

caciquismo but also of Spanish *caciquismo*, i.e. that of the *encomendero*, in which an *individual* can hold a *community* to ransom. Wayne A. Cornelius, Jr, explains how this is possible:

> [The cacique] possesses de facto authority to make decisions binding upon the community under his control, as well as informal police powers and powers of taxation. Thus in some respects the *cacicazgo* represents a sort of informal government-within-a-government, controlled by a single domi-nant individual who is not formally accountable either to those residing in the community under his control or to external political and governmental authorities.[71]

This is a hybrid form of indigenous and European patriarchy in which indi-vidualism and communality are combined to favour exploitation. The state can do little to inject democracy into the countryside against such a power-fully despotic system, whilst the Church is unable to contest the power of a *cacique* who is seen by the inhabitants of his town to embody their destiny. The lack of democratic spirit or even any idea of resistance to Pedro Páramo's will is testament to the tenacity of this system in the novel. When Abundio kills the *cacique*, he achieves nothing but the creation of a ghost town; when Rentería fights for the Cristeros, he is merely avoiding the struggle against *caciquismo*; when Perseverancio attempts to gain better terms for his band of revolutionaries, he is brushed aside.

However, this form of *caciquismo* is even more dangerous in the post-Revolutionary world when it is allied to the strength of institutions. As Rulfo explains, *Pedro Páramo* is not a metaphor but a kind of permanent and direct reflection of a real system and real people, changing only to evolve, never to die: 'No hay en ello pues ninguna metáfora, si acaso cierta metamorfosis que los convierte, por asociación, en consorcios o en sociedades anónimas al servicio de determinados intereses.'[72] This appears to be borne out by histor-ical investigations. Luisa Paré describes how a cycle of political domination by local *caciques* in Puebla is successfully maintained until the 1970s by the relationships between the main local *caciques* and the 'supercaciques' (the Ávila Camacho brothers).[73] Could Pedro Páramo have followed the same path? To some extent, the answer to this question does not matter. Even though he does not physically exist in this period, the *spirit* of *caciquismo* – its legacy or, rather, its continued evolving existence – clearly does and

---

[71] Wayne A. Cornelius, Jr, 'Contemporary Mexico: A Structural Analysis of Urban Caci-quismo', in Kern, *The Caciques*, p. 138.

[72] Rulfo, *Los murmullos*, p. 49.

[73] Paré, pp. 46–48.

this is what Paré's study seems to demonstrate. What is more, it appears that *Pedro Páramo* shows us one way in which *caciquismo* might be replicated in the figure and behaviour of el Tilcuate who could, according to Paré's model, be one of those 'hombres de confianza' who, having benefited from the favour of a local *cacique*, would then proceed to acquire political influence through the institutionalised party.[74] This type of state-sponsored *caciquismo* is referred to by Ugalde as 'institutional factionalism', a non-violent legacy of factional *caciquismo* whereby 'political bosses ... began to seek offices for their followers after they realised that offices had become seats of power'.[75] Such was the success of the *Partido Revolucionario Institucional* (PRI) in adapting *caciquismo* and other village traditions to its own ends that Ugalde feels moved to praise the effort: 'It is to the credit of the PRI to have successfully adopted reformed traditional institutions in villages for the achievement of its goals.'[76]

In Ugalde's case study, meanwhile, we have excellent centrifugal evidence for the kind of *cacique* behaviour we see in 'Nos han dado la tierra':

> It was not until 1924 that a government resolution arrived authorizing the expropriation of the hacienda that had in the past controlled the life and the economy of Díaz Ordaz. The hacendado was strongly opposed to the expropriation of his land. The first engineer sent by the government to carry out the expropriation was bought off by the hacendado and attempted to give only the poor rocky land and the slopes of the hills to the village.[77]

The peasants resist this interference through a self-styled representative called Pablo Reyes, as Ugalde's informant proceeds to tell us: 'Pablo Reyes ... saw the trick and he said that he did not want *pedregales*, that we already had enough stones, that what we wanted was land, land to seed, land to harvest.'[78] His efforts, after some difficulties and violent opposition from the *hacendado* and local police, paid off as the village was able to make 'the beginning of the ejido'.[79] However, the very name of Rulfo's *cacique*, Pedro Páramo, gives us the impression that these stones – the *pedregales* – are the legacy of the Revolution. Even if the Revolution destroyed the physical *cacique*, the ruins are little to build on and provide no means of sustenance, allowing him to live on in spirit: 'Dio un golpe seco contra la tierra y se fue desmoronando como si fuera un montón de piedras' (195). So ends the novel, but the crumbling

[74] Paré, p. 49.
[75] Ugalde in Kern, *The Caciques*, p. 134.
[76] Ugalde, p. 134.
[77] Ugalde, p. 125.
[78] Ugalde, p. 125
[79] Ugalde, p. 125.

of the mountain of stones is centrifugally-ironic because the crumbling of the physical manifestation of the cacique, his body, is irrelevant if *caciquismo* still exists in the world of the modern reader, if rural Mexicans are still subservient to those in authority and if there is little democratic legitimacy in the governments of many rural areas.

This pessimistic conclusion is more convincing if we consider that Reyes, having become municipal president in 1927, turned out to be just as violent as the *hacendado*: 'Pablo Reyes was a cacique because he had a near total control of the village ... he used violence when convenient; he was recognized by outside higher political leaders as the village's authority.'[80] It is in this latter aspect of Reyes's behaviour that Ugalde sees the real difference between pre-Revolution *caciquismo* (of which we may say Pedro Páramo is an example) and post-Revolutionary neo-*caciquismo* which sprang from its ruins: 'Neo-*caciquismo* differs from pre-Revolution *caciquismo* and should be considered a subtype. The power base of the new cacique was much weaker and he was more dependent on recognition and legitimation from outside powers than were his predecessors.'[81] Could neo-*caciquismo* be the ironic result of Revolution, the fallen stones of Pedro Páramo? Perhaps what the death of the *cacique* indicates in *Pedro Páramo* is not the demise of *caciquismo* but the transition from pre-Revolutionary, isolated *caciquismo* to post-Revolutionary *integrated caciquismo*, with the newly-propertied el Tilcuate as the neo-*cacique* in the making.

Another variation of *caciquismo*, discussed by Wayne Cornelius, Jr, is 'urban' *caciquismo*. The particular skills of this new *cacique* have far more to do with organisation, political negotiating skills and maintaining unity among the community. The importance of political contacts ('derivative power'[82]) in a 'supra-local' context therefore distinguishes the new urban from the old rural *cacique* represented by Pedro Páramo, who relies for legitimacy and authority on the guarantee of 'a constant flow of concrete, material benefits to the settlement as a whole as well as to individual residents'.[83] Cornelius shows how urban and rural *caciquismo* are nevertheless linked in the ways that they each rely on retinues, *compradazgo* and the formation of a 'cohesive "political family" which supports, protects, and insulates the *cacique* against harassment by dissatisfied residents or predatory aliens'.[84] Furthermore, a probable reason for urban *caciquismo* is the fact that many of the low-income inhabitants of a city are of rural

---

80 Ugalde, pp. 125–27.
81 Ugalde, p. 127.
82 Cornelius, in *The Caciques*, p. 142.
83 Cornelius, p. 143.
84 Cornelius, p. 141.

origins and their behaviour is therefore an example of 'residual ruralism
… the transference from the rural areas of institutions, values and behavior
patterns and their persistence or adaptation to the specific requirements
of the urban setting'. Therefore, factors in urban *caciquismo* include 'the
strong predisposition [of the peasant] toward authoritarianism and a propensity to enter into paternalistic dependency relationships'[85]
    In the light of such overwhelming evidence for the continuation of *caci-
quismo* in various forms, decades after the Revolution, it bears repeating
that Pedro Páramo's death as a *cacique* could not be the death of *caciquismo* and his murder by Abundio is not any meaningful kind of revenge,
for, as Rulfo himself suggests, the ghosts of the *cacique* and the inhabitants
of Comala represent the continuation of political factors which continue to
intimidate Mexicans. In the journalist Máximo Simpson's original inquiry,
referred to at the start of ths chapter, it is put to Rulfo that perhaps Juan
Preciado's question '¿están ustedes muertos?' is intended primarily as a
meditation on life and death rather than on *caciquismo*. Rulfo dismisses
the suggestion out of hand:

> Con la pregunta '¿están ustedes muertos?' se quiere encontrar una respu-
> esta al por qué las fuerzas del poder, no obstante que operan en todas direc-
> ciones, permanecen en la oscuridad. Hay ocasiones en que uno desearía
> saber dónde se oculta aquello que causa a veces tanto daño. Por ejemplo,
> ignoramos cómo se produce y cunde la pobreza; quién o qué la causa y
> por qué. Yo no me preguntaría por qué morimos, pongamos por caso; pero
> sí quisiera saber qué es lo que hace tan miserable nuestra vida. Usted dirá
> que ese planteamiento no aparece nunca en *Pedro Páramo*; pero yo le digo
> que sí, que allí está desde el principio y que toda la novela se reduce a esa
> sola y única pregunta: ¿dónde está la fuerza que causa nuestra miseria? Y
> hablo de miseria con todas sus implicaciones.[86]

What Rulfo's comments indicate to us here is the political and social urgency
of the question he himself poses and that I have attempted to answer. In this
chapter, I have argued that the answer to his question lies in the historical
ramifications of *caciquismo* and its living spirit in the present day. Rulfo
argues as much when he tells us that, 'en otras palabras, son los represent-
antes del antiguo coloniaje al que aún estamos sometidos'.[87] This makes the
novel centrifugally-ironic because it suggests an awkward rebuttal of the
rhetoric of Revolution in its insistence on the death of *caciquismo* and a
new beginning for the country, even in the post-2000 Mexico heralded as

---

[85] Cornelius, p. 149.
[86] Rulfo, *Los Murmullos*, p. 49.
[87] Ibid.

one of change by Vicente Fox. Indeed, the degree to which we perceive the irony of the *cacique*'s physical death in *Pedro Páramo* increases with time as *caciquismo* refuses to die away, instead renewing itself in the form of neo-*caciquismo*, urban *caciquismo* or, as Rulfo suggests, national *caciquismo*: 'Aún en nuestros días, los hay que son dueños hasta de países enteros.'[88]

[88] Ibid.

CONCLUSION

Rulfo's fiction can be read as a series of 'centripetally-efficient' works of irony but his allusions to context through centrifugal irony are given a heuristically useful framework in the form of postcolonial theory, which emphasises the urgency of analysing fictional narratives within the context of political projects of economic and cultural dominance. Postcolonial Studies has not yet dealt adequately with the benefits and limitations of its application to Latin American cultures partly because its growth as a field was related principally to the legacy of British and French empires. One could argue, of course, that Latin American Studies has always dealt with the issues addressed by this field but many concepts, such as Bhabha's 'mimicry', (colonial) 'fetish' and 'ambivalence', have not yet been applied directly to Latin American culture in any systematic way. This study represents a partial attempt to meet this challenge but the task is made much easier by Rulfo's irony. This irony creates a relationship between the writer, the characters, and the reader which facilitates a greater understanding between Self and Other, Coloniser and Colonised, West and non-West.

The irony works because Rulfo is economical to the point of self-effacement. As Self, he suppresses his objectivising voice to inflict a Barthesian 'suicide', thus enabling the subjective response of his characters, his Other. There is much evidence in the original manuscripts that the restraining of the authorial voice was a painstaking process involving brutal editing. Rulfo admits as much:

> Quería no hablar como se escribe, sino escribir como se habla. Buscar personajes a los que pudiera darles tratamiento más simple … No es cuestión de palabras. Siempre sobran, en realidad. Sobran un qué o un cuándo, está un de o un más de más, o algo así.[1]

Such a process results in work typical of what Sontag would call a 'stubborn' author, as I discussed in the introduction. With a 'stubborn' author, the reader must modify his or her acquired reading conventions in order to accept the

---

[1] Reina Roffé and Juan Rulfo, *Autobiografía armada*, p. 25.

absence of the more 'over-cooperative' author who narrates and interprets simultaenously. The reader is then invited to *interact* with the fragmented, often chaotic, nature of a fictionalised oral history, constructing a vision of the past that is inclusive of this history and the characters that represent it. In the process, the reader will become aware of the values that she or he brings to this relationship with the text and learn to continue to modify them, rather than passively repeat them in the way that the interlocutor might do in the story 'Luvina'. Reading, in one sense, becomes a process of critical self-reflexivity.

The political implication of such writing is that the colonising state, just like the author, and just like the teacher in 'Luvina', should also abandon its objectivising forms of control and rationalisation over events and people to replace them with a meaningful dialogue in which the peasant is active and equal, not objectified. This is a radical call for equality in a world character-ised by diversity as opposed to an insistence on hierarchy in a world charac-terised by (supposedly inferior) alterity. In this call, postcolonial theory can play a key role for, as Robert Young asserts, it concerns inequality:

> Postcolonialism claims the right of all people on this earth to the same material and cultural well-being. The reality, though, is that the world today is a world of inequality, and much of the difference falls across the broad division between people of the west and those of the non-west.[2]

Such differences between Western and non-Western peoples can be ideologi-cally entrenched, leading to poor communication. If one is fed on Western values without ever questioning them, one could end up interpreting the violence, lack of education and poverty in much of Rulfo's work as evidence of a backward peasantry. Rulfo's centripetal irony, as I have repeatedly argued and demonstrated here, prevents the reader from falling into this trap by training us to read between the lines and explore alternative, *centrifugal* meanings and explanations. With postcolonial readings, for example, the reader is expected to interact with and question powerful but ambiguous words such as 'tierra', 'país', 'padre', 'patria', 'pecado' and, indeed, 'revolu-ción'.

There is ample scope for extending the centripetal/centrifugal analytical model to other Latin American authors: Carlos Fuentes, Manuel Puig and Gabriel García Márquez, particularly, make use of centripetal and (highly political) centrifugal irony in works such as *Aura* (1966), *El beso de la mujer araña* (1976) and *El general en su laberinto* (1989), respectively. Even with

---

[2]   Robert J. C. Young, *Postcolonialism: A Very Short Introduction* (Oxford: Oxford Univer-sity Press, 2003), p. 2.

Rulfo, the project is not yet complete, for I have not had space or time to analyse all of Rulfo's stories in the light of irony, but 'Anacleto Morones', 'La noche que lo dejaron solo' and 'Es que somos muy pobres' stand out as suitable subjects for study within the model used in this book. As well as this, we have largely untapped resources in, for example, his cinematic writing and his descriptions of architecture. Most importantly, although I have managed to refer to some of Rulfo's photographs in support of the present study, very little detailed criticism has been written on this subject. In the context of postmodern irony discussed in the first chapter, the question which seems open to investigation is whether Rulfo's photographs of indigenous people in dances, festivals and processions are exotic and sentimental or ironic and challenging. This observer has heard highly educated members of the Mexican middle and upper classes describe such photos as representative of Mexico's 'beautiful history'. Such superficial reactions suggest that perhaps Rulfo's photos are in danger of falling into the trap of postmodern irony where there is not sufficient centripetal commentary for the viewer to access any centrifugal context, with the result that the irony – if it is there – is lost. What could this context be? One suspects that the context, like that of Rulfo's fiction, is related to colonial discourse: early architecture dominates Rulfo's photographic output and he wrote reams of unexplored work on colonial buildings.[3] The centrifugal context here would include biographical details which have been largely absent from the mainly literary reading in the present study. For example, Rulfo worked as an official movie censor in the 1950s and in Mexico City's *Instituto Nacional Indigenista* for most of the period after the 1950s until his death. His work here is yet to be investigated and would surely provide a fruitful avenue of inquiry, for we can then perhaps answer the problem of whether Rulfo was happy to be working for the government and merely 'preserving Mexico's "good image"' or if, in reality, he wished to counter this image with a more powerful photographic vision requiring the use of irony.[4]

If colonialism and its legacy on the indigenous population is the centrifugal context, and centripetal irony is necessary – as I have argued – for postmodern, detached irony to avoid the trap of non-perception, what are the

---

[3] See Víctor Jiménez, 'Metztitlán, La geografía, la historia y la arquitectura de México en Juan Rulfo', in *Los murmullos*, pp. 68–71. For photographs, more commentary and more of Rulfo's writings on colonial architecture, see *Juan Rulfo, Letras e imágenes*, ed. by Víctor Jiménez (Mexico City: Editorial RM, 2002).

[4] See Elena Poniatowska's Foreword in Joseph, Rubenstein and Zolov, *Fragments*, p. xiv: 'One must remember that in those years [the 1950s] writers like Carlos Fuentes and Juan Rulfo worked as movie censors under the orders of then national director of Cinematographic Affairs Jorge Ferretis, preserving Mexico's "good image." Censorship consisted of shouting "cut" each time a scrawny dog walked on the set because its presence denigrated Mexico.'

mechanics of centripetal irony which prepare us for this context in Rulfo's photography? Do they lie in the choice of subject? Or in the direction of the subject's gaze? For example, could Rulfo's unusually generous devotion of photographic space to skies represent a kind of cosmic irony in relation to nature? Is there any correlation between this and the equally generous photographic space allotted to colonial buildings, when they are the subject? In other words, is colonial discourse represented in Rulfo's photography through an association of dominating skylines with dominating colonial ruins? This is an area of criticism on Rulfo that requires urgent investigation and the observations made, in turn, would almost certainly enrich our understanding of his fiction.

BIBLIOGRAPHY

Alemán, Miguel, *Discursos de Alemán* (Mexico City: Partido Revolucionario Institucional, 1946).

Álvarez, Nicolás Emilio, *Análisis arquetípico, mítico y simbólico en Pedro Páramo* (Miami: Universal, 1983).

Amat, Nuria, *Juan Rulfo* (Barcelona: Omega, 2003).

Anderson, Benedict, *Imagined Communities: Reflection on the Origins and Spread of Nationalism* [1983] (London: Verso, 1987).

Antolín, Francisco, *Los espacios en Juan Rulfo* (Miami: Universal, 1991).

Aparicio de Rulfo, Clara and Yvette Jiménez de Báez, eds, *Los cuadernos de Juan Rulfo* (Mexico: Era, 1994). Notes, fragments and drafts written by Juan Rulfo.

Archivo General de la Nación, Colección Carteles, Ávila Camacho: C/993/75 (Collection of Government Posters from the 1930s, 1940s and 1950s).

Arenas Saavedra, Anita, *Juan Rulfo, el eterno: caminos para una interpretación* (Maracaibo: Astro Data, 1997).

Arias Urrutia, Ángel, 'Juan Rulfo: los cristeros de Comala', in *Entre la cruz y la sospecha, Los Cristeros de Revueltas, Yáñez y Rulfo* (Madrid: Iberoamericana, 2005), 159–205.

Arizmendi, A. L., 'Alrededor de *Pedro Páramo*', *Cuadernos Americanos*, 30:2 (1971), 184–96.

Ascensio, Juan Antonio, *Un extraño en la tierra: biografía no autorizada de Juan Rulfo* (Mexico City: Debate, 2005).

Bailey, David C., *¡Viva Cristo Rey!: The Cristero Rebellion and Church–State Conflict in Mexico* (Austin: University of Texas Press, 1974).

Bakhtin, Mikhail, *The Dialogic Imagination* (Austin: University of Texas Press, 2000).

Baldick, Chris, *The Concise Oxford Dictionary of Literary Terms* (Oxford: Oxford University Press, 2001).

Barbe, Katharina, *Irony in Context* (Amsterdam and Philadelphia: John Benjamins, 1995).

Barry, Peter, *Beginning Theory, An Introduction to Literary and Cultural Theory* (Manchester: Manchester University Press, 2002).

Bartra, Roger, ed., *Caciquismo y poder político en el México rural* (Mexico City: Siglo Veintiuno, 1975).

Beardsell, Peter, 'Juan Rulfo: Pedro Páramo', in *Landmarks in Modern Latin American Fiction*, ed. by Philip Swanson (London: Routledge, 1990), 74–96.

Befumo Boschi, Liliana, 'La locura de Susana San Juan', *Cuadernos Hispanoamericanos*, 421–23 (1985), 433–47.

Beltrán, Rosa, 'La revolución congelada: *Pedro Páramo* de Juan Rulfo', *Mester*, 21:1 (1992), 23–30.

Benítez Rojo, Antonio, ed., *Recopilación de textos sobre Juan Rulfo* (Havana: Casa de las Américas, 1969).

Benjamin, Thomas, *La Revolución: Mexico's Great Revolution as Memory, Myth and History* (Austin: University of Texas Press, 2000).

Bermejo, Ernesto González, 'Pedro Páramo: un cacique del desierto', *El Nacional*, 10 July 1979, pp. 1–3.

Bhabha, Homi K., *The Location of Culture* (London: Routledge, 1994).

Blanco Aguinaga, Carlos, 'Realidad y estilo de Juan Rulfo' [1955], in *Para cuando yo me ausente*, ed. by Juan Rulfo (Mexico City: Grijalbo, 1982), 175–203.

———, 'Introducción', in Juan Rulfo, *El llano en llamas* (Madrid: Cátedra, 1997), 11–32.

Boldy, Steven, 'The Use of Ambiguity and the Death(s) of Bartolomé San Juan in Rulfo's *Pedro Páramo*', *Forum for Modern Language Studies*, 19:3 (1983), 224–35.

———, 'The Death of the Father, Language, and Others in Juan Rulfo's *Pedro Páramo*', *Romance Quarterly*, 33:4 (1986), 463–75.

Booth, George C., *Mexico's School-Made Society* [1941] (New York: Greenwood, 1969).

Borges, Jorge Luis, *El Aleph* (Buenos Aires: Emecé, 1957)

Brennan, Timothy, 'The National Longing for Form', in *Nation and Narration*, ed. by Homi K. Bhabha (London: Routledge, 1990), 44–71.

Brushwood, John S., *Narrative Innovation and Political Change in Mexico* (New York: Peter Lang, 1989).

Burkholder, Mark A. and Lyman L. Johnson, *Colonial Latin America* [1990] (New York: Oxford University Press, 1998).

Burton, Julianne, 'Sexuality and the Mythic Dimension in Juan Rulfo's *Pedro Páramo*', *Symposium*, 28 (1974), 228–47.

Butler, Matthew, 'Keeping the Faith in Revolutionary Mexico: Clerical and Lay Resistance to Religious Persecution, East Michoacán, 1926–1929', *The Americas*, 59:1 (July 2002), 9–33.

Calviño Iglesias, Julio, '*Pedro Páramo*: texto e ideología', *Cuadernos Hispanoamericanos*, 421–23 (1985), 355–79.

Campbell, Federico, ed., *La ficción de la memoria: Juan Rulfo ante la crítica* (Mexico City: Ediciones Era, 2003).

Canfield, Martha L., 'Dos enfoques de *Pedro Páramo*', *Revista Iberoamericana*, 55:148–49 (1989), 965–88.

Cantu, Roberto, 'De nuevo el arte de Juan Rulfo: *Pedro Páramo* reestructura(n) do', *Cuadernos Hispanoamericanos*, 421–23 (1985), 305–54.

Cárdenas, Lázaro, *La unificación campesina* (Mexico City: Partido Revolucionario Institucional, 1934).

_____, *Ideario agrarista del General de División Lázaro Cárdenas* (Mexico City: Departamento Agrario, 1935).

Cardoza y Aragón, Luis and Antonio Rodríguez, *Diego Rivera, Los murales de la Secretaría de Educación Pública* (Mexico City: SEP, 1986).

Childs, Peter and Patrick Williams, *An Introduction to Post-Colonial Theory* (Harlow: Pearson, 1997).

Colebrook, Clare, *Irony*, The New Critical Idiom series (London: Routledge, 2004).

Cornelius, Wayne A., Jr, 'Contemporary Mexico: A Structural Analysis of Urban Caciquismo' in *The Caciques, Oligarchical Politics and the System of Caciquismo in the Luso-Hispanic World*, ed. by Robert Kern (Albuquerque: University of New Mexico Press, 1973), 135–63.

Cosgrove, Ciaran, 'Abstract Gestures and Elemental Pressures in Juan Rulfo's *Pedro Páramo*', *The Modern Language Review*, 86:1 (1991), 79–88.

Cuadernos Hispanoamericanos, Revista Mensual de Cultura Hispánica (Madrid, Spain), July–Sept. 1985, 421.

D'Lugo, Carol Clark, '*Pedro Páramo*: The Reader's Journey through the Text', *Hispania*, 70:3 (1987), 468–74.

_____, *The Fragmented Novel in Mexico: The Politics of Form* (Austin: University of Texas Press, 1997).

Doremus, Anne T., *Culture, Politics and National Identity in Mexican Literature and Film, 1929–1952* (New York: Peter Lang, 2001).

Dove, Patrick, 'Reflections on the Origin, Transculturation and Tragedy in *Pedro Páramo*', *Angelaki, Journal of the Theoretical Humanities*, 6:1 (April 2001), 91–110.

Dragón, Antonio, *El martirio del Padre Pro* [1940] (Mexico City: Populibros, 1972).

Durand Gasta, Silvia, 'Lo que pasa es que no me conocen bien: Juan Rulfo', *El Nacional*, 11 January 1986, Second Section, p. 6.

Eagleton, Terry, *The Idea of Culture* (Oxford: Blackwell, 2000).

Echavarren, Roberto, '*Pedro Páramo*: la muerte del narrador', *INTI*, 13–14 (1981), 111–25.

El Nacional, 17 May 1945, pp. 1–8.

El Universal, 1 November 1936, Photographic Supplement, p. 1.

Embeita, María J., 'Tema y estructura en *Pedro Páramo*', *Cuadernos Americanos*, 26:2 (1967), 218–23.

Espinosa Tamayo, Alfredo, *Psicología y sociología del pueblo ecuatoriano* [1918] (Quito: Banco Central del Ecuador, Corporación Editora Central, 1979).

Estrada Cárdenas, Alba Sovietina, *Estructura y discurso de género en Pedro Páramo* (Mexico City: Eón, 2005).

Excelsior, 12 May 1938, p. 5.

_____, 2 September 1944, pp. 1 and 12.

_____, 16 July 1950, Second Section, p. 3.

Ezquerro, Milagros, *Lecturas rulfianas* (Jalisco: University of Guadalajara Press, 2006).

Fares, Gustavo C., 'Juan Rulfo: crítica reciente', *Revista Iberoamericana*, 55:148–49 (1989), 989–1003.

_____, *Imaginar Comala: el espacio en la obra de Juan Rulfo* (New York: Peter Lang, 1991).

_____, *Juan Rulfo: la lengua, el tiempo y el espacio* (Buenos Aires: Almagesto, 1994).

Fernández, Sergio, '*Pedro Páramo*: una sesión espiritista', *Revista Iberoamericana*, 55:148–49 (1989), 953–63.

Ferrer Chivite, Manuel, *El laberinto mexicano en/de Juan Rulfo* (Mexico City: Novaro, 1972).

Fiddian, Robin, ed., *Postcolonial Perspectives on the Cultures of Latin America and Lusophone Africa* (Liverpool: Liverpool University Press, 2000).

Filer, Malva E., 'Sumisión y rebeldía en los personajes de *Pedro Páramo*', *INTI*, 13–14 (1981), 64–72.

Fiorillo, Heriberto, 'Los muertos en libertad', *La Jornada Semanal*, 28 January 1996. Previously unpublished interview conducted in 1983.

Franco, Jean, 'Rulfo y el *ressentiment*', in *Revista Canadiense de Estudios Hispánicos* (Montreal), XXII:2 (Invierno, 1998), 273–82.

Frye, Northrop, *The Anatomy of Criticism: Four Essays by Northrop Frye* (Princeton: University of Princeton Press, 1957).

Fuego, Emilio, 'De chamanes e informantes', *México Indígena*, 4 (May–June 1985), 37–44.

Fuentes, Carlos, *La nueva novela hispanoamericana* (Mexico City: Cuadernos Joaquín Mortiz, 1969).

_____, 'Mugido, muerte y misterio: El mito de Rulfo', *Revista Iberoamericana*, 47:116–17 (1981), 11–21.

_____, et al., *Mexico: Juan Rulfo fotógrafo* (Mexico City: Lunwerg, 2001).

Gamio, Manuel, *Forjando patria* (Mexico City: Editorial Porrúa, 1960).

García Bonilla, Roberto, 'Juan Rulfo y la ciudad de México', in *La ficción de la memoria, Juan Rulfo ante la crítica*, ed. by Federico Campbell (Mexico City: Ediciones Era, 2003), 379–93.

_____, *Un tiempo suspendido. Cronología de la vida y obra de Juan Rulfo* (Mexico City: CONACULTA, 2009).

Garrido, Felipe, '*Pedro Parámo* y *El llano en llamas* de Juan Rulfo', in *Para cuando yo me ausente*, ed. by Juan Rulfo (Mexico City: Grijalbo, 1982), 13–35.

_____, 'La sonrisa de Juan Rulfo' in *Tierra con Memoria* (Mexico City: Punto Fino, 1997), 29-41.

_____, *Voces de la tierra, La lección de Juan Rulfo* (Mexico City: Universidad Nacional Autónoma de México, 2004).

Gazarai Karlenovich, Grigori and Sorel Scarlet Contreras Meyemberg, *Juan Rulfo* (Mexico City: Tomo, 2004).

Giacoman, Helmy F., *Homenaje a Juan Rulfo* (New York: Anaya-Las Américas, 1974).

Gibson, Charles, 'Caciques in Postconquest and Colonial Mexico' in Robert Kern, ed., *The Caciques, Oligarchical Politics and the System of Caciquismo in the Luso-Hispanic World* (Albuquerque: Univeristy of New Mexico Press, 1973), 18-26.

González Alonso, Javier, 'Susana San Juan: función y significado textuales en *Pedro Páramo*', *Revista Canadiense de Estudios Hispánicos*, 15:2 (1991), 209–21.

González Boixo, José C., *Claves narrativas de Juan Rulfo* (León: Universidad de León, 1984).

_____, 'El factor religioso en la obra de Juan Rulfo', *Cuadernos Hispanoamericanos*, July–Sept 1985, vol. 421–423 pp. 165–77.

_____, 'Introducción', in Juan Rulfo, *Pedro Páramo* (Madrid: Cátedra, 1989), 9–61.

_____, 'The Underlying Currents of Caciquismo in the Narratives of Juan Rulfo', in *Structures of Power: Essays on Twentieth-Century Spanish-American Fiction*, ed. by Terry J. Peavler and Peter Standish (New York: State University of New York Press, 1996), 107–25.

González Casillas, Magdalena, *La sociedad en la obra de Juan Rulfo* (Jalisco: Secretaría de Cultura, 1998).

Grande, Guadalupe, 'El silencio en la obra de Juan Rulfo', *Cuadernos Hispanoamericanos*, 467 (May 1989), 61–70.

Gutiérrez, Mouat, 'Un personaje olvidado de *Pedro Páramo*', *Revista Iberoamericana*, 51:130–31 (1985), 235–39.

Gyurko, Lanin A., 'Rulfo's Aesthetic Nihilism: Narrative Antecedents of *Pedro Páramo*', *Hispanic Review*, 40 (1972), 451–66.

Hart, Stephen M., 'Juan Rulfo's *Pedro Páramo* and the Dream of the Dead Father', *Forum for Modern Language Studies*, 26:1 (1990), 62–74.

_____, *A Companion to Spanish American Literature* (Woodbridge: Tamesis, 1999).

_____, *A Companion to Latin American Literature* (Woodbridge: Tamesis, 2007).

Hayes, Aden W., 'Rulfo's Counter-Epic: *Pedro Páramo* and the Stasis of History', *Journal of Spanish Studies*, 7 (1979), 279–96.

Hodges, Donald C. and Ross Gandy, *Mexico: The End of the Revolution* (Westport: Praeger, 2002).

'Homenaje a Juan Rulfo', *Mexicanísimo* (Mexico City), 2:16 (2009).

Hutcheon, Linda, *Irony's Edge: The Theory and Politics of Irony* (London: Routledge, 1994).

INTI: Revista de Literatura Hispánica (Providence: Providence College), 13–14 (Spring–Fall 1981).

Jiménez, Víctor, ed., *Juan Rulfo, Letras e imágenes* (Mexico City: Editorial RM, 2002).

_____, Alberto Vital and Jorge Zepeda, *Tríptico para Juan Rulfo* (Mexico City: Editorial RM and Fundación Juan Rulfo, 2006).

Jiménez de Baez, Yvette, 'Juan Rulfo, del páramo a la esperanza: estructura y sentido', *Nueva Revista de Filología Hispánica*, 36:1 (1988), 501–66.

_____, *Juan Rulfo, del páramo a la esperanza, una lectura crítica de su obra* (Mexico City: El Colegio de México, 1990).

Joseph, Gilbert M., 'Caciquismo and the Revolution: Carillo Puerto in Yucatán', in *Caudillo and Peasant in the Mexican Revolution*, ed. by David Brading (Cambridge: Cambridge University Press, 1980), 193–221.

_____, Anne Rubenstein and Eric Zolov, eds, *Fragments of a Golden Age* (Durham: Duke University Press, 2001).

_____, and Timothy J. Henderson, eds, *The Mexico Reader: History, Culture and Politics* (Durham: Duke University Press, 2002).

Jurado Valencia, Fabio, *Pedro Páramo, de Juan Rulfo: Murmullos, susurros y silencios* (Bogotá: Común Presencia Editores, 2005).

Karic, Pol Popovic and Fidel Chávez Pérez, *Juan Rulfo: perspectivas críticas* (Mexico City: Siglo XXI, 2007).

Kern, Robert, ed., *The Caciques, Oligarchical Politics and the System of Caciquismo in the Luso-Hispanic World* (Albuquerque: University of New Mexico Press, 1973).

King, John, ed., *Modern Latin American Fiction: A Survey* (London: Faber and Faber, 1987).

Klahn, Norma, 'La ficción de Juan Rulfo: nuevas formas del decir', in *Toda la Obra* (Colección Archivos, Mexico City: 1997), 521–30.

Knight, Alan, 'Popular Culture and the Revolutionary State in Mexico, 1910–1940', *Hispanic American Historical Review*, 74:3 (August 1994), 393–444.

_____, *The Mexican Revolution* (Cambridge: Cambridge University Press, 1986).

Larsen, Neil, 'Más allá de lo "transcultural": Rulfo y la conciencia histórica', in *Revista Canadiense de Estudios Hispanicos* (Montreal), XXII:2 (Invierno, 1998), 267–71.

Leal, Luis, *Juan Rulfo* (Boston: Twayne, 1983).

Leinhard, M., 'El substrato arcaico en *Pedro Páramo*: Quetzalcoatl y Tlaloc', in *Iberoamérica: historia, sociedad, literatura: Homenaje a Gustav Siebenman*, ed. by J. M. López de Abiada (Munich: Wilhelm Fink, 1983), 473–90.

Lioret, Kent E., 'A Matter of Life and Death in *Pedro Páramo*', *Romance Notes*, 17 (1976), 99–102.

Longo, Teresa, '*Pedro Páramo*: Love and the Illusion of Paradise', *Hispanófila*, 35:2 (1992), 65–75.

López Mena, Sergio, *Los caminos de la creación en Juan Rulfo* (Mexico City: Universidad Nacional Autónoma de México, 1993).

_____, ed., *Revisión crítica de la obra de Juan Rulfo* (Mexico City: Praxis, 1998).

_____, *Perfil de Juan Rulfo* (Mexico City: Praxis, 2001).

Lorente-Murphy, Silvia, *Juan Rulfo: realidad y mito de la Revolución Mexicana* (Madrid: Pliegos, 1988).

Los murmullos, Boletín de la Fundación Juan Rulfo, First and Second Semester, 1999 (Mexico City: Quadrata, 1999).

Loyo, Aurora, *La Unidad Nacional* (Mexico City: M. Casillas, 1983).

Luraschi, I. A., 'Narradores en la obra de Juan Rulfo: estudio de sus funciones y efectos', *Cuadernos Hispanoamericanos*, 308 (1976), 5–29.

Magnarelli, Sharon, 'Women, Violence, and Sacrifice in *Pedro Páramo* and *La muerte de Artemio Cruz*', *INTI*, 13–14 (1981), 44–54.

Mallon, Florencia E., *Peasant and Nation: The Making of Postcolonial Mexico and Peru* (Los Angeles: University of California Press, 1995).

Martin, Gerald, 'Narrative Since 1920', in *A Cultural History of Latin America*, ed. by Leslie Bethell (Cambridge: Cambridge University Press, 1998), 133–227.

Martin, Sabas, 'El libro inexistente de Comala', *Cuadernos Hispanoamericanos*, 421–23 (1985), 27–33.

McLeod, John, *Beginning Postcolonialism* (Manchester: Manchester University Press, 2000).

Mena, Lucila Inés, 'Estructura narrativa y significado social de *Pedro Páramo*', *Cuadernos Americanos*, 217 (1978), 165–88.

Merrell, Floyd, 'Some Considerations of Bird Imagery in Rulfo's *Pedro Páramo*', *Romance Notes*, 17 (1977), 255–59.

Mexicanísimo (Mexico City), 'Homenaje a Juan Rulfo', 2:16 (2009).

Meyer, Jean, *The Cristero Rebellion: Mexican People between Church and State* (Cambridge: Cambridge University Press, 1976).

Muecke, D. C., *Irony* (London: Methuen, 1970).

Muñoz, Mario, 'Dualidad y desencuentro en *Pedro Páramo*', *Cuadernos Hispanoamericanos*, 421–23 (1985), 385–98.

Obregón, Álavaro, 'The Revolution was Fought for Democracy', in *The Meaning of the Mexican Revolution*, ed. by Charles C. Cumberland (Boston: D. C. Heath, 1967), 9–15.

O'Malley, Ilene, *The Myth of the Revolution, Hero Cults and Institutionalisation of the Mexican State, 1920–1940* (Westport, CT: Greenwood Press, 1986).

Ortega, Julio, '*Pedro Páramo*: A Metaphor for the End of the World', *Studies in Twentieth Century Literature*, 14:1 (1990), 21–26.

Ortega, María Luisa, *Mito y poesía en la obra de Juan Rulfo* (Bogotá: Siglo del Hombre, 2004).

Palacio, Antonio, 'Juan Rulfo: la revolución cubana desencadenó el "boom" americano', *ABC*, 22 April 1982, p. 31.

Paré, Luisa, 'Caciquismo y estructura de poder en la Sierra Norte de Puebla' in *Caciquismo y poder político en el México rural*, ed. by Roger Bartra (Mexico City: Siglo Veintiuno, 1975).

Pavia Crespo, José, *El Nacional*, 2 May 1955, p. 10.

Paz, Octavio, *El laberinto de la soledad* (Mexico City: Fondo de Cultura Económica, 1950).

Peavler, Terry J., *El texto en llamas: El arte narrativo de Juan Rulfo* (New York: Peter Lang, 1988).

Peralta, Violeta and Liliana Befumo Boschi, *Rulfo: La soledad creadora* (Buenos Aires: Cambeiro, 1975).

Pérez, César P., *Análisis de Pedro Páramo* (Bogotá: Panamericana, 2003).

Pimentel, Luz Aurora, 'Los caminos de la eternidad: El valor simbólico del espacio en *Pedro Páramo*', *Revista Canadiense de Estudios Hispánicos*, 16:2 (1992), 267–91.

Poinsett, Joel, 'The Mexican Character', in *The Mexican Reader: History, Culture, Politics*, ed. by Gilbert M. Joseph and Timothy J. Henderson (Durham: Duke University Press, 2002), 11–14.

Polic Bobic, Mirjana, 'La recepción del personaje Pedro Páramo', *Cuadernos Hispanoamericanos*, 421–23 (1985), 399–403.

Portal, Marta, *Rulfo: dinámica de la violencia* (Madrid: Instituto de Cooperación Iberoamericana, 1984).

Portes Gil, Emilio, *La escuela y el campesino* (Mexico City: Instituto de Estudios Sociales, Políticos y Económicos, 1936).

Price, David W., *History Made, History Imagined, Contemporary Literature, Poiesis and the Past* (Illinois: University of Illinois Press, 1999).

Pupo Walker, C. Enrique, 'Personajes y ambiente en *Pedro Páramo*', *Cuadernos Americanos*, 28:6 (1969), 194–204.

Ramírez, Rafael, *El Porvenir, Plan Sexenal Infantil*, 4 (Mexico City: Secretaría de Educación Pública (SEP), Biblioteca Cuauhtémoc, 1937).

Revista Canadiense de Estudios Hispanicos (Montreal), XXII:2 (Invierno, 1998).

Riveiro Espasandín, José, *Pedro Páramo: Juan Rulfo* (Barcelona: Laia, 1984).

Robles, Humberto E., 'Variantes en Pedro Páramo', *Nueva Revista de Filología Hispánica*, 31:1 (1982), 106–16.

Rodríguez-Alcalá, Hugo, *El arte de Juan Rulfo: historias de vivos y difuntos* (Mexico City: Bellas Artes, 1965).

_____, 'Rulfo y la Crítica', in *INTI: Revista de Literatura Hispánica* (Providence: Providence College), 13–14 (Spring–Fall 1981), 9–24.

_____, and Jean-Pierre Barricelli, 'Dante and Rulfo: Beyond Time through Eternity', *Hispanic Journal*, 5:1 (1983), 7–27.

Rodríguez-Luis, Julio, 'Algunas observaciones sobre el simbolismo de la relación entre Susana San Juan y Pedro Páramo', *Cuadernos Hispanoamericanos*, 270 (1972), 584–94.

_____, 'La función de la voz popular en la obra de Rulfo', *Cuadernos Hispanoamericanos*, 421–23 (1985), 135–50.

Roffé, Reina, *Autobiografía Armada* (Buenos Aires: Corregidor, 1973).

_____, *Las mañas del zorro* (Madrid: Espasa-Calpe, 2003).

Rorty, Richard, *Contingency, Irony and Solidarity* (Cambridge: Cambridge University Press, 1989).

Rosales, Nilda, 'El tema del caudillismo en *Pedro Páramo* de Juan Rulfo', in *'Cuadillos', 'Cacique'» et dictateurs dans le roman hispano-américain*, ed. by Paul Verdevoye (Paris: Éditions Hispaniques, 1978), 280–95.

Ross, Stanley R., ed., *Is the Mexican Revolution Dead?* (New York: Alfred A. Knopf, 1966).

Rowe, William, *El llano en llamas* (London: Grant & Cutler, 1986).

_____, and Vivian Schelling, eds, *Memory and Modernity* (London: Verso, 1991).

_____, and Jens Andermann, eds, *Images of Power: Iconography, Culture and State in Latin America* (New York and Oxford: Berghahn, 2006).

Rufinelli, Jorge, *El lugar de Rulfo y otros ensayos* (Xalapa: Universidad Veracruzana, 1980).

Rulfo, Juan, *El llano en llamas* [1953] (Madrid: Cátedra, 1997).
_____, *Pedro Páramo* [1955] (Madrid: Cátedra, 1989).
_____, *El gallo de oro y otros textos para el cine* [1980] (Mexico City: Ediciones Era, 2000).
_____, ed., *Para cuando yo me ausente* (Mexico City: Grijalbo, 1982).
_____, *Inframundo: el México de Juan Rulfo* (Mexico City: Ediciones del Norte, 1983).
Sabugo Abril, Amancio, 'Comala o una lectura en el infierno', *Cuadernos Hispanoamericanos*, 421–23 (1985), 417–32.
Said, Edward, *Orientalism: Western Conceptions of the Orient* [1978] (London: Penguin, 1995).
Saragoza, Alex, 'The Selling of Mexico: Tourism and the State, 1929–1952', in *Fragments of a Golden Age*, ed. by Gilbert Joseph, Anne Rubenstein and Eric Zolov (Durham: Duke University Press, 2001), 91–116.
Schwerin, Karl H., 'The Anthropological Antecedents: Caciques, Cacicazgos and Caciquismo', in *The Caciques, Oligarchical Politics and the System of Caciquismo in the Luso-Hispanic World*, ed. by Robert Kern (Albuquerque: University of New Mexico Press, 1973), 5–17.
Secretaría de Educación Pública, *Serie SEP 3er año* (Mexico City: SEP, Comisión Editorial Popular, 1938).
Selden, Raman, and Peter Widdowson, *A Reader's Guide to Contemporary Literary Theory* (London: Harvester Wheatsheaf, 1993).
Soler Serrano, Joaquín, 'Entrevista con Juan Rulfo' (Video), *A Fondo* (Madrid: Editrama), 17 April 1977.
Sommers, Joseph, 'Los muertos no tienen tiempo ni espacio (un diálogo con Juan Rulfo)', *¡Siempre!, La Cultura en México*, 1051 (15 August 1973), vi–vii.
_____, ed., *La narrativa de Juan Rulfo: interpretaciones críticas* (Mexico City: SEP, 1974).
Sontag, Susan, 'Against Interpretation' (1964), in *A Susan Sontag Reader* (London: Penguin Books, 1982).
Sosnowski, Saul, '*Pedro Páramo*: clausura de un proceso histórico', *INTI*, 13–14 (1981), 55–62.
Sousa, Ronald W., 'The Father Figure Motif in the Worlds of Pedro Páramo and Pascoa Feliz', *Bulletin of Hispanic Studies*, 54 (1977), 29–39.
Stanton, Anthony, 'Estructuras antropológicas en *Pedro Páramo*', *Nueva Revista de Filología Hispánica*, 36:1 (1988), 567–606.
Swanson, Philip, ed., *Landmarks in Modern Latin American Fiction* (London: Routledge, 1990).
Tatard, Béatrice, *Juan Rulfo, photographe: esthétique du royaume des âmes* (Paris: L'Harmattan, 1994).
Thakkar, Amit, 'Ambivalence and the Crisis of the Mimic Man: Centrifugal Irony in Juan Rulfo's "Luvina"', *Journal of Iberian and Latin American Studies* (Cardiff), 11:1 (2005), 65–89.
_____, 'Irony and the Priest in Fragment 14 of Juan Rulfo's *Pedro Páramo*', *The Bulletin of Hispanic Studies* (Liverpool), 83:3 (2006), 203-223.

_____, 'One Rainy Market Day: Integration and Indigenous Peoples in the Fiction and Thought of Juan Rulfo', in *(Re)Collecting the Past, History and Collective Memory in Latin American Narrative*, ed. by Victoria Carpenter (Oxford: Peter Lang, 2009), 191–216.

_____, 'Juan Rulfo'. *The Literary Encyclopedia*. First publishesd 27 August 2009, http://www.litencyc.com/php/speople.php?rec=true&UID=11993.

Tittler, Jonathan, '*Pedro Páramo*: Nihilismo fracasado', *INTI*, 13–14 (1981), 73–82.

_____, *Narrative Irony in the Contemporary Spanish-American Novel* (Ithaca and London: Cornell University Press, 1984).

Torres, Rafael Ramírez, *Miguel Agustín Pro* (Mexico City: Tradición, 1976).

Trabulse, Elías, 'Juan Rulfo y las crónicas coloniales', in *La ficción de la memoria: Juan Rulfo ante la crítica*, ed. by Federico Campbell (Mexico City: Ediciones Era, 2003), 485–89.

Turner, Paul, *The Life of Thomas Hardy*, Blackwell Critical Biographies (Oxford: Blackwell, 1998).

Ugalde, Antonio, 'Contemporary Mexico: From Hacienda to PRI', in *The Caciques, Oligarchical Politics and the System of Caciquismo in the Luso-Hispanic World*, ed. by Robert Kern (Albuquerque: University of New Mexico Press, 1973), 119–34.

Uzquiza González, José Ignacio, 'Simbolismo e historia en *Pedro Páramo*', *Revista Iberoamericana*, 58:159 (1992), 639-55.

Valdés, María Elena de, 'Sexuality and Insanity in Rulfo's Susana San Juan', *Revista Canadiense de Estudios Hispánicos*, 18:3 (1994), 491–501.

Vasconcelos, José, *La raza cósmica* (1925) and *De Robinson a Odiseo* (1935), in *Obras Completas II* (Mexico: Libreros Mexicanos Unidos, 1957).

Vaughan, Mary Kay, *The State, Education, and Social Class in Mexico, 1880–1928* (DeKalb: Northern Illinois University Press, 1982).

_____, 'Cambio ideológico en la política educativa de la SEP: programas y libros de texto, 1921–40', in *Escuela y sociedad en el periodo cardenista*, ed. by Susana Quintanilla y Mary Kay Vaughan (Mexico City: Fondo de Cultura Económica, 1997).

_____, *Cultural Politics in Revolution: Teachers, Peasants and Schools in Mexico, 1930–1940* (Tucson, AZ: University of Arizona Press, 1997).

Veas Mercado, Luis Fernando, *Los modos narrativos en los cuentos en primera persona de Juan Rulfo* (Mexico City: Universidad Nacional Autónoma de México, 1984).

Vital, Alberto, *Lenguaje y poder en Pedro Páramo* (Mexico City: Consejo Nacional para la Cultura y las Artes, 1993).

_____, *Noticias sobre Juan Rulfo* (Mexico City: Editorial RM, 2004).

Volek, Emil, '*Pedro Páramo* de Juan Rulfo: Una obra aleatoria en busca de su texto y del género literario', *Revista Iberoamericana*, 56:150 (1990), 35–47.

Volpi, Jorge, 'Me mataron los murmullos', in *La ficción de la memoria: Juan Rulfo ante la crítica*, ed. by Federico Campbell (Mexico City: Ediciones Era, 2003), 506–09.

Wagner, C., *El Nacional*, 5 June 1943, p. 3.

White, Hayden, *Metahistory: The Historical Imagination in Nineteenth-Century Europe* (Baltimore: Johns Hopkins University Press, 1973).

Wilkie, James, Michael C. Meyer and Edna Monzón de Wil, eds., *Contemporary Mexico: Papers of the IV International Congress of Mexican History* (Berkeley: University of California Press, 1976).

Young, Robert, *Postcolonialism: An Historical Introduction* (Oxford: Blackwell, 2001).

_____, *Postcolonialism: A Very Short Introduction* (Oxford: Oxford University Press, 2003).

Zepeda, Jorge, *La recepción inicial de Pedro Páramo* (Mexico City: Editorial RM and Fundación Juan Rulfo, 2005).

INDEX